Ethics of the Urban

Ethics of the Urban

The City and the Spaces of the Political

Edited by Mohsen Mostafavi

**Harvard University
Graduate School of Design**

Lars Müller Publishers

Neighborhoods and Neighborliness

Public Space and Public Sphere

Borders and Boundaries

This book considers the reciprocities between our ethical and political responsibilities and capabilities and their spatial and situational manifestations. A series of themes or headings—cities and citizenship, monuments and memorials, neighborhoods and neighborliness, public space and public sphere, borders and boundaries— are used as prompts to help develop a more grounded approach towards the ethical and political discussion and unfolding of the urban today. Photographs have also been used to add greater nuance to the topics. The aim is to stimulate greater conversation between scholars and designers. There is also the hope that the essays presented here will not only add to our deeper understanding of the urban but also inspire the next generation of designers. Architects and urbanists need to imagine cities that both contribute to the quality of life of the citizens and have the necessary spatial character to provide the framework for agonistic pluralism in action.

Mohsen Mostafavi

Agonistic Urbanism

Mohsen Mostafavi

The contemporary city is in a constant state of transition. What we think of as the city, whether large or small, is itself part of a greater process of urbanization that is both a "territorial artifact" and a "socio-economic organism," albeit one with physical consequences. The dynamics of the relationship between the physical and the social dimensions of the urban is one of the key factors that help define our everyday interactions with others.

Designers, including architects, landscape architects, and urbanists, provide plans and blueprints for the physical manifestation of this relationship. But the settings of our everyday lives are invariably shaped by a much larger list of contributors, which includes experts in areas such as infrastructure, finance, transportation, development, and construction. It is the collaboration between these groups that supplies the knowledge—and the creative possibilities—that inform a specific design proposal for a particular location. In this schema the urban, as a physical artifact, is the built representation not just of our creative and technical knowledge but also of our societal values.

In actuality, however, there is always a tension between socio-economic forces and design solutions. For one thing, there is never a single outcome for a particular brief or program. Equally, every solution should have the potential to be used or occupied in a variety of different ways. But beyond this, it is the capacity of design to question, interpret, or rethink a given program which is of such relevance in our contemporary culture, particularly in relation to the modes and practices of urbanization. The imaginative construction of the relationship between the design and the brief of any project can turn the tension between them into a productive outcome.

It is in part the responsibility of the designer to imagine alternative ways of actualizing the relationship between various dimensions of society. To understand both the given condition of things and their potential transformation, however, requires constant collaborations and reciprocities between the users and the designer. These interactions and understandings are necessary catalysts for imaginative and unexpected design proposals and solutions.

In the case of the urban, the de facto assumption is that there will always be a multiplicity of users with different needs and interests. The provision of an urban environment that is responsive to pluralism is what enables the citizens to locate themselves within certain physical and social conditions that promote their rights and engender their potential participation in a democratic society.

The responsiveness of the urban to pluralism enables the diversity of interests and differences within the population to be both manifested and accommodated as part of the physical fabric of the city. In as much as the urban is the representation of a collective, it demands that we question the balance or relational articulation between sameness and difference as it pertains to the shaping of the urban environment.

To take an obvious example, most major American and European cities have their own versions of Chinatown. These areas are frequently distinguished by the use of Chinese symbols such as gateways, lions, and lanterns that tend to densify and transform the existing fabric of the city into a hybrid of Western and Chinese visual and olfactory references. Food and its associated aromas and colors usually feature large.

We are attracted to these places even though they do not necessarily represent an "authentic" Chinese city. What they do provide is a displaced version, which is nevertheless just as authentic in its own invariably kitsch way. This appealing cultural hybridity, which extends to their Korean, Indian, Bangladeshi, or Russian counterparts, is often made possible by the way in which the building stock in most older cities has the capacity to accommodate change.

The potential for adaptive reuse, from one function to another, plays a crucial part in allowing and incorporating difference. These sites—urban palimpsests—are often initially located within the marginal zone of the city where property values are relatively low and change is not difficult to manage. Then gradually the programmatic transformation creates additional demand and interest in these neighborhoods, which in turn leads to a form of gentrification and a significant increase in property values. This is as much the case in New York City as it is in London or Paris.

But beyond the incorporation of the "other" in places such as Chinatown, and the promotion of a certain type of exoticism, there is a more general question of how the urban can and must accommodate a diversity of interests more broadly, and not just in relation to the culture of the immigrant population. The interests of the general populace cannot be defined solely in terms of entrepreneurial activities. Rather, we must consider, amongst other things, the provision of housing, public space, and diversity of institutions as a factor in creating equitable and just cities and societies. It is also the combination of these factors and their performance that helps define the quality of life of a district or a city.

This situation is blatantly clear in many major American cities. In Los Angeles and San Francisco, for example, the issue of homelessness is so acute that it is hard to walk around any part of the central districts without encountering large numbers of homeless people. An ad hoc tent city has established itself near LA's Union Station and along its freeway overpasses. The freeways have become the city's new extraterritorial spaces for the dispossessed. Similarly, it is bewildering to read of the level of success of some of San Francisco's young entrepreneurs and then witness the scale of homelessness in the downtown area. Politicians are now taking steps to enable the police to forcibly remove these encampments. But the erasure of homelessness from public view does nothing to rectify the cause of the problem.

The stark reality of homelessness is in contrast to the increasing bureaucracy that constantly hinders any attempt at radical urban transformation, whether by developers or the cities themselves. In the face of these bureaucratic obstacles, the emphasis has shifted from proposals to procedures with many stakeholders and negotiating partners. And the bigger picture—the interests of the general populace—has been lost in the process. In LA, very few people seem to know the precise boundaries of the city. The County of Los Angeles is made up of 88 incorporated cities and many unincorporated areas covering over 4,000 square miles. In this context the mechanisms for decision-making are so fragmented that they make a coherent model of planning almost impossible to envisage.

How did we get to this point? How is it possible for one of the world's richest nations to find itself in such a complex ethical conundrum, apparently unable to afford to provide its citizens with basic shelter?

It would seem that the last thing many of the planning agencies in cities such as LA need is more planning or design. Rather, they believe they first need new forms of organization and new models of governance to enable them to benefit from the values that design can then bring to bear. But waiting for such transformations, while a necessary goal, is like waiting for Godot. In the absence of a holistic and integrated approach, what remains is the tactical and the strategic, which can at least demonstrate a fragment of what is possible now.[1]

The Star Apartments for the Skid Row Housing Trust, by Michael Maltzan, is an example of the type of mixed-use project, including a health center, exercise facilities, and a community garden, that can be built with relatively modest means.[2] The 102 efficiency apartments are exclusively for the homeless, but the building has a wider reach through the community services and retail units housed in it. It would not be hard to imagine a collection of such projects all over the city. There are obvious benefits to developing a range of design approaches, incorporating innovations in architecture, landscape architecture, and urban design that can then be utilized as part of a larger and more comprehensive planning and design approach. These efforts could be extended more systematically into the affordable housing sector and public institutions such as libraries and schools. The creation of public spaces, parks, and other places of leisure and pleasure would further demonstrate the city's hospitality toward its citizens.

The specific example of Los Angeles shows the inseparability of the ethical from the political. In the case of the urban, the ethical addresses the question of our values and our code of conduct as individuals and as a community and beyond, while the political represents the structural means by which we can address the potential actualization of values that matter to us. But since our society is made up of conflicting interests it would be naïve to consider the political as a means of achieving consensus in any sphere of social life. Acknowledging the conflictual condition of the political is therefore one of the realities architects and urbanists has to face in conceiving contemporary urban projects.

Superkilen is a public park in the Nørrebro district of Copenhagen. Designed by the arts group Superflex, the architects BIG (Bjarke Ingels Group), and the landscape architecture practice Topotek 1 in collaboration with the local—largely immigrant—population, the park is articulated into distinct areas, in terms of character and potential use. One area with a smooth gray hill covered in white lines is primarily devoted to sport, while another provides a shockingly colorful promenade with benches for gathering and conversation. There is also a more traditional type of green space suited as a promenade and place of exchange, rather than sports activity or play.[3]

The gift of this public space to a marginalized part of the city has had a significant impact, drawing not just younger locals but also tourists to the area. Furthermore, the park recognizes the nuances of cultural difference. Its uncommon playground equipment and street furniture was sourced from a variety of different countries, representing the home nations of the local inhabitants. These affiliations further enhance the sense of community and ownership of the space.

Superkilen is the outcome of a set of competing negotiations between various activities and people—an outcome that does not seek a singular resolution, but instead provides a set of different stages for the participatory actions and the sharing of life of its multitude of users. In this respect, the approach and method adopted by the designers show the spatial possibilities of what Chantal Mouffe has called agonistic pluralism.[4] Agonism—from the Greek word agon, meaning struggle—is in one sense a political theory that accommodates the conflictual conditions embodied in the very notion of pluralism. As opposed to the materialist conception of history, which sees struggle as a precondition for the establishment of a harmonious society, agonistic pluralism is a form of ongoing yet positive struggle. Agonistic, but not antagonistic.

Mouffe, both alone and sometimes together with her late partner Ernesto Laclau, has helped develop a set of arguments which seem particularly relevant to the ongoing conflictual conditions faced by many diverse communities and societies today. Mouffe is in agreement with philosophers such as John Rawls or Jürgen Habermas on the need to think in a new way about democracy, but considers their model of deliberative democracy to be an inadequate response. In her view, their approach ultimately calls for rational consensus and, by continuing to place the emphasis on the "rational" citizen, it neglects the indispensable role played by passions and emotions in shaping our decisions. Accordingly, "what is precluded in these rationalistic approaches is the very question of what are the conditions of existence of the democratic subject."[5] To address this dichotomy, Mouffe argues, will require the "multiplying of the institutions, the discourses, the forms of life that foster identification with democratic values."[6] This is why the urban artifact, with all that it has to offer in terms of institutions, public spaces, transportation systems, etc., provides such a crucial setting for promoting democratic values.

Projects such as Superkilen are important for the way in which they engender the types of everyday practices, the sharing of and participation in "forms of life," that characterize Agonistic Urbanism. The physical and public spaces of the city have the capacity to bring people together for cultural and emotional exchange. They are also the places where difference and disagreement can be accommodated. An active engagement with the other, and consequently with the experience of difference, is a prerequisite for a pluralist society.

At its best, the city provides the arena for these ongoing encounters and disagreements. But the urban can also be the instigator of further struggles, as in the case of homelessness or lack of infrastructure or appropriate civil institutions. The inability of our society to provide such basic amenities is therefore a marker of our inability to construct a truly pluralistic democracy. The urban is a means of demonstrating our commitment to democracy and the sites of its practices.

What does an awareness and acceptance of these conditions mean for those involved with the design and transformation of the built environment? It is true that an architect's or landscape architect's urban projects have the potential to enhance the quality of everyday life. But there is the further potential to redescribe the urban—to see it in terms other than its current condition. Such an effort would require a more coherent and collaborative approach, with a shift from single projects to the consideration of a more relational and interconnected set of initiatives. The links between infrastructure and urban development, or between housing and the provision of new forms of public space, are examples of this type of hybrid approach.

Such an approach does not underestimate the importance of singular projects. Rather it seeks to explore ways in which the creativity and imagination of the designer can be utilized in order to propose new and enhanced settings for our social life and interactions. Reimagining, and hence redescribing, the urban also shares parallels with seeking alternative forms of democracy. The association between the political and the spatial, the influence of the one on the other, can become a positive force in how design both responds to and shapes potential forms of social relations.

From the perspective of the design professions this is an opportune moment to see what can be learned from both best practices and past failures in the areas of planning and urban design. Urban planning models of the late 19th and early 20th centuries all tended to share a criticism of the 19th-century city's lack of hygiene, pollution, overcrowding, poor housing conditions, and insufficient open space. This is perhaps why most examples of planning from that time include what might be called a dimension of "anti-urbanity." Projects such as Ebenezer Howard's garden city movement (1898), Patrick Geddes' valley section form of regional planning (1909), Le Corbusier's Radiant City (1924), or Frank Lloyd Wright's Broadacre City (1932) all look beyond the city to the countryside or nature as the location for new forms of human settlement.

But the optimistic belief in the socially restorative powers of the tabula rasa site has been repeatedly undermined by the inability of many of these projects to create diversity and dynamic environments that are often associated with the traditions of dense and compact cities. Ironically, many of the concerns regarding the 19th-century city are still with us today, though they invariably have different causes and require different solutions for contemporary urbanization; many cities, such as Beijing, for example, suffer from severe forms of pollution caused not just by manufacturing but also by the ever-increasing number of automobiles.[7] Many of today's ethical questions also remain much the same as they were in the 19th century. In considering how to make cities healthy, there is a need for constant attention to the diversity of environmental, legal, and social issues that affect the lives of the citizens. The considered combination of these forces is a necessary factor for constructing a network of spatial relations guided by equity, fairness, and justice.

Susan Fainstein, among others, has used the concept of the just city to remind us of the need for "recognition and just distribution," whereby social justice is incorporated as a key component of urban policy.[8] Particularly in societies where private development provides the vast majority of a nation's housing stock, this means viewing cities in terms other than their economic development, or rather in addition to their economic viability.

The increasing segregation of communities according to their income level has had a devastating impact on the provision of services such as schools and hospitals—a situation made worse by an overreliance on local real-estate taxes as a way of funding educational and other local programs. Financial inequity, combined with racial and political tensions, has stoked social and physical antagonism in many parts of the world.

Despite their distant geographies, there are similarities between the conditions of an eastern suburb of Paris like Clichy-sous-Bois, say, and a suburb of St. Louis like Ferguson, Missouri. Though Ferguson has historically been a town with median levels of income, the shift from a majority white population—and white police force—to a predominantly African-American population has resulted in the city's administration being accused of "constitutional violations" after the 2014 killing of Michael Brown.

The increasing racialization of space, reflected in the growing focus on the number of African-Americans incarcerated or killed by the police, lends further credence to the call for a broad and holistic approach toward spatial justice.

Iris Marion Young's Justice and the Politics of Difference reminds us of the need for a form of justice that is geographically, historically, and institutionally located. Instead of placing emphasis on outcomes that lead to the de-spatialization of justice, an abstract phenomenon, she argues for the importance of processes that promote difference and pluralistic solidarity. For Young, "social justice ... requires not the melting away of difference, but institutions that promote reproduction of and respect for group difference without oppression."[9]

Spatial justice, like its architectural counterpoint, agonistic urbanism, is highly dependent on specific and concrete situations. Injustice is not solely a matter of one's legal rights. It also extends to the equitable distribution of services and resources available to citizens. The call for a return to spatial justice is a recognition of how the settings of our everyday actions and relations, infrastructure, retail, housing, places of work and leisure are all components of how justice is practiced in actuality, and not only in an abstract and generalizable fashion. Furthermore, Young's articulation of the politics of difference recognizes the importance of differentiated networks of urban life, and hence of group-differentiated politics.

The recent case of the 2016 Brexit referendum and the decision of the UK to leave the European Union, a decree largely influenced by questions over immigration policy, points to the difficulties of constructing a society that can genuinely promote "difference and pluralistic solidarity."[10] Clearly the question of immigration is an important, emotional topic that requires significant careful attention. But it is equally the case that the failure of many countries to carefully and honestly address contentious issues has led to the rise of anti-immigrant, xenophobic movements, not just in Europe, but in the United States as well. In The Right to the City, David Harvey writes, "The question of what kind of city we want cannot be divorced from that of what kind of social ties, relationship to nature, lifestyles, technologies, and aesthetic values we desire. The right to the city is far more than the individual liberty to access urban resources: it is a right to change ourselves by changing the city. It is, moreover, a common rather than an individual right since this transformation inevitably depends upon the exercise of a collective power to reshape the process of urbanization."[11]

The productive tension embodied in the idea of "the right to change ourselves by changing the city" is of utmost importance for those invested in the reciprocities between urban design and its social, cultural, and political consequences. For one thing this concept makes the character and quality of the urban artifact crucial factors in assessing a project's performance. A performance that can contribute to the right to change ourselves.

1 See for example, Krzysztof Wodiczko, "Art, Trauma, and *Parrhesia*," in this volume. Wodiczko describes his Homeless Vehicle project as "a shock-absorbing mechanism" that mediates between the homeless population and passersby (see p. 125).
2 See photograph by Iwan Baan on pages 20–21 of this volume.
3 See photograph by Iwan Baan on pages 216–17 of this volume.
4 See "Radical Politics as Counter-Hegemonic Intervention: The Role of Cultural Practices" by Chantal Mouffe, in this volume. Mouffe suggests that urban conflicts can take an "agonistic" rather than an "antagonistic" form (see p. 225).
5 Chantal Mouffe, The Democratic Paradox (London; New York: Verso, 2000), 95.
6 Ibid., 96.
7 See photograph by Hannes Zander on page 242–43 of this volume.
8 Susan Fainstein, The Just City (Ithaca, NY: Cornell University Press, 2011). See also, Susan Fainstein, "Planning and the Just City," Searching for the Just City: Debates in Urban Theory and Practice, ed. Peter Marcuse (London; New York: Routledge, 2009), 35.
9 Iris Marion Young, Justice and the Politics of Difference (Princeton, NJ: Princeton University Press, 1990), 47.
10 Edward W. Soja on Iris Marion Young's proposal to concentrate our efforts on structural forces that promote inequality and injustice in order to move away from distributive justice. Edward W. Soja, Seeking Spatial Justice (Minneapolis: University of Minnesota Press, 2010), 78.
11 David Harvey and Andrew Herod, Social Justice and the City (Athens: University of Georgia Press, 2009), 315.

NIGHT AND DAY

How does the feeling of a city change from night to day? In an interview with the Leica Internet Team on July 1, 2015, Johannesburg-based photographer Mack Magagane explained, "Personally, I feel there is nothing that beats the orange-yellowish-tinted color of nighttime."

Bangkok's Khao San Road is filled with tourists from night to day. Tours begin in the morning as food vendors open; at night, music and lights transform the space. How can the passage of a day serve as a means of measurement to understand more deeply how a city matrix is commodified and consumed, both temporally and spatially? How can design exploit this knowledge? For example, can the commercial presence of street vendors and markets increase public safety at night?

Providing 102 efficiency apartments for formerly homeless individuals, Skid Row Housing
Trust's Star Apartments, designed by Michael Maltzan Architecture, is a mixed-use development
combining new community spaces amid the residences.

Photographer Maciej Dakowicz tells us that Saint Mary Street in Cardiff, Wales, transforms on a Saturday night from a street for shopping and offices to a party stage fueled by alcohol and emotions, a not uncommon phenomenon in other cities too. Dakowicz observes that "Nobody seems to worry about tomorrow, what matters is here and now."

Photograph by Antoine Rose, "Crossroads," 2014, www.antoinerose.com

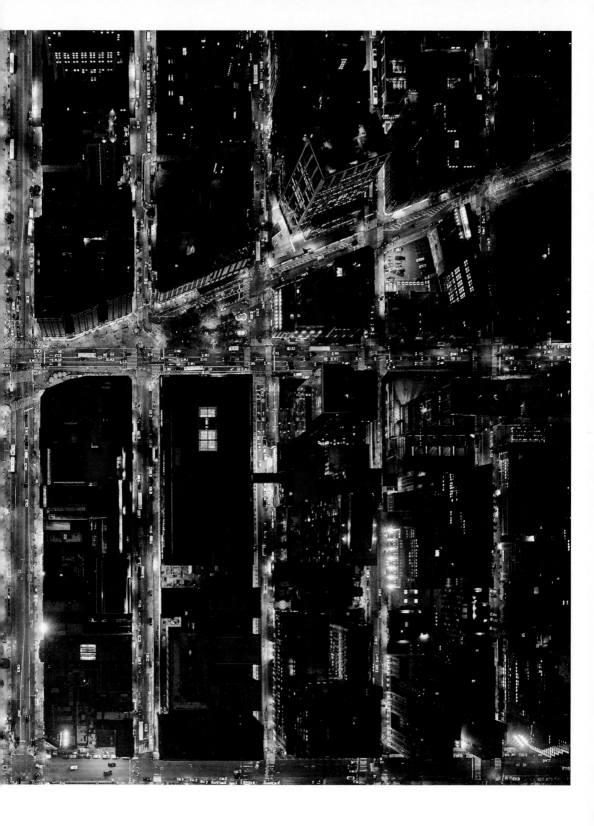

In 1920, when permanent traffic lights appeared in the city that never sleeps, the pulsing, nocturnal soundscape drastically changed. A study from Columbia University states 98 percent of public space in Manhattan experiences unhealthy levels of noise. What is heard and seen at night? What is hidden and drowned out?

WALKING THROUGH

From 2007 to 2009, a team from Gehl Architects collaborated with the New York City Department of Transportation to pedestrianize Times Square. Above, New Yorkers and tourists walk, sit, and stand at Broadway; only a few years prior, this same space was clogged with cars.

WALKING THROUGH

The Allianz Arena in Munich, designed by Vogt Landscape Architects, hosts approximately two million visitors per season. Distinctive winding pathways extend from the stadium. In designing the surroundings, Günther Vogt stated, "The resulting dialogue with the decisive features of this space was deliberate." How does this dialogue influence the urban traveler?

In 2008, Boston's Rose Kennedy Greenway opened as a linear park. Historically, the space was an elevated highway through Boston until 1991, when the Central Artery/Tunnel Project, or "Big Dig," began construction for its relocation underground. Does the park act to unify? Or does it act to divide?

Trees are spaces of respite: providing trunks for support, air for breathing, and shade as a sanctum. During spring, streets around Athens are infused with the aroma of bitter orange trees. How do seasonal smells and changes of foliage, and daily dances of shade, influence experiences of the urban?

Cities and Citizenship

Beyond Differences of Race, Religion, Class:
Making Urban Subjects

Saskia Sassen

Cities have distinctive capacities to transform conflict into the civic. In contrast, national governments tend to militarize conflict. This does not mean that cities are peaceful spaces. On the contrary, cities have long been sites for conflicts, from war to racisms and religious hatreds. Yet militarizing conflict is not a particularly urban option: cities have tended to triage conflict through commerce and civic activity. Even more important, the overcoming of urban conflicts has often been the source for an expanded civic sense. And more generally, the daily dynamics and interdependences of life in the city contribute to the making of an *urban* subject, as distinct from an ethnic, religious, or racialized subject. I think of the possibility of an urban subject not as one that erases these powerful markers, but repositions them. This repositioning is likely to take on many diverse forms and involve diverse spaces, depending on a city's trajectory. Notwithstanding this variability, we can conceive of the urban subject as one who can experience the urban context as such, as urban. It signals that urban space is an actor in these dynamics, a thesis I explore in "Does the City Have Speech?"[1]

Today cities are at risk of losing this capacity and becoming sites for a range of new types of conflicts, such as asymmetric war, ethnic and social "cleansing," and class wars. Dense urbane spaces can easily become conflictive spaces in cities overwhelmed by inequality and injustice. The major environmental disasters looming in our immediate futures could lead cities to become the sites for a variety of secondary, more anomic conflicts, such as drug wars and other non-urban conflicts that merely use the city as a deployment space. All of these challenge the traditional commercial and civic capacity that has given cities tools to avoid falling into armed conflict, and to incorporate diversities of class, culture, religion, ethnicity.

The question I examine here is whether this emergent urban future of expanding conflicts and racisms contains within it those conditions and urban capabilities that have historically allowed cities to transform conflict. In the past, urban capabilities and urban subjects were often crafted through the struggle to address challenges larger than our differences, our hatreds, our intolerances, our racisms. Out of this dialectic came the open urbanity that made many cities historically spaces for the making of the civic and commerce, from historic Jerusalem, Baghdad, and Istanbul to modern Chicago and New York. One factor feeding these positives was that cities became strategic spaces also for the powerful and their needs for self-representation and projection onto a larger stage. Both the modest social classes and the powerful found in the city a space for their diverse "life projects." None of these cities and projects were perfect. All of them saw hatreds and injustices. But the complex interdependence of daily life in cities was the algorithm that made them thrive.

I will argue that today's unsettling of older urban orders is part of a larger disassembling of existing organizational logics and hence unlikely to produce urbanities that resemble the shapes of our recent past. This disassembling is also unsettling the logic that assembled territory, authority, and rights into the dominant organizational format of our times—the modern nation-state.[2] All of this is happening even as both cities and national states continue to be major building blocks of the familiar geopolitical landscape and the material organization of territory. In this sense, the urban order that gave us, for instance, the open city in Europe is still there, but increasingly as mere visual order and less so as social order, an order that can enable the making of urban subjects.

In what follows I first elaborate on dynamics that are altering the familiar urban order and then argue that this is also a moment of challenges larger than our differences. Confronting these challenges will require that we transcend those differences. Therein lies a potential for reinventing that capacity of cities to transform conflict into openness rather than war. But it

© Hilary Koob-Sassen, artist and filmmaker

"Layering," from Transcalar Vehicles, a film premiered at London Film Festival 2014 (above and opposite)

is not necessarily going to be the familiar order of the open city and of the civic as we have come to represent it, especially in the West.

Where Powerlessness Becomes Complex

Cities are one of the key sites where new norms and new identities are *made*.[3] They have been such sites at various times and places, and under diverse conditions. This role can become strategic in particular times and places, as is the case today in global cities. Current conditions in these cities are creating not only new structurations of power but also operational and rhetorical openings for new political actors who may long have been invisible or without voice. A key element of the argument here is that the localization of strategic components of globalization in these cities means that the disadvantaged can engender new forms of contesting globalized corporate power, including right there in their neighborhoods.

© Hilary Koob-Sassen, artist and filmmaker

Critical in this process is the capability of urban space to produce a difference: that being powerless does not necessarily mean being invisible or impotent. The disadvantaged, especially in global cities, can gain "presence" in their engagement with power but also vis-à-vis each other. This differs from the 1950s–1970s period in the United States, for instance, when white flight and the significant departure of major corporate headquarters left cities hollowed out and the disadvantaged in a condition of abandonment. Today, the localization of the most powerful global actors in these cities creates a set of objective conditions for engagement. Examples here are the struggles against gentrification—an encroachment into minority and modest neighborhoods that led to growing numbers of homeless people beginning in the 1980s—the struggles for the rights of the homeless, or demonstrations against police brutality against minorities.

Elsewhere I have developed the case that while these struggles are highly localized, they actually represent a form of global engagement; their globality takes the form of a horizontal, multi-sited recurrence of similar struggles in hundreds of cities worldwide. These struggles are different from the ghetto uprisings of the 1960s, which were short, intense eruptions confined to the ghettos and causing most of the damage in the neighborhoods of the disadvantaged themselves. In these ghetto uprisings there was no direct engagement with power on its terrain. In contrast, current conditions in major, especially global, cities are creating spatial openings for new political actors, including the disadvantaged and those who were once invisible or without voice.

The conditions that today make some cities strategic sites are basically two, and both capture major transformations that are destabilizing older systems organizing territory and politics. One of these is the re-scaling of strategic territories that articulate the new politico-economic system and thereby at least some features of power. The other is the partial unbundling or at least weakening of the national as container of social process due to the variety of dynamics encompassed by globalization and digitization. The consequences for cities of these two conditions are many: what matters here is that cities emerge as strategic sites for major economic processes and for new political actors.[4]

Against the background of a partial disassembling of empires and nation-states, the city becomes a strategic site for making elements of new, perhaps less partial orders. In this larger disassembling new socio-political orderings can coexist with older orderings such as the nation-state, the interstate system, and the older urban order of a hierarchy dominated by the national state. Among the new orderings are global cities: these have partly exited that national, state-dominated hierarchy and become part of multi-scalar, regional, and global networks. The last two decades have seen an increasingly *urban* articulation of global logics and struggles, and an escalating use of urban space to make political claims not only by the citizens of a city's country but also by foreign firms and the global rich.

What is being engendered today in terms of political practices in the global city is quite different from what it might have been in the medieval city of Weber. The medieval city was a space that enabled the burghers to set up systems for owning and protecting property against more powerful actors, such as the king and the church, and to implement various defenses against despots of all sorts. Today's political practices, I would argue, have to do with the production of "presence" by those without power and with a politics that claims rights to the city rather than protection of property. What the two situations share is the notion that urban space enables also the weaker actor and that through urban practices new forms of political subjectivity (i.e., citizenship) are being constituted. Both the medieval and today's city are leading sites for this type of political work. The city is, in turn, partly constituted through these dynamics. Far more so than a peaceful and harmonious suburb, it is the contested city where the civic is getting built. After the long historical phase that saw the ascendance of the national state and the scaling of key economic dynamics at the national level, the city is once again a scale for strategic economic and political dynamics.

Two rescalings have repositioned cities. On the one hand, several strategic components of economic globalization and digitization concentrate in global cities and produce dislocations and destabilizations of existing institutional orders that go well beyond cities.[5] On the other hand, some of the major legal, regulatory, and normative frames for handling urban conditions are now part of national framings—much of what is called urban development policy *is* national economic policy. The concentration of such global and national dynamics in these cities forces the need to craft new types of responses and innovations on the part of both the most powerful and the most disadvantaged, albeit for very different types of survival.

But what happens to these urban capabilities when war goes asymmetric and when racisms grow in cities where increasing numbers become poor and have to struggle for survival? Here follows a brief discussion of two cases that illustrate how cities can enable powerlessness to become complex. In this complexity lies the possibility of making the political, making history.

Urbanizing War: Making Visible the Limits of Military Power

The pursuit of national security has become a source for urban insecurity.[6] In earlier wars, large armies needed large open fields or oceans to meet and fight. But nowadays, when conventional armies go to war their enemy is likely to consist of irregular combatants, and major cities are likely to become frontline space. This turns the traditional security paradigm based on national state security on its head. What may be good to protect the national state apparatus may come at a high price to major cities since that is where most asymmetric war is enacted. One component of asymmetric war is terrorism. Since 1998 most terrorist attacks have been in cities. This produces a disturbing map. Access to urban targets is far easier than access to planes for hijacking or to military installations. The U.S. Department of State *Annual Report on Global Terrorism* allows us to establish that today cities are the key targets for terrorist attacks, a trend that began before the September 2001 attacks on New York.[7] From 1993 to 2000, cities accounted for 94 percent of the injuries resulting from all "terrorist attacks," according this report, and for 61 percent of the deaths. Second, in this period the number of incidents doubled, rising especially sharply after 1998. In contrast, in the 1980s hijacked airplanes accounted for a larger share of terrorist deaths and destruction than they did in the 1990s.

We can see this urbanizing of war in the invasion of Iraq, which became largely an urban war theater. But we also see the negative impacts of this war on cities that are not even part of the immediate war theater—the bombings in Madrid, London, Casablanca, Bali, Mumbai, Lahore, and so many others. The new urban map of war is expansive: it goes far beyond the actual nation-states involved. The bombings in each of these cities have their own specifics and can be explained in terms of particular grievances and instruments. These are localized actions by local armed groups, acting independently. Yet they are also clearly part of a new kind of multi-sited war—a distributed and variable set of actions that gain larger meaning from a particular conflict with global projection, the so-called War on Terror, beginning most visibly with the invasion of Afghanistan and Iraq.

A defining feature of asymmetric wars is that they are partial, intermittent, and lack clear endings. There is no armistice to mark their end. They are one indication of how the center no longer holds—whether the center is the imperial power of a period or the national states of our modernity. We can see all these features in the U.S. war on Iraq. It took the U.S. conventional military aerial bombing only six weeks to destroy the Iraqi army and enter the country. But then asymmetric war set in, with Baghdad, Mosul, Basra, and other Iraqi cities the sites of conflict. A second feature of contemporary wars, especially evident in the less-developed areas, is that they often involve forced urbanization. Contemporary conflicts produce significant population displacement into cities; however, when the armed conflict takes over the whole city (e.g., Mogadishu in the 2000s), we also see flight out of cities. Also common today is for the warring bodies to avoid battle or direct military confrontation, as Mary Kaldor has de-scribed in her work on the new wars.[8] Their main strategy is to control terri-tory by expelling people of a different identity (ethnicity, religion, politics). The main tactic is terror—conspicuous massacres and atrocities, pushing people to flee.

These types of displacement—with ethnic/religious "cleansing" the most virulent form—have a profound impact on the cosmopolitan character of cities. Cities have long had the capacity to bring together people of differ-ent classes, ethnicities, and religions through commerce, politics, and civic practices. Contemporary conflicts unsettle and weaken this cultural diversity of cities when they lead to forced urbanization or internal displacement. Belfast, Baghdad, or Mostar each is at risk of becoming a series of urban ghettoes, with huge implications for infrastructure, the local economy, and the civic. Baghdad has undergone a deep process of such "cleansing," a criti-cal component of the (relative) "peace" the U.S. government claimed it had secured in the mid-2000s.

The systemic equivalent of these types of "cleansing" in the case of very large cities may well be the growing ghettoization of the poor and the rich—albeit in very different types of ghettoes. It leaves to the middle classes, the task of bringing urbanity to these cities. The risk is that they will supplant traditional urban cosmopolitanisms with narrow defensive attitudes in a world of growing economic insecurity and political powerlessness. Under these conditions also, displacement from countryside to town or within cities becomes a source of insecurity rather than of rich diversity.

Today's urbanizing of war differs from histories of cities and war in modern times. In the two so-called world wars, large armies needed large open fields or oceans to meet and fight and to carry out invasions. These were the frontline spaces of war. In World War II, the city entered the war theater not as a site for war making but as a technology for instilling fear: the full destruction of cities as a way of terrorizing a whole nation, with Hiroshima and Dresden the iconic cases.

This comparison of conventional and asymmetric war brings up a critical dimension: under certain conditions, such as asymmetric war, cities can function as a type of weak regime. The countries with the most powerful conventional armies today could flatten a city whether Baghdad, Gaza, the Swat valley, or so many other urban conflict zones.[9] Yet in many ways they cannot. They can engage in all kinds of activities, including violations of the law: rendition, torture, assassinations of leaders they don't like, bombing of civilian areas, and so on, in a history of brutality that can no longer be hidden and seems to have escalated the violence against civilian populations. But superior military powers stop short of pulverizing a city, even when they have the weapons to do so. The United States could have pulverized Baghdad, and Israel could have pulverized Gaza. But they didn't.[10]

It seems to me that the reason was not respect for life or the fact that killing unarmed civilians is illegal according to international law—they do this all the time. It has more to do with a vague constraint that remains unstated: the notion that the mass killing of people in a city is a different type of horror from allowing the deaths of massive numbers of people year after year in jungles and villages due to, for instance, a curable disease such as malaria. I would posit that pulverizing a city is a specific type of crime, one that elicits a horror that people dying from malaria does not. The mix of people and buildings—in a way, the civic—has the capacity to temper destruction, if not to stop it. History repeatedly shows us the limits of superior power.[11] In an increasingly interdependent world, the most powerful countries find themselves restrained through multiple interdependencies. To this I add the city as a weak regime that can obstruct and temper the destructive capacity of a superior military power. It is one more capable for systemic survival in a world where several countries have the capacity to destroy the planet.[12] Under these conditions the city becomes both a technology for containing conventional military powers and a technology of resistance for armed insurgencies. The physical and human features of the city are an obstacle for conventional armies—an obstacle wired into urban space itself.[13]

Cities as Frontier Spaces: The Hard Work of Keeping Them Open
Historically cities have evinced capacities to go beyond conflicts—conflicts that result from racisms, governmental wars on terror, and more. This implies the possibility of making new subjectivities and identities. For instance, often it is the urbanity of the subject and the setting that mark a city, rather than ethnicity, religion, or phenotype. But that marking urbanity of subject and setting does not simply fall from the sky. It is made, through hard work and painful trajectories. One question is whether it can also come out of the need for new solidarities in cities that confront major challenges, such as violent racisms or environmental crises. Their acuteness and overwhelming character can serve to create conditions where those challenges are bigger and more threatening than a city's internal conflicts and hatreds. This might force us into joint responses and from there to emphasizing an urban rather than individual or group subject and identity (such as an ethnic or religious subject and identity).

Immigration gives us a window into these types of possibilities. It helps make visible the work of making norms, of making open cities, and of repositioning both the immigrant and the citizen as urban subjects. In becoming urban subjects they can transcend this differentiation of immigrant versus citizen in spaces where it does not help or is not necessary. In the daily routines of a city the factors that rule are work, family, school, public transport, and so on, and this holds for both immigrants and citizens. Perhaps the sharpest marking difference in a city is between the rich and the poor, and each of these classes includes both immigrants and citizens. It is when the law and the police enter the picture that the differences of immigrant status versus citizen status become the determining factor, but most of daily life in the city is not ruled by this differentiation.

Here I address this issue from the perspective of the capacity of urban space to generate norms and subjects that can escape the constraints of dominant power systems—such as the nation-state, the War on Terror, the growing weight of racism in a national political culture. The particular case of immigrant integration in Europe over the centuries is one window into this complex and historically variable process, with diverse outcomes.

In my reading, both European and Western hemisphere history shows that the challenges of incorporating the "outsider" often became instruments for developing the civic and, at times, for expanding the rights of the already included.[14] Responding to claims made by the excluded has often had the effect of expanding the rights of citizenship. And restricting the rights of immigrants has been part of a loss of rights by citizens. This was clearly the case with the immigration reform act passed by the Clinton administration in the United States, which shows that a Democratic Party legislative victory for an "immigration law" had the effect of taking away rights from immigrants *and* citizens.[15]

Anti-immigrant sentiment has long been a critical dynamic in Europe's history, one mostly overlooked in standard European historiographies until the 1960s.[16] Anti-immigrant sentiment and attacks occurred in each of the major immigration phases of the last 200 years across Europe. No labor-receiving country has a clean record—not Switzerland, with its long admirable history of international neutrality, and not even France, the most open to immigration, refugees, and exiles. Critical is the fact that there have always been individuals, groups, organizations, and politicians who believe in making our societies more inclusive of immigrants. History suggests that those fighting for incorporation have succeeded in the long run, even if only partially. Just to focus on the recent past, one-quarter of the French have a foreign-born ancestor three generations removed, and 34 percent of Viennese are either born abroad or have foreign parents. It took active making to transform the hatreds toward foreigners into the urban civic. But it is also the result of constraints in a large city; for instance, to have a reasonably fast public transport system means that it is not feasible to check on the status of all users. A basic and thin rule needs to be met: pay your ticket and you are on. That is the making of the civic as a material condition: all those who meet the thin rule—pay the ticket—can use the public bus or train, regardless of whether they are citizens or tourists, good people or not-so-good people, local residents or visitors from another city.

"European history," is dominated by the image of Europe as a continent of emigration, never of immigration. Yet in the 1700s, when Amsterdam built its polders and cleared its bogs, it brought in workers from northern Germany; when the French developed their vineyards, they brought in Spaniards; workers from the Alps were brought in to help develop Milan and Turin; as were the Irish when London needed help building water and sewage infrastructure. In the 1800s, when Haussmann rebuilt Paris, he brought in Germans and Belgians; when Sweden decided to become a monarchy and needed some good-looking palaces, they brought in Italian stoneworkers; when Switzerland built the Gotthard Tunnel, it brought in Italians; and when Germany built its railroads and steel mills, it brought in Italians and Poles.

At any given time there were multiple significant flows of intra-European migration. All of the workers involved were seen as outsiders, as undesirables, as threats to the community, as people that could never belong. The immigrants were mostly from the same broad cultural group, religious group, and phenotype. Yet they were seen as impossible to assimilate. The French hated the Belgian immigrant workers, saying they were the wrong type of Catholics, and the Dutch saw the German immigrant workers as the wrong type of Protestants. This is a telling fact. It suggests that it is incorrect to argue, as is so often done, that today it is more difficult to integrate immigrants because of their different religion, culture, and phenotype. When all of these factors were similar, anti-immigrant sentiment was as strong as today, and it often led to physical attacks on immigrants.

Yet all along, significant numbers of immigrants did become part of the community, even if it took two or three generations. They often maintained their distinctiveness, yet were still members of the community—part of the complex, highly heterogeneous social order of any developed city.

Today the argument against immigration may be focused on questions of race, religion, and culture, and might seem rational—that cultural and religious distance is the reason for the difficulty of incorporation. But in sifting through the historical and current evidence, we find only new variations on an old passion: the racializing of the outsider as Other. Today the Other is stereotyped by differences of race, religion, and culture. These are equivalent arguments to those made in the past when migrants were broadly of the same religious, racial, and cultural group. Migration hinges on a move between two worlds, even if within a single region or country—such as East Germans moving to West Germany after 1989, where they were often viewed as a different ethnic group with undesirable traits.

What is today's equivalent challenge, one that can force us to go beyond our differences and transform ourselves into urban subjects?

Conclusion

The particularity of today's emergent urban landscape is profoundly different from the old European tradition. This is so even though Europe's worldwide imperial projects remixed European traditions with urban cultures that belonged to other histories and geographies. Yet it shares with that older time the fact of challenges larger than our differences. Therein lies a potential for reinventing that capacity of cities to transform conflict and difference into at least relative openness rather than war and intolerance. But it is not going to be the familiar order of the open city and of the civic as we have come to represent it, especially in the European tradition.

My sense is rather that the major challenges that confront cities (and society generally) have increasingly strong feedback loops that in fact contribute to the disassembling of the old civic urban order. Asymmetric war, as discussed earlier, is perhaps one of the most acute versions of this dynamic in cities that are part of the active theater of war. And the "War on Terror" at home extends the distortions of war deep inside the United States and Europe.

Yet this mix of conditions can generate ironic turns of events. These challenges affect both rich and poor, immigrants and citizens, women and men, and thereby contain their own specific potential for making novel platforms for urban action. Addressing them will demand that everybody joins the effort. Further, while sharp economic inequalities, racisms, and religious intolerance have long existed, they are also local mobilizers for civic participation in a context where the center—whether the imperial center, the national state, or the city's rich and powerful—no longer holds in the old ways. Similarly, the abuses of power by the state on its own people in the name of fighting terrorism can create coalitions, bringing together residents who may have thought they could never collaborate.

These negative conditions can forge a process that can transcend class, race, and religion in particular settings and dynamics. But it cannot easily do this in a large California corporate farm or a suburb. It is a process that needs the city, and there it can make subjects that are above all urban subjects.

This text is based on several publications in which the reader can find extensive bibliographic and empirical materials: Saskia Sassen, *Territory, Authority, Rights: From Medieval to Global Assemblages* (Princeton, NJ: Princeton University Press, 2008, especially chapters 6, 7, and 8); Sassen, "When the City Itself Becomes a Technology of War," *Theory, Culture & Society*, vol. 27, no. 6 (2010): 33–50 ; "The Global City: Enabling Economic Intermediation and Bearing Its Costs" *City &* *Community* 15, no. 2 (June 2016); http://www.theguardian.com/cities/2015/nov/24/who-owns-our-cities-and-why-this-urban-takeover-should-concern-us-all; http://www.huffingtonpost.com/2015/01/17/paris-attacks-frontline_n_6479120.html; and Digital formations of the powerful and the powerless, http://dx.doi.org/10.1080/1369118X.2012.667912.

1 Saskia Sassen, "Does the City Have Speech?" *Public Culture* 25, 2 (2013): 209–21.

2 The emergent landscape I am describing promotes a multiplication of diverse spatio-temporal framings and diverse normative (mini)orders where once the dominant logic was oriented toward producing (grand) unitary national spatial, temporal, and normative framings (Sassen, *Territory, Authority, Rights*, chapters 8 and 9). This proliferation of specialized orders extends even inside the state apparatus. I argue that we can no longer speak of "the" state, and hence of "the" national state versus "the" global order. There is a novel type of segmentation inside the state apparatus, with a growing and increasingly privatized executive branch of government aligned with specific global actors, notwithstanding nationalist speeches, and a hollowing out of the legislature whose effectiveness is at risk of becoming confined to fewer and more domestic matters (Sassen, *Territory, Authority, Rights*, chapter 4).

3 With globalization and digitization–and all the specific elements they entail–global cities do emerge as such strategic sites for making norms and identities. Some reflect extreme power, such as the global managerial elites, and others reflect innovation under extreme duress, notably much of what happens in immigrant neighborhoods. While the strategic transformations are sharply concentrated in global cities, many are also engendered (besides being diffused) in cities at lower orders of national urban hierarchies.

4 In contrast, in the 1930s until the 1970s, when mass manufacturing dominates, cities had lost strategic functions and were not the site for creative institutional innovations. The strategic sites were the large factory at the heart of the larger process of mass manufacturing and mass consumption. The factory and the government were the strategic sites where the crucial dynamics producing the major institutional innovations of the epoch were located. The large Fordist factory and the mines emerge as key sites for the making of a modern working class and a syndicalist project; it is not always the city that is the site for making norms and identities.

5 Emphasizing this multiplication of partial assemblages contrasts with much of the globalization literature that has tended to assume the binary of the global versus the national. In this literature the national is understood as a unit. I emphasize that the global can also be constituted inside the national–that is, the global city. Further, the focus in the globalization literature tends to be on the powerful global institutions that have played a critical role in implementing the global corporate economy and have reduced the power of "the" state. In contrast, I also emphasize that particular components of the state have actually gained power because they have to do the work of implementing policies necessary for a global corporate economy. This is another reason for valuing the more encompassing normative order that a city can (though does not necessarily) generate.

6 For a fuller development of this subject, see Sassen, "When the City Itself Becomes a Technology of War."

7 I derived these numbers from the annual country reports. U.S. Department of State, *Annual Report on Global Terrorism* (Washington, D.C.: Bureau of Public Affairs, Office of Strategic Communications).

8 Mary Kaldor, *New and Old Wars,* 2nd ed. (Cambridge, MA: Polity Press, 2006).

9 Even if the nuclear threat to cities has remained hypothetical since 1945, cities remain highly vulnerable to two kinds of very distinct threats. The first one is the specialized aerial attack of new computer-targeted weaponry, which has been employed "selectively" in places like Baghdad or Belgrade. The second is terrorist attacks.

10 One exception is the past two years of intensive destruction of Aleppo's section controlled by the uprising; it is an extreme case of horrifying mass murder and Assad will most probably be treated by history far more harshly than the U.S. government, which brought about much more destruction and death since WWII.

11 A separate source for unilateral restraint is tactical: Thus theorists of war posit that also the superior military force should, for tactical reasons, signal to its enemy that it has not used its full power.

12 Sassen, *Territory, Authority, Rights*, chapter 8. And, from a larger angle than the one that concerns me here, when great powers fail in this self-restraint we have what John Mearsheimer has called the tragedy of great powers. See Mearsheimer, *The Tragedy of Great Power Politics* (New York: W.W. Norton, 2001).

13 This dual process of urbanization of war and militarization of urban life unsettles the meaning of the urban. Peter Marcuse writes that "the War on terrorism is leading to a continued downgrading of the quality of life in U.S. cities, visible changes in urban form, the loss of public use of public space, restriction on free movement within and to cities, particularly for members of darker skinned groups, and the decline of open popular participation in the governmental planning and decision-making process." See Marcuse, "Urban Form and Globalization after September 11th: The View from New York," *International Journal of Urban and Regional Research* 26, no. 3 (2002): 596–606.

Second, it questions the role of cities as welfare providers. The imperative of security means a shift in political priorities. It implies a cut or a relative decrease in budgets dedicated to social welfare, education, health, infrastructure development, economic regulation, and planning. These two trends, in turn, challenge the very concept of citizenship (Sassen, *Territory, Authority, Rights*, chapter 6).

14 Sassen, *Guests and Aliens* (New York: New Press, 1999).

15 Sassen, *Territory, Authority, Rights*; see also chapters 4 and 5 for a diversity of other domains, besides immigration, where this holds.

16 This section is based on Sassen, *Guests and Aliens*.

Insurgent Urbanity and the Political City

Erik Swyngedouw

"The people is those who, refusing to be the population, disrupt the system."[1]

"Change life! Change Society! These ideas lose completely their meaning without producing an appropriate space."[2]

Insurgent Architects: Staging Equality

The Taksim Square revolt in Istanbul and the Brazilian urban insurgencies were in full swing at the time of writing, with uncertain and largely unpredictable outcomes. Tahrir Square—where a revolutionary transformation of Egypt took root—later experienced a much rawer form of insurgency, finally crushed when tanks and soldiers marched in and a coup d'état displaced the first democratically elected government of Egypt in decades. While Western leaders boldly applauded the Egyptian insurgents in 2011, claiming that "the Egyptian people" had finally risen up against a dictatorship (long held in place by Western powers) and demanded democracy, these same leaders remained conspicuously moderate in their critique of the military takeover and deafeningly silent on the Turkish revolts.

These urban rebellions are part of a long sequence of political insurgencies that erupted rather unexpectedly after Mohamed Bouazizi's self-immolation on December 17, 2010 sparked the Tunisian Revolution. During the magical year of 2011, a seemingly never-ending proliferation of urban rebellions of many kinds and in a wide range of different historical and geographical contexts profoundly disturbed the apparently cozy neoliberal status quo and disquieted various economic and political elites. The end of history, boldly proclaimed by Francis Fukuyama in the early 1990s, proved to be rather short-lived as incipient political movements reflected, albeit in often contradictory and confusing manners, a profound discontent with the state of the situation and choreographed—in spectacular Bakhtinian outbursts—new urban modes of being-in-common. Such urban uprisings have continued to erupt ever since, as the recent examples of Hong Kong, Santiago de Chile, or St. Louis testify.

Indeed, 2011 was an extraordinary urban year. Not since the 1960s have so many people in vastly different cities across the world taken to the streets, occupying squares and experimenting with new ways of organizing the urban commons. There is an uncanny choreographic affinity between the eruptions of discontent in cities as diverse as Istanbul, Cairo, Tunis, Athens, Madrid, Lyon, Lisbon, Rome, New York, Tel Aviv, Chicago, London, Berlin, Thessaloniki, Stockholm, Barcelona, Montreal, Oakland, São Paulo, or Hong Kong, among many others. A wave of deeply political protest is rolling through the world's cities, whereby those who do not count demand a new constituent process for producing space politically. Under the generic name of "real democracy now," the heterogeneous mix of gatherers exposed the variegated "wrongs" and spiraling inequalities of neoliberalization and actually existing instituted democratic governance. The era of urban social movements, celebrated by Manuel Castells's seminal *The City and the Grassroots,* seems to be over, as a much more politicized mobilization, animated by insurgent urban architects, is increasingly choreographing the contemporary theater of urban struggle and conflict.[3]

For Jacques Rancière, democratizing the polis is inaugurated when those who do not count stage the count, perform the process of being counted and, thereby, initiate a rupture in the order of things, "in the distribution of the sensible," such that things cannot go on as before.[4] From this perspective, democratization is a performative act that both stages and defines equality, exposes a "wrong," and aspires to a transformation of the senses and of the sensible, to render common sense what was non-sensible before. Democratization, he contends, is a disruptive affair whereby the *ochlos* (the rabble, the scum, the outcasts, "the part of no part") stage to be part of the *demos* and, in doing so, inaugurate a new ordering of times and places, a process by which those who do no count, who do not exist as part of the polis, become visible and audible, stage the count, and assert their egalitarian existence.

There are many uncounted today. Alain Badiou refers to them as the "inexistent," the masses of the people that have no say, "decide absolutely nothing, have only a fictional voice in the matter of the decisions that decide their fate."[5] The scandal of actually existing instituted (post-)democracy in a world choreographed by oppression, exploitation, and extraordinary inequalities resides precisely in rendering masses of people inexistent, politically unheard, without a recognized voice.

For Badiou, "a change of world is real when an inexistent of the world starts to exist in the same world with maximum intensity."[6] In doing so, the order of the sensible is shaken and the kernel for a new common sense, a new mode of being in common, becomes present in the world, makes its presence sensible. It is the appearance of another world in the world. Was it not precisely the sprawling urban insurgencies and rebellions since 2011 that sparked off with rarely seen intensity that ignited a new sensibility about the polis as a democratic and potentially democratizing space? This appearance of the inexistent, staging the count of the uncounted, is precisely, it seems to me, what the polis, the political city, is all about.

As Foucault reminds us, the people (as a political category) are those who, refusing to be the population, disrupt the system. The notion of democracy introduced above is one that foregrounds intervention and rupture, sustained by an axiomatic assumption of equality. Democratization, then, becomes the act of the few who become the material and metaphorical stand-in for the many, the 99 percent; they stand for the dictatorship of the democratic—direct and egalitarian—against the despotism of the "democracy" of the elites—representative and inegalitarian. Is it not precisely these spiraling urban insurgencies that brought to the fore the irreducible distance between the democratic as the immanence of the presumption of equality and its performative spatialized staging on the one hand, and democracy as an instituted form of oligarchic governing on the other? Do the urban revolts of the past few years not foreground the abyss between "the democratic" and "democracy"? Is it not precisely the reemergence of the proto-political in the urban revolts that signals an urgent need to reaffirm the urban, the polis, as a political space, and not just a space for the bio-political governing of city life?

Of course the resistance against the Morsi regime, the attacks on Erdogan's combination of religious conservatism with a booming neoliberalization of the urban process (stunningly well captured in the documentary *Ecumenopolis: City Without Limits*[7]), the spiraling discontent over the public bailouts and severe austerity regimes mounted by assorted states and international organizations to save the global financial system (and the very socially embodied agents that sustained its growth) from imminent collapse after the speculative bubble that had nurtured unprecedented inequalities and extraordinary concentration of wealth finally burst in 2008. The quilting points that sparked the rebellions were highly variegated too. A threatened park and a few trees in Istanbul, a religious-authoritarian but nonetheless democratically elected regime in Egypt, massive austerity in Greece, Portugal, and Spain, social and financial mayhem in the United Kingdom or the United States, a rise in the price of public transport tickets in São Paulo, the further commodification of higher education in Montreal.

Yet the urban insurgents quickly turned their particular grievances into a wholesale attack on the instituted order, on the unbridled commodification of urban life in the interests of the few, on the unequal choreographies of existing representational democracy. The particular demands transformed seamlessly into a universalizing staging for something different, however diffuse, inchoate, and unarticulated this may be. The assembled groups ended up without particular demands and thereby demanded everything, nothing less then the wholesale transformation of the instituted order. They staged in their sociospatial acting new ways of practicing equality and democracy, experimented with innovative and creative ways of being together in the city, and prefigured, both in practice and in theory, new ways of distributing goods, accessing services, producing healthy environments, organizing debate, managing conflict, practicing ecologically saner lifestyles, and negotiating urban space in an emancipatory manner.

These insurgencies are decidedly urban; they may be the embryonic manifestation of the immanence of a new urban commons, one always in the making, aspiring to produce a new urbanity through intense meetings and encounters of a multitude, one that aspires to spatialization, that is to universalization. Such universalization can never be totalizing, as the lines of demarcation are clearly drawn—lines that separate the "us" (as multitude) from the "them," those who mobilize all they can to make sure nothing really changes, captured neatly in the slogan of the 99 percent versus the 1 percent. The democratizing minority stands here in strict opposition to the majoritarian rule of instituted democracy.

These proto-political but decidedly urbanized attempts to produce a new commons offer perhaps a glimpse of the theoretical and practical urban agenda ahead. Do they not call for an urgent reconsideration of both urban theory and urban praxis? Does their acting not signal a clarion call to radically displace what has hitherto been defined as urban studies? To return the intellectual gaze to consider again what the polis has always been—the site for political encounter and place for enacting the new, the improbable, things often considered impossible by those who do not wish to see any change? To invest the site for experimentation with the staging and production of new radical imaginaries for what urban democratic being-in-common might be all about? Recentering the urban political therefore is for me one of the fundamental intellectual demands made by today's urban life.

The insurgencies surely troubled the assembled elites of the world. The 2012 Davos World Economic Forum's Risk Report considered these proliferating political movements—what the report referred to as "seeds of dystopia"— among the key risks affecting the world.[8] The assembled elites at the annual Davos Forum were clearly shaken by this intrusion in what had been for years a rather smooth and rarely contested process of organizing the world's social and ecological geographies according to their neoliberal fantasies. For Badiou, in contrast, these movements represent a potential "rebirth of history" in the form of a new democratizing and egalitarian political sequence, unfolding in the interstices of a hegemonic process of depoliticization and post-democratization. The insurgents' rallying cry for "Democracy Now!," rather than articulating specific social or economic demands addressed to the elites, turns them into explicitly "political" insurgent movements. Henri Lefebvre's 1960s call for "The Right to the City" is translated here in directly political demands, claiming "The Right to the Polis," a new democratic constituent process, as political space. These insurgent movements call indeed for revisiting the nature of "the political," its theorization and configuration—a call that brings to the fore the dialectic between depoliticization and repoliticization and its inscription in the dynamics of urban space. This politicization of space is of course precisely what Lefebvre had in mind when he wrote:

> What, then, of the political status of space? No sooner has
> space assumed a political character than its depoliticization
> appears on the agenda. A politicized space destroys
> the political conditions that brought it about, because the
> management and appropriation of such a space run counter
> to the state as well as to political parties; they call for
> other forms of management—loosely speaking, for "self-
> management"—of territorial units, towns, urban communi-
> ties, regions, and so on. Space thus exacerbates the
> conflict inherent in the political arena and in the state *per
> se*. It lends great impetus to the introduction of the anti-
> political into the political, and promotes a political critique
> which lends its weight to the trend towards the self-
> destruction of the "moment of politics."[9]

The budding reinscription of the political in the urban landscape, articulated around the signifier of "equality," demands revisiting the recent history of critical urban theory and its emphasis on "sociological" markers of inequality and the dynamics of their production. There is widespread agreement today that urban theory and its multiple allied practices of planning, architecture, design, urban policy, and urban economic development are in a serious crisis (together with so many other acute environmental, social, cultural, and economic crises that we face). This indeed calls for an urgent reconsideration of what we, urban intellectuals, think and—perhaps more important—do.

From Urban Critical Theory to the Political City

Much of the recent history (since the 1970s) of critical urban theory has been marked by a commitment to a politics of emancipatory transformation and to the creation of socially just urban geographies.[10] Successive bodies of critical thought intervened in the existing state of urban theory and practice, reframed and transgressed how urban theory ought to be done, and what kind of urbanism ought to be practiced. Implicit and occasionally explicit reference to normative notions of equality, justice, and freedom motivated the impulse to further the formation, both theoretically and practically, of a genuinely humanizing urbanity.

Of course, the epistemological and ontological parameters of what constitutes proper and properly critical emancipatory enquiry and politics have shifted over the past decades, as indeed did the contours and dynamics of the urbanization process itself. Many of the theoretical and philosophical foundations of critical emancipatory thought have been examined, reexamined, reformulated, and often radically changed as an early emphasis on class and the political-economy of class-based urbanization was gradually extended to include (and occasionally replaced by) a wider range of other, often competing, theoretical accounts and political claims, most notably around identitarian inscriptions like race, ethnicity, age, sexual preference, subalterity, and gender, or around attempts to produce more inclusive and participatory forms of urban governing.

Surprisingly enough, relatively little critical reflection has been devoted to what constitutes the political domain, to what and where "the political" is or might be. In most of urban theory's critical theoretical apparatuses, the political is usually assumed to emerge from what I would call a broadly "socio-spatial" analysis. Put simply, a critical theory of the "social" (despite the wide-ranging dispute over what exactly constitutes "the social") is considered to be the foundational basis from which an urban politics can (or will) emerge, both theoretically and practically. It is the socio-spatial condition and the excavation of the procedures of its inauguration that opens up and charts the terrain of political intervention and that striates the political subject. Substantive critical social theory, whether Marxist or post-Marxist, structuralist or post-structuralist, essentialist or non-essentialist, centered or decentered, presumably opens the terrain for proper political intervention and action; the debate usually focusing on how exactly one or the other epistemological framework constitutes the foundation for a more or less empowering, emancipatory, and/or transformative urban politics.

And every twist and turn in the meandering of critical theory over the last decades announced its own transformative political subject with its geographically constituted tactics: the figure of the proletarian for Marxists, woman for feminists, the creative class/cosmopolitan multitude for (neo-) liberals, the subaltern subject for post-colonial theorists, heterogeneously assembled human/post-human actants for Latourians, the decentered subject for Lacanians. From these perspectives, the political is seen as an emergent field that derives from substantive analysis: politically correct tactics flow from theoretically correct analysis, and critical urban theory proposes both the frame and the location of the properly political. Emancipatory politics, so it seems, arise out of substantive analysis, of grasping the contours and dynamics of the states we are in. Such analysis situates the intellectual, the philosopher-king, in the driver's seat of radical urban politics.

These perspectives do not present the political as an autonomous domain of engagement and a practice. On the contrary, its contents and practices "derive" from processes operative in other domains. Put in philosophical terms, the political is viewed as ontic, that is the perceptible organization, tactics, and strategies of actors such as political parties, politicians, institutions, civil society organizations, urban social movement, unions, business elites, artefacts, and the like. These "perceptible" dynamics, in turn, shape and are shaped by the ephemeral dynamics of a restless urban landscape that is increasingly taking planetary forms. Their acting can be understood and hence interfered with through the mobilization of the correct urban substantive theory.

In contrast to this, I contend, together with Badiou, that there is nothing that can any longer be done with social theory as a basis for recentering the political. The various insurgent urban movements that dot the landscape of planetary urbanism testify precisely to the bankruptcy of critical urban thought and urge us to think "the political" again as an autonomous and immanent field of action. Indeed, for Badiou, socioeconomic "analysis and politics are absolutely disconnected": the former is a matter for expertise and implies hierarchy; the latter is not. An absolute separation has to be maintained, he argues, between "science and politics, of analytic description and political prescription."[11] For Badiou, the political is not a reflection of something else, like the cultural, the social, or the economic. Instead, it is the affirmation of the capacity of each and all to act politically. It is a site open for occupation by those who call it into being, claim its occupation and stage "equality," irrespective of the "place" they occupy within the social edifice. It is manifested in the process of subjectification, in the "passage to the act." This is precisely what the new (urban) political movements practice.

The (Urban) Political Re-scripted

In what follows, I shall explore further this post-foundational understanding of the political that foregrounds the notion of equality as the axiomatic yet contingent foundation of democracy, that considers égaliberté as an unconditional democratic demand, and that sees the political as immanent process expressed in the rupture of any given socio-spatial order by exposing a "wrong" and staging "equality."[12] This "wrong" is a condition in which the axiomatic principle of equality is perverted through the institution of an order —what Rancière refers to as "police"—that is always necessarily oligarchic.

The political, therefore, is not about expressing demands to the elites to rectify inequalities or unfreedoms, the daily choreography of interest and conflict intermediation in public policy arrangements, or a call on "the state" to undertake action, but, in contrast, it is the demand to be counted, named, and recognized, theatrically and publicly staged by those "that do not count." It is the articulation of a voice that demands its place in the spaces of the police order: it appears, for example, when undocumented workers shout "we are here, therefore we are from here" and demand their place within the socio-political edifice, or when the Spanish *indignados* demand "Democracia real ya!" and the Occupy movements claim to be the 99 percent that have no voice. These are the evental time-spaces from where a new democratizing political sequence may unfold. Insurgent democratic politics, therefore, are radically anti-utopian; they are not about fighting for a utopian future, but are precisely about bringing into being, spatializing, what is already promised by the very principle upon which the political is constituted: equalitarian emancipation.

The political act, then, is the voice of "floating subjects that deregulate all representations of places and portions"[13] and that occupies, organizes, and restructures space:

> In the end everything in politics turns on the distribution
> of spaces. What are these places? How do they function?
> Why are they there? Who can occupy them? For me, political
> action always acts upon the social as the litigious distri-
> bution of places and roles. It is always a matter of knowing
> who is qualified to say what a particular place is and what
> is done to it."[14]

The political, therefore, always operates from a certain minimal distance from the State/the police and invariably meets with the violence inscribed in the functioning of the police. Its spatial markers are not the parliament, meeting room, or council chamber, but the square, the housing estate, the people's assembly, the university campus, the factory floor. Insurgent urbanity cannot be other than provoking the wrath of the state and has to confront, stare in the face, the violence that marks the rebirth of history. Insurrectional interruption precisely incites the objective inegalitarian violence of the instituted order to become subjective, to become visible. Politics is indeed the moment or process of confrontation with the police order, the meeting ground between police and the political when the principle of equality confronts a wrong instituted through the police order.

The space of the political is to disturb the socio-spatial ordering by rearranging it with those who stand in for "the people" or the community.[15] It is a particular that stands for the whole of the community and aspires toward universalization. The rebels on Tahrir or Taksim Square were not the Egyptian or Turkish population; while being a minority, they stood materially and metaphorically for the Egyptian and Turkish people. The political emerges when the few claim the name of the many, the community as a whole, and are recognized as such. The emergence of political space is always specific, concrete, particular, but stands as the metaphorical condensation of the universal.

And of course, politics is about the production of spaces and the recognition of the principle of dissensus. Politics understood in the above terms rejects a naturalization of the political, signals that a political "passage à l'acte" does not rely on expert knowledge and administration (the partition of the sensible), on rearranging the choreographies of governance, on organizing "good governance," but on a disruption of the field of vision and of the distribution of functions and spaces on the basis of the principle of equality. This view of politics as a space of dissensus, for enunciating difference and for negotiating conflict, stands in sharp contrast to the consolidating consensual "post-politicizing" rituals of contemporary neoliberal "good" governance that combines a politicization of "the economy" with an economization of "politics" under the aegis of a naturalized market-based configuration of the production and distribution of goods and services. It unhinges a deep-seated belief that expert knowledge and managerial capacity can be mobilized to enhance the democratic governance of urban space, to limit the horizon of intervention to consensualizing post-democratic management of the state of affairs.[16] Of course, the above argument raises the question of what to do. How to reclaim the political from the debris of consensual autocratic post-democracy?

"Democracia Real Ya!": The Return of the Political

The notion of the political presented above centers on interruption, dissensus, polemic, and the performative practices of staging equality, articulated around the constitutive dissensual heterogeneities that split "the people," traverse the myth of the One, the singular. It rejects the myth of an archae-political possibility of an organic, sutured, nonfractured community.

The form of politicization predicated upon universalizing egalitarian demands cuts directly though the radical politics that characterize so much of the current forms and theorizations of urban resistance. Rather than embracing the multitude of singularities and the plurality of possible modes of becoming, rather than considering the ethical stance as the ultimate horizon of and for political action, this approach starts from the suturing attempts of the existing police order and its associated social relations; rather than reveling in the immanence of imperial transformation, an immanence to which there is no outside (à la Hardt and Negri[17]), rather than the micropolitics of dispersed resistances, alternative practices, and affects (à la Holloway[18] or Critchley[19]), the view explored in this contribution foregrounds division and exclusion and emphasizes the passage to the act through a political truth procedure that necessitates taking sides.[20]

Such egalitarian-democratic demands and practices, scandalous in the representational order of the police, are nonetheless eminently realizable. These passions for the Real can be thought and practiced irrespective of any substantive urban social theorization—it is the urban political in itself at work.[21] It is an active process of intervention through which (public) space is reconfigured and through which—if successful—a new socio-spatial order is inaugurated. The taking and remaking of urban public spaces has indeed always been the hallmark of emancipatory geopolitical trajectories.

In *The Rebirth of History*, Badiou considers the proliferation of these urban rebellions and their insurgent architecture to be a sign of a potential return of the universal idea of freedom, solidarity, equality, and emancipation.[22] In his dissection of the events, he argues that these events are marked by procedures of *intensification, contraction, and localization*. A political idea/imaginary cannot find grounding without localization. A political moment is therefore always placed, localized, in a public space, a housing estate, a factory occupation. Squares and other common spaces have historically always been the sites for performing and enacting emancipatory practices. Such localization of the proto-political event invariably mobilizes enormous vital energies for a sustained period of time. All manner of people come together in an intensive explosion of Bakhtinian acting, of an intensified process of being that inaugurates a process of political subjectification. And finally, this intensity operates in and through the collective

PERFORMING PLAY

How do we perform play in public? In 2015, the *Brisbane Times* ran a story on the Brisbane Ultimate Chess Battle. One interviewee noted the liberating, energizing feeling of playing outside, surrounded by music and markets. Where is play located? What rules are taught, perpetuated, or challenged through play?

PERFORMING PLAY

Historically the summer residence for the Tappan and Ward families of Boston, Tanglewood's
250 acres of land attracts people from around the world to hear world-class musical performances
on the large, manicured lawns.

PERFORMING PLAY

In 2009, *The Guardian* described how, "As the sun dips behind the skyscrapers … Kabukichō, the Japanese capital's red light district, has come out to play." Who loses? Who wins? Vying to be the location for the Olympics resulted in a mandate to close hostess bars and sex clubs at midnight.

PERFORMING PLAY

In 1986, HSBC headquarters in Hong Kong was the most expensive building on the planet. With pressure to construct more than one million square feet, Norman Foster used global prefabrication. In 2015, *The Guardian* noted, "the project conceived as a city-sized Meccano set." How does building design play into geopolitics?

PERFORMING PLAY

On the weekends, Filipino maids use the public granite plaza on the ground floor of HSBC headquarters in Hong Kong for picnicking. What politics are performed and challenged through picnicking in the underbelly of a bank?

Rocinha, the largest *favela* in Brazil, is located in Rio de Janeiro. The 2010 Census quotes a population of 70,000; unofficial estimates are around 180,000. With growing density, where are safe spaces to play? Who performs on what stage? Who is being played? Meanwhile, not far away, the Olympic Games played on.

PERFORMING PLAY

How can spaces be imagined for play? How can spaces of play further promote imagining? Brooklyn Bridge Park, spanning 1.3 miles between Jay Street and Atlantic Avenue, had once been the location of an out-of-use complex for storage and cargo shipping near both the Brooklyn and Manhattan bridges.

The 85 acres of Brooklyn Bridge Park are used day and night. Performances in the park highlight the importance of accessible, open, public spaces. Located adjacent to the East River, the design of the park takes into account the relation between city and water. How can water facilitate play within the urban?

Drawing with chalk on the road, jumping-rope on the sidewalk, or taking photographs from
a stoop—play has the power to create a sense of ownership, safety, and neighborliness.
How have places of play changed or stayed the same throughout generations? What can we
learn from children, of present day or yesteryear?

togetherness of a wide variety of individuals who in their multiplicity and intense process of becoming political subjects stand for the metaphorical condensation of The People (as political category).

However, such intense and contracted localized practices can only ever be an event, original but ultimately pre-political. It does (not yet) constitute a political sequence. A political truth procedure or a political sequence, for Badiou, unfolds when in the name of equality, fidelity to an event is declared, a fidelity that, although always particular, aspires to become public, to universalize. It is a wager on the truth of the egalitarian political sequence staged in the event, a truth that can be only verified ex-post. A political event can only be discerned as such retroactively.

Such political sequence concentrates the enunciation of demands that lie beyond the symbolic order of the police; demands that cannot be symbolized within the frame of reference of the police and, therefore, would necessitate a transformation in and of the police to permit symbolization to occur. Yet these are demands that are eminently sensible and feasible when the frame of the symbolic order is shifted, when the parallax gap between what is (the constituted symbolic order of the police) and what can be (the reconstituted symbolic order made possible through a shift in vantage points, one that starts from the partisan universalizing principle of equality) is clear for all to see and fully endorsed. It is the sort of demand that "restructure[s] the entire social space."[23] And this requires sustained politicization. The key political question then is what happens when the squares are cleared, the tents removed and energies dissipated, when the dream is over and the dawn of everyday life breaks again. In other words, what is required now in the aftermath of the eruptions since 2011 and what needs to be thought through is if and how these proto-political localized events can turn into a spatialized political "truth" procedure.

Answering this revolves squarely around questions of political organization, the arena of struggle and the construction of new political collectivities. While the 19th- and 20th-century markers of emancipatory political struggle centered on the party as organizational conduit, the state as the arena to conquer, and the proletarian as political subject, these markers do not appear to be performative today. They may have to be relegated to the dustbin of history. The urgent tasks to undertake now for those who maintain fidelity to the political events choreographed in the new insurrectional spaces revolve around inventing new modes and practices of collective political organization: organizing the concrete modalities of spatializing and universalizing the Idea provisionally materialized in these localized insurrectional events; mobilizing a wide range of new political subjects who are not afraid to imagine a different commons; demanding the impossible;

staging the new and confronting the violence that will inevitably intensify as those who insist on maintaining the present order realize that their days might be numbered. The political successes of firebrand political movements like Syriza in Greece and Podemos in Spain may point in this direction, as do the unexpected victories of new political movements in Barcelona and Madrid. While staging equality in public squares and commons space is a vital moment, the process of transformation requires the slow but unstoppable production of new forms of spatialization quilted around materializing the claims of equality, freedom, and solidarity. This is the promise of the return of the political embryonically manifested in insurgent urban practices.

1 Michel Foucault, *Security, Territory, Population: Lectures at the Collège de France 1977–1978* (London: Palgrave Macmillan, 2007), 43–44.

2 Henri Lefebvre, *The Production of Space* (Oxford: Blackwell, 1991), 59.

3 Manuel Castells, *The City and the Grassroots: A Cross-Cultural Theory of Urban Social Movements* (Berkeley: University of California Press, 1993).

4 Jacques Rancière, *Disagreement: Politics and Philosophy* (Minneapolis: University of Minnesota Press, 1998).

5 Alain Badiou, *The Rebirth of History: Times of Riots and Uprisings* (London: Verso, 2012), 56.

6 Ibid.

7 See http://www.ekumenopolis.net/#/en_US, accessed 22 July 2013.

8 World Economic Forum, *Global Risks 2012 – Seventh Edition* (Geneva: Risk Response Network, 2012).

9 Lefebvre, *Production*, 416.

10 Emblematically initiated by David Harvey, *Social Justice and the City* (London: E. Arnold, 1973), and Manuel Castells, *The Urban Question* (London: E. Arnold, 1977).

11 Alain Badiou, *La Organisation Politique*, 28, no. 2, cited in Peter Hallward, *Badiou – A Subject to Truth* (Minneapolis: University of Minnesota Press, 2003).

12 Etienne Balibar, *La Proposition de l'Égaliberté* (Paris: Presses Universitaires de France, 2010).

13 Rancière, *Disagreement,* 99–100.

14 Jacques Rancière, "Politics and Aesthetics: An Interview," *Angelaki* 8 (2003): 201.

15 Jacques Rancière, "Ten Theses on Politics," *Theory & Event* 5 (2001).

16 For a more in-depth discussion of the processes of post-politicization and post-democratization, see Erik Swyngedouw, "The Antinomies of the Post-Political City: In Search of a Democratic Politics of Environmental Production," *International Journal of Urban and Regional Research* 33 (2009): 601–620; Erik Swyngedouw, "Interrogating Post-Democracy: Reclaiming Egalitarian Political Spaces," *Political Geography* 30 (2011): 370–380.

17 Michael Hardt and Antonio Negri, *Multitude* (London: Penguin Books, 2004).

18 John Holloway, *Change the World without Taking Power: The Meaning of Revolution Today* (London: Pluto, 2002).

19 Simon Critchley, *Infinitely Demanding: Ethics of Commitment, Politics of Resistance* (London: Verso, 2007).

20 Jodi Dean, *Žižek's Politics* (New York: Routledge, 2006).

21 See Alain Badiou, *The Century* (Cambridge, UK: Polity Press, 2007).

22 For further details, see Badiou, *Rebirth*.

23 Slavoj Žižek, *The Ticklish Subject: The Absent Centre of Political Ontology* (London: Verso, 1999), 208.

The Fair City: Can We Design Neighborhood Equality?

Robert J. Sampson

That income inequality has risen sharply in recent times is undisputed. What is surprising is that inequality has quickly risen to the forefront of both academic and public debate.[1] Embodied by the "Occupy" protests on Wall Street in late 2011 that rippled outward to many countries, a populist movement emerged that continues to agitate for reforms to reduce inequality. Major policy elites have also entered the debate. In the United States, the issue of how to respond to inequality has been raised by President Obama, and, with the election of Mayor Bill de Blasio in New York City as one highly visible example, leaders at the local level are taking bold aim at policies to reduce inequality. Housing in particular has come under scrutiny, and urban planning is suddenly in play more generally: Can we design the "fair city?"[2]

In this essay, I place the quest for equity against the backdrop of existing evidence. Although I am not an expert on urban planning, social movements, or housing, as a sociologist my inclination is to think first about the structural impediments to designing equality. To be sure, I am fully in support of efforts to reduce inequality by trying new policies and reinforcing ones that work. But to be effective, policies need to be cognizant of deep structures, often many years in the making. With this in mind, I offer five propositions for consideration as cities go about the hard business of confronting inequality. I focus on neighborhood inequality in the United States, starting with general observations that bear implications for urban design before turning to the rise of mixed-income housing policies as a proposed mechanism for inducing more equitable cities.

Inequality Is Multidimensional

There is considerable social inequality between neighborhoods, especially in terms of socioeconomic position and racial segregation. Particularly in the United States, these factors are connected, in that concentrated disadvantage often coincides with the geographic isolation of racial minority and immigrant groups. But violence, incarceration, and multiple health-related problems tend to come bundled together at the neighborhood level as well. These problems are also predicted by neighborhood characteristics such as the concentration of poverty, racial isolation, and single-parent families, and, to a lesser extent, rates of residential and housing instability. I have come to think of this as the "social matrix of adversity" at the community level, a phenomenon that contradicts the growing tendency to isolate clean causal estimates or manipulate single causes.[3] Something more like a matrix of hyper-advantage exists at the upper end of the spectrum: multiple social indicators of what many would consider progress, such as affluence, computer expertise, and elite occupational attainment, are also clustered geographically. These patterns are seen in many global cities.

Inequality Is Surprisingly Persistent

Although there is always population turnover of individual residents, and poverty and its correlates fluctuate over time, it turns out that if we know where a neighborhood starts out statistically, we can do rather well predicting where it will end up relative to other neighborhoods. Many poor neighborhoods get stuck for decades. The "stickiness" of inequality by place is also notable at the high end. The Gold Coast of Chicago is as golden as ever, and elite neighborhoods from the Upper East Side of New York to Bel Air in Los Angeles are in no danger of even relative decline.

These durable inequalities seem surprising or even paradoxical when we consider the changing American landscape. Poverty is increasing most rapidly in the suburbs, crime has decreased just about everywhere, and gentrification is reshaping many working-class and poor areas of central cities. New York is the poster child these days for crime reduction and a new type of urban renewal. The media and popular culture have focused attention on Brooklyn, for example, highlighting gentrifying neighborhoods that were in despair not long ago. The phenomenon is real, but the fact that it makes the news is precisely the point—"rags to riches" is no more common among neighborhoods than it is among people. For every poor neighborhood on the move, more struggle out of the media glare: durable inequality is the norm.

Residential Selection Is an Engine of Inequality Reproduction

Enduring inequality in the United States is reinforced by homophily, or the tendency of many people to choose to live near others who have similar valued characteristics, and distant from those with disvalued or different characteristics. One might think of this as the "demand" side of inequality, leading to spatial forms of *hierarchy maintenance*. Structural features, such as changes in racial or economic composition, bear on individual appraisals and decisions to move, but so do perceptual and symbolic cues, such as perceived disorder. It may even be that symbolic forms of stigmatization and implicit biases are more pervasive today than direct forms of discrimination in reproducing spatial inequality.

In a kind of self-fulfilling prophecy, neighborhoods thus have effects in part because people and institutions act *as if* neighborhoods matter, further reinforcing the reproduction of inequality by place. Crime, perceived safety, disorder, and school rankings lead to reputations with real consequences. I have argued that neighborhood reputations may well be sturdier than those of individuals (a point not lost on real estate agents), which in turn reinforces inequality.

There is a more general point to be made. The tendency of humans to segregate by place along dimensions of social status (and race or ethnicity, depending on the larger context such as country) has persisted across long time spans and eras despite the transformation of specific boundaries, political regimes, and the physical layout of cities. There are variations, to be sure, but research by archaeologists indicates that spatial divisions were even found in ancient cities.[4] The neoliberal state may exacerbate, but it does not explain, the long spatial divide.

The State Can Mitigate Neighborhood Inequality

Despite individual selection mechanisms, state policies and national contexts nonetheless do induce variations in neighborhood inequality.[5] In Chicago, for example, I have shown that the range of variation in neighborhood concentration at both the bottom and top of the income distribution is greater than in Stockholm. We can think of this as "inequality compression" in Stockholm. Indeed, Chicago's extended range of concentrated disadvantage is unmatched by Stockholm.[6] High-violence neighborhoods in Chicago also have no counterpart in Stockholm. Part of the difference in ecological distributions is arguably due to Swedish policies on community planning, more equitable service allocation, and progressive taxation. The implication is that housing policies and mixed-income policies set by the government are potentially powerful tools for reducing inequality.

But this does not deny local effects. In the Chicago-Stockholm comparison, as neighborhood disadvantage rises, violence does as well, in both cities and in a similar nonlinear way. The collective efficacy of residents is also negatively related to violence in both cities, independent of traditional demographic and socioeconomic controls.[7] Pitting neighborhood against the state is thus unproductive. Both "top down" and "bottom up" processes are at work, and even national policies (e.g., the Affordable Care Act in the United States) are mediated by local institutions.

Mixed-Income Housing Policies Need to Confront Neighborhood Dynamics

Based on a combination of faith in government (or "State") approaches and considerable research linking concentrated poverty to compromised well-being, policymakers and academics have argued that increasing the presence of higher-income neighbors through the mixed-income redevelopment of high-poverty neighborhoods—along with the movement of poor people out of concentrated public housing—will improve the lives of the poor. In other words, by designing the income mix of neighborhoods through policy levers available to the government, the idea is that behavior can be changed and inequality lessened.

Although often implicit and not a theory in the formal sense, this popular policy move reflects a set of theoretical assumptions about neighborhood change.[8,9] First, it assumes that low-income residents benefit from having higher-income neighbors as models of middle-class behavior in the realms of family, education, and employment that are not available in the absence of redevelopment. Second, it assumes that proximity to higher-income neighbors leads to the formation of social ties, which residents will use to obtain social leverage or social support. Third, it assumes that higher-income residents will enforce informal social control and participate in formal neighborhood organizations. Fourth, at the aggregate level, it assumes that improvements in social organization due to declining neighborhood poverty rates will not be offset by residential instability and ethnic heterogeneity, which can undermine social organization. Finally, mixed-income policy implicitly assumes a static equilibrium with regard to intervention effects; it also does not account for the interdependencies among neighborhoods in social mechanisms, and the macro-level political and social environment, that can reinforce economic and ethnic segregation.

I would suggest that none of these assumptions is well founded in the research literature at present. In fact, several assumptions are contradicted. For example, recent ethnographic research has examined the unintended consequences of the HOPE VI housing intervention (designed by the Department of Housing and Urban Development, or HUD) in targeted developments and residents of nontargeted developments in the vicinity. In the Boston neighborhoods of Mission Main (a reconstructed HOPE VI development) and Alice Taylor (a public housing development that did not receive a HOPE VI grant), Jonke shows that the policy led to *decreased* interactions between Mission Main and their neighbors in public housing across the street.[10] Jonke attributed this to a schism created by the intervention itself, with residents of the adjacent project, Alice Taylor, stigmatized as "disorderly" and disreputable, which produced different cultural meanings and sense of community on each side. A similar lack of social interactions across class lines was found in another mixed-income development in Boston.[11]

Or consider the potential displacement of criminal activity or poverty following the demolition and redevelopment of high-poverty neighborhoods, such as the teardown of large-scale public housing that occurred in Chicago under the auspices of the Chicago Housing Authority and the federal government. If mixed-income redevelopment lowers crime in one area by shifting it to another area, either through the movement of people or gang-related activity, the overall welfare gains for the city are lower than what one would predict from studying only the revitalized neighborhood(s). Similarly, if poverty is simply shifted to the suburbs or other city neighborhoods, the net policy gain is not clear.

Another example of durable inequality and urban design is provided by the "Moving to Opportunity" (MTO) housing experiment in Chicago. Despite the good intentions of the HUD-based MTO intervention, over half (55 percent) of the experimental group in the study ended up in just 4 percent of all tracts in the Chicago metropolitan area. An equivalent 55 percent of the control group ended up in only 3 percent of all tracts.[12] The tracts for both groups were also well above the national average of poverty and typically in decline. This highly constricted movement conforms to the pattern of mobility among non-MTO poor families.[13]

In short, the urban planning efforts and policy levers available to the State operate within highly constrained environments. Poor families, whether or not subsidized by housing vouchers, tend to move within metropolitan structures of sharp inequality and racial segregation[14,15]—a process I called "Moving to Inequality."[16] Furthermore, compositional changes in surrounding neighborhoods of the sort induced by housing design policies (e.g., changes in poverty and racial status) predict the probability of residential out-migration.[17]

Conclusion

The burgeoning efforts to reduce neighborhood inequality by design are laudable and refreshing, but the powerful legacies of history and the multidimensional reach of inequality present formidable challenges. In addition, the lesson for urban design coming out of housing voucher policies is that neighborhoods are not static entities that can be presumed to passively receive treatments without change; rather, like individuals, neighborhoods are spatially embedded and interdependent. Combined with the powerful forces induced by individual choice mechanisms and residential migration flows, the consequences of policy interventions to modify the environment are difficult to anticipate and even harder to control. The fair city is thus a goal that will take efforts as persistent as the inequality it seeks to reduce.

Note: A version of this essay was presented at "Cities and Design," a meeting held at the Social Science Research Council (December 2013), and the Ethics of the Urban Conference at the Harvard University Graduate School of Design (March 2012); it is also based in part on an essay in the *New York Times* ("Division Street, USA"), October 2013.

1 Thomas Piketty, *Capital in the Twenty-First Century* (Cambridge, MA: Harvard University Press, 2014).

2 Mireya Navarro, "Affordability Will Be Focus for New Housing Leaders," *New York Times*, February 8, 2014.

3 Robert J. Sampson, "Criminal Justice Processing and the Social Matrix of Adversity," *ANNALS of the American Academy of Political and Social Science* 651, 296–301 (2014).

4 Michael E. Smith, "The Archaeological Study of Neighborhoods and Districts in Ancient Cities," *Journal of Anthropological Archaeology* 29, 137–154 (2010).

5 Loïc Wacquant, "Marginality, Ethnicity, and Penality in the Neoliberal City: An Analytic Cartography," *Racial and Ethnic Studies Review* 10, 1687–1711 (2014).

6 Robert J. Sampson, *Great American City: Chicago and the Enduring Neighborhood Effect* (Chicago: University of Chicago Press, 2012).

7 Ibid.

8 Mark L. Joseph, Robert J. Chaskin, and Henry S. Webber, "The Theoretical Basis for Addressing Poverty through Mixed-Income Development," *Urban Affairs Review* 42, 369–409 (2007).

9 Henry G. Cisneros and Lora Engdahl, eds., *From Despair to Hope: Hope VI and the New Promise of Public Housing in America's Cities* (Washington, D.C.: Brookings Institution Press, 2009).

10 Kevin Michael Jonke, (thesis, Social Studies, Harvard University, 2009).

11 Laura M. Tach, "More than Bricks and Mortar: Neighborhood Frames, Social Processes, and the Mixed-Income Redevelopment of a Public Housing Project," *City & Community* 8, 273–303 (2009).

12 Robert J. Sampson, "Moving to Inequality: Neighborhood Effects and Experiments Meet Social Structure," *American Journal of Sociology* 114, 189–231 (2008).

13 Sampson, *Great American City.*

14 Douglas S. Massey and Nancy Denton, *American Apartheid: Segregation and the Making of the Underclass* (Cambridge, MA: Harvard University Press, 1993).

15 Susan Clampet-Lundquist and Douglas S. Massey, "Neighborhood Effects on Economic Self-Sufficiency: A Reconsideration of the Moving to Opportunity Experiment," *American Journal of Sociology* 114, (2008): 107–43.

16 Sampson, "Moving to Inequality."

17 Kyle Crowder and Scott J. South, "Spatial Dynamics of White Flight: The Effects of Local and Extralocal Racial Conditions on Neighborhood Out-Migration," *American Sociological Review* 73, (2008): 792–812.

Bottom-Up Is Not Enough

Michelle Provoost

Is democracy spatial? Are the physical aspects of our cities, houses, streets, and public spaces the bearers of our values? Or is it rather the way our cities are being conceptualized, built, and managed that determines their democratic content?

Some interesting shifts have become apparent in the architecture world that relate to these questions. In contrast to the stream of iconic buildings commissioned by commercial developers, designed by the likes of Zaha Hadid, Jean Nouvel, OMA, Foster, etc., other types of practice have become increasingly popular. These approaches are the opposite of their antecedents in all respects. Characterized by small-scale projects that have originated from a direct need, their architecture is both bottom-up and cheap. They range from collective housing blocks to urban agriculture, (many) public space projects, and a variety of temporary self-built structures. Offices such as Urban-Think Tank, Teddy Cruz, Atelier Bow-Wow, ZUS, and countless lesser known collectives and ad hoc groups are creating a boom in small-scale, bottom-up projects worldwide. It has become an international

ZUS, ongoing development of squatted Schieblock into creative industries' offices, rooftop garden, shops, restaurant, and bar, Rotterdam, 2009–present

movement that not only celebrates successes at biennales and related professional events but has also completed many concrete projects. And the movement is still growing. These context-specific "urban acupuncture" projects challenge the public, bureaucratic planning institutions as well as icon-driven starchitecture. As the product of designers together with residents and local businesses, their democratic content is higher and more direct than that of the previous generation of urban projects that were determined by large commercial interests and global trends that largely evade democratic control.

The economic crisis was responsible for the boom in bottom-up projects insofar as the collapse of the construction economy made space, literally and figuratively: a lack of building both freed up locations and increased governments' and companies' willingness to tolerate bottom-up projects. But there is a snake in the grass: starting out as a countermovement, these projects are now embraced by governments and businesses as the ideal, cheap instrument to create value as long as "business as usual" remains impossible. Temporary parks are welcomed as "place making" and give wastelands a valuable new identity; artists' projects in derelict neighborhoods provide an attractive narrative; guerilla stores and pop-up bars project a positive image and are stimulated as a stepping stone toward commercial development. Many temporary projects are supported by institutional partners, and there is an emerging industry of temporality—pop-up, participatory planning and crowdsourcing that is used by and for the institutional parties directly, without any ambition to achieve a greater goal.

In this sense, the do-it-yourself and self-organization movement risks losing its critical potential. The projects are inexpensive, often tempo-

Stad in de Maak, cooperation of residents taking over vacant buildings in Rotterdam-North, redeveloping them to create a network of neighborhood services as well as housing, 2016

rary, and therefore harmless. Their contagious energy is ideally constructed for potential abusers. The bottom-up method is now extensively promoted by planning services and commercial real estate developers, and sociologists have warned against the unilateral participation of certain groups and the risk of inequality and segregation in such projects: the well-educated creative class dominates bottom-up processes, while other populations remain barred from this "Garden of Eden of politically correct hipster pastoralism."[1]

Again, architecture seems to have created a path for itself that has no critical meaning. Despite its initial ambitions, this movement plays merely a supporting function for the powers that be. Can this bottom-up dynamic have a real impact that transcends each individual project? Can the increased democratic content of this architecture movement be perpetuated, even in a post-crisis future? How can this generation make the transition from the avant-garde to the center, from the exception to the standard, from the elite to the society? Can it become the new modus operandi?

The next step in this process should be to build a bridge from single projects to civic institutions and link bottom-up initiatives to public, democratic structures—in other words, to connect the bottom to the top. It will be necessary to go deeper into the political, financial, and economic fundamentals of urban development. The reclaiming of these foundations is a tough and tedious job—one that not every designer has the talents to pursue. It is far more complicated and labor-intensive work than a single intervention, but also much more influential. To be truly effective and continue, these efforts must grow strong roots, so that their effects become long term and operate at larger scales. Otherwise this "movement" becomes reduced to a series of forgettable pinpricks rather than acquiring the profound cumulative effect of targeted acupuncture.

1 Justus Uitermark, "De zelforganiserende stad,"
in *Toekomst van de stad* (The Hague: Raad voor de
leefomgeving en infrastructuur, 2012), 5–9. Quote
from Wouter Vanstiphout, "Dark Matter, Ditch Urbanism
Revisited," *Harvard Design Magazine,* no. 37, 2014.

Monuments and Memorials

The Public Image of Demos

Erika Naginski

DEMOS. In its most standard meaning, this Greek word designates the people; it implies the idea of a sovereign and deliberative assembly, such as the people of Athens as opposed to the magistrates and Areopagus [or high court of appeals]. However, when not used in the context of the language of the law, one cannot hide the fact that authors repeatedly employ another meaning of the word *demos* in the sense of the common people.

—*Encyclopédie des gens du monde* (1836)[1]

Democratic peoples have a passion for generic terms and abstract words because these expressions enhance thought and, as they allow a few words to capture many objects, help intellectual work.... Democratic authors constantly create abstractions of this type in which they amplify the abstract meaning of already abstract language. More than this, in order to render discourse more fluid, they personify these abstractions and make them act like a real individual.

—Alexis de Tocqueville (1840)[2]

To anyone familiar with the programmatic aspects of French revolutionary public monuments and the urban spaces for which they were intended, the fact that these were enlisted to function as allegories of democratic principles seems self-evident. Goddesses of Reason, Liberty, Equality, and Justice emerged as the new political lingua franca, invading everything from proposals for triumphal arches to paper money. According to political philosopher Alexis de Tocqueville, democracy displays a tendency to personify abstractions and even give them agency (to "make them like a real individual"). In this, he was following Enlightenment writers such as Jean-François Marmontel, who underscored allegory's communicative capacities. Marmontel held in high regard allegory's professed ability to create a significant link between ideas and things and, furthermore, took allegory to be the cultural sign of an enlightened public sphere. With the Athenian polis and Greek mythology in mind, he proposed that the "more a people possess a vivid imagination, the more *allegory* is familiar to them; it is this ability to understand the link between an abstract idea with a sensible object, and to conceive of the former in the shape of the latter … as this ingenious people becomes more philosophically inclined, its *allegories* present a more just and profound meaning."[3]

Viewed from this angle, the French Revolution, its public spaces, and its representation of a newly formed body politic can be taken as a test case for the coalescence of the political and the aesthetic in urban contexts. The coalescence was far from seamless, however, for what remains unclear in all of this is what it means to construe "the people" as both agents and recipients of a process of signification called allegory. This short essay aims to foreground some noteworthy aspects of the public monument and its transformation during the French Revolution. It offers a brief reflection on the concept of commemoration through two manifestly different examples, which nonetheless both grappled with the public image of the people, or *demos*.

The first concerns the state-sponsored transformation of architect Jacques-Germain Soufflot's church of Sainte Geneviève into a Pantheon for revolutionary martyrs. This conversion of a Catholic church, originally commissioned by the crown, into a secular temple of heroes was overseen by Antoine Chrysostome Quatremère de Quincy, architectural theorist of the ideal. The program he devised exemplified the revolutionary reliance on allegory.[4] The second example concerns a landscaped tumulus erected near the royal church of Saint Denis in 1793 made with the debris of the

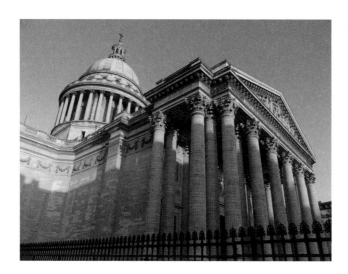

Panthéon, Paris, France

MAKING MONUMENTS

In 2015, the mayor of Tehran, Mohammad Bagher Ghalibaf, covered the city's 1,500 billboards with images of famous artwork. Over 30 percent of the art chosen was foreign and largely European. According to one official, citizens were too busy to go to galleries, so they made the city into one large gallery.

How does memory of the past inspire the future of cities? Both man and statue, above, stand
on Akadimias Avenue in Athens after the capital was monumentally impacted by the global financial
downfall in 2012.

MAKING MONUMENTS

Christ the Redeemer (*Cristo Redentor*), built in 1931, stands 30 by 28 meters, illuminated against the sky and city of Rio de Janeiro. Often monuments become symbols of a city, tangibly representing a past and looking toward a collective future. Who looks up? Who is watched? Who is made invisible?

Construction in Mecca brings together Muslims from around the world working to build the city. Who gets to construct, maintain, and view a monument, etched into the muscle and memory of the urban? What is being preserved, and what is being forgotten?

After 150 years of debate, the Vacant Plinth Committee designated the fourth plinth in London's Trafalgar Square as a space for contemporary installations. In 2009, Antony Gormley's "One & Other" showcased 2,400 people from across the UK, each for an hour.

On October 27, 2009, YAK Films posted a powerful turfing (Taking Up Room on the Floor) performance in memory of RichD, including dancing by, from left to right, Dreal, BJ, Man, and No Noize. The film, taken outside in the rain, is a memorial for the brother of one of the dancers.

latter's vandalized royal tombs. The tumulus appears as a popularly inscribed approach to the monument as well as an early manifestation of what we might today call a "counter-monument."[5] Despite the contrast between high and low, between official and popular, both the temple and the mound take us to the urban and monumental aspects of the French Revolution and the image these afforded of a newly formed body of citizens whose ambiguous definition stood at the center of events.

If "the people" made manifest an unstable category, this was because it had not existed as a clear political entity before 1789: what was citizenship, and how to constitute the legitimate terms of belonging to the polity? By the same token, the aesthetic emergence of "the people" is found in one of art history's founding myths: the celebrated *Demos* painted by Parrhasius of Ephesus and recorded by Pliny the Elder: "[In] his allegorical picture of the People of Athens, he has displayed singular ingenuity in the treatment of his subject; for in representing it, he had to depict it as at once fickle, choleric, unjust, and versatile; while, again, he had equally to show its attributes of implacability and clemency, compassionateness and pride, loftiness and humility, fierceness and timidity— and all these at once."[6] What this image actually looked like was, for centuries, the subject of speculation including for Quatremère, who came up with a "polycephalic monster of democracy" juxtaposing multiple expressive heads on the body of Athena's owl of wisdom. His astonishing caricature conveyed, he wrote, how the "People, or *Demos* in Greek indicated ... that political collective of people claiming sovereignty, a truly mysterious body whose totality has the right to impose its laws on parts that have the power to disobey."[7]

Anonymous, *View of the Mountain of Saint-Denis,* ink wash drawing, n.d.

The image of *demos* in the French revolutionary context was propelled into being by the destruction of the divinity of the royal sovereign. The execution of Louis XVI took place on January 21, 1793, at Place de la Révolution (namely Place Louis XV designed by the architect Ange-Jacques Gabriel that we know today as Place de la Concorde). Print after print depicting that fateful moment insists on the empty pedestal nearby that had previously held up Edmé Bouchardon's bronze equestrian statue of Louis XV—such emptiness a means of registering the highly orchestrated destruction of royal statues in the city's squares as a symbolic redundancy of the death of the monarch. Up to this point, as historian Lynn Hunt has proposed, kingship was "the sacred center that made possible social and political mapping. It gave the members of its society their sense of place. It was the heart of things, the place where culture, society, and politics came together."[8] As an image of political radicalism, *demos* filled the vacuum left behind by the violent demise of kingship only, in turn, to inaugurate—and this is Hunt again—a "crisis of representation."

Demos, that is, was nothing if not an unstable abstraction, and as the requisite backdrop for our two examples, it prompts some initial reflections on how its image intervened in the spaces of the city and the actions that unfolded there. Take the Third Estate or proverbial 99 percent as it appeared in *ancien régime* France. This is how Abbé Emmanuel Joseph

Anonymous, *A Peasant Carrying a Prelate and a Noble,* color engraving, 1789

Sieyès explained its status in the pamphlet he published in January 1789 just prior to the convocation of the Estates General: "What is the Third Estate? EVERYTHING. What has it been until now in the political order? NOTHING. What does it demand? To become SOMETHING."[9] That "something" remains obscure for the simple reason that Sieyès turns it into an abstraction: "the Third Estate constitutes the nation," he writes simply. "Being" and "becoming" function differently in Sieyès's pamphlet. If the outcome of "becoming" remains an abstraction—something called the nation, whatever this meant in 1789—it's quite clear what the common people of France *are* in 1789: something akin to a beast of burden, which needs to be freed from the dead weight of the privileged orders, the nobility, and the clergy—a familiar theme in period caricatures.

Interestingly if logically, the uncertainty of what the Third Estate would become increased pressure to *see* citizenship in the public sphere: to *see* "belonging" in the political sense, to *see* membership in the citizenry—in other words, to mark the collective body of the people as visible, recognizable, and transparent. This is where the Jacobin painter Jacques-Louis David stepped up as pageant master of the Republic, designing everything from clothing for the new citizen to the iconographies of the festivals that ritualized and rescripted public spaces: with his designs for the clothes of the citizen and the government functionary, for example, or with the decorative

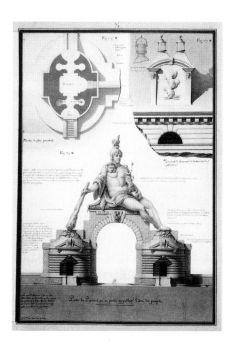

scheme of the Festival of the Supreme Being on June 8, 1794, used by Max-imilien Robespierre to inaugurate his new state religion, a form of Deism erected in the name of reason and nature.[10]

The uncertainty triggered by the concept of the Third Estate ulti-mately translated into a realm of visual abstractions, into that retinue of alle-gories, mostly female, personifying concepts such as liberty, equality, justice, reason, nature, and motherland. As Quatremère put it in his reports on the transformation of the church of Sainte Geneviève into the Pantheon:

> It is to sculpture that we owe this metamorphosis ...
> It also became too risky to entrust sculpture with the task of representing some of the events of the Revolution, which history has not yet placed at a distance from the individuals who were their instruments in order to grant them completely to the populace who was their motor. ... The traits of history copied at such close vantage resemble objects seen in a magnifying glass; it became necessary to sacrifice local and accidental truths to the general truth ...
> Allegory alone can accomplish this task.[11]

The Pantheon was the Revolution's most ambitious monument, and so it is worth taking note of its iconographic overhaul. Quatremère envisioned the edifice at the center of a landscaped precinct—a heroic sanctuary in its sacred wood—that would preserve the site's serenity and provide a setting for cer-emonies, festivals, and other public events. On the exterior, he planned for a pedimental bas-relief, five portico bas-reliefs (two of which are extant on the façade today), exterior statues, thirty-two statues over each of the col-umns of the drum, and a crowning allegory of Fame. Inside, he planned for twenty pendentives in the cupolas, an allegorical frieze suspended in the gal-lery of the central cupola, and an altar group he drew up in his own hand enthroning the reigning allegory of the French Republic.[12] The allegorical image of the people as Hercules appeared throughout his program: Hercu-lean clubs were brandished by a Genius of Liberty near the center of the pediment, in one of the exterior bas-reliefs titled Patriotic Devotion, and by the male figure dominating an interior pendentive called, simply, Strength; yet another winged Genius of Virtue in the guise of Patriotic Devotion "wears the lion skin on his head, holds the club and the pike staff that has just pierced the monster at its feet"; and a seated figure of Strength was set in the portico under a bas-relief depicting the Empire of Laws.[13]

One of revolutionary allegory's great achievements, cultural histo-rian Antoine de Baecque has remarked, is that it "succeeded in channeling its power toward ambitious pedagogical ends."[14] It was by means of allegory that the alarming contingencies, political splintering, and unsettling temporality of revolution could best be filtered—appearing on the other side of the mediating pellicle as a visually streamlined version of the new social order. The problem, of course, was that allegory hardly functioned as a universally accessible language. As Quatremère admitted: "[T]he language of figures and the writing of signs ceases to be useful, because there are no longer enough whole figures, nor enough complete signs to express all the possible combinations of thought. What results is the reign of abstractions . . . I know well that allegory can be made to say anything."[15]

Perhaps nowhere was such confounding equivocation more tangible than in the public image of *demos*. For the people, a new and resolutely masculine allegory had inverted the traditional Gallic Hercules previously deployed as monarchical propaganda.[16] The new Hercules was a buff demigod, as examples in Quatremère's Pantheon demonstrated, a colossal ideal nude grasping Liberty and Justice in one hand and the club in the other—a figure, most of all, whose equivocal status rested on the fact that he represented strength, impulsive violence, and, potentially, anger. This allegory was, in short, all brawn and no brains, all action and no talk, and suggested a populace lacking the capacity for forethought and instead ruled by chaos and force. That violence inevitably lurked at the fringes here is wittingly recorded

MOYEN EXPÉDITIF DU PEUPLE FRANÇAIS POUR DÉMEUB-
'LER UN ARISTOCRATE. 13 novembre 1790.

Anonymous, *Expeditious Means by which the French People Move an Aristocrat Out of His Residence,* after November 13, 1790

by the French visionary architect Jean-Jacques Lequeu in his proposed Arch of the People, a monumental rusticated gateway over which the colossal Hercules reclines, propped up by his club and donning the Phrygian cap crowned by a rooster. This, Lequeu wryly scribbled on the page, was "a project to save me from the guillotine. Everything for the Motherland."[17]

Much has been written on the allegory of Hercules and on the ways in which it signaled the anxieties of a nascent political structure claiming its right to exist on the very basis of what it apparently feared most: itself.[18] So let us simply retain the idea that Hercules was couched in fierceness, and that its invention as an image of the people was necessarily a reflection on violence and representation. What is interesting to contemplate are the ways in which the allegorical expression of Herculean potency in public monuments functioned as the flip slide of urban events and the spaces of public occupation. On the one hand, allegories were deployed in what was officially defined as the roster of new public spaces such as the Place de la Revolution, the Pont-Neuf, and the Pantheon. On the other hand, what can be set against the official image of *demos* were events unfolding as flashpoints in the city.

How to read images of destruction, for instance? What are they representing? (One needs to insist on the representational aspect, as such images always necessarily fictionalize the real.) Take the example of *Expeditious Means by which the French People Move an Aristocrat Out of His Residence*, a small anonymous engraving published as frontispiece to an issue of a revolutionary journal—influential politician and journalist Camille Desmoulins's *Revolutions de France et de Brabant*.[19] Such an image establishes clear guidelines for how to orchestrate the sack of an architectural space that, under pre-revolutionary conditions, would have been deemed both imposing and impregnable: the Hôtel de Castries on the Rue de Varennes. Begin, so the image instructs, by opening a window through which to display the domestic treasures you are about to hurl from the sanctuary of affluence: bed sheet after bed sheet, a cracked mirror in a gilt frame, or an overstuffed chair waiting to meet its embroidered twin below. It is crucial that the display allow for a brief moment of contemplation. What thereby gets signaled to the outside world is an internal struggle between a desire to possess and an ethos of refusal. Your companions will accordingly be vulnerable to flashes of indecision: a note of regret in the young woman on the lower right who fingers the heavy drape; the hats coming off to salute to the king's likeness on the second floor; and maybe a tinge of longing for the lady in the oval frame held, for the first time, at arm's length.

While individual encounters with luxury are successively captured in each window, ensuing propulsion ensures that debris from the everyday life of privilege will continue to accumulate in the courtyard: a commode beyond repair, a shattered window, a frying pan, an enema syringe there as indecorous metaphor for purging France of its elite—and thrown in as junk along with the rest, a single worthless bill of paper money. This destruction of valued objects functioned to subvert ongoing attempts by the government to identify and appraise France's newly nationalized patrimony. Instead, the propulsion of things through windows mediating inside and outside, private and public, instigates a spatial metonymy of dispersion.

We should take note of those windows. Windows (like doors and mirrors), explained philosopher and sociologist Henri Lefebvre, are transitional objects or thresholds bearing a ritual significance. In selecting descriptive terms like "transitional" and "threshold," Lefebvre was speaking to the capacity of architectural openings and reflective surfaces to breach the physical boundaries they demarcate (with frame, sill, ledge, balcony, or roofline). Those architectural openings negotiate an exchange between interiority and exteriority by collapsing various spatialities, bringing the room (and the objects it contains) to the street and vice versa. The concept of ritual adds another dimension to this ongoing process of two-way transference. For Lefebvre, thresholds can localize sacred precincts (temples, palaces, churches) and, by extension, can inaugurate life-defining rites of passage. Thus his argument seeks to demonstrate how localizations themselves, as they work to produce social spaces, "derive not only from ideology but also from the symbolic properties of space, properties inherent to that space's practical occupation."[20]

This inherent hybridity of space—cast in terms of both symbolics and practices—brings us back to the window as it is figured in the image of

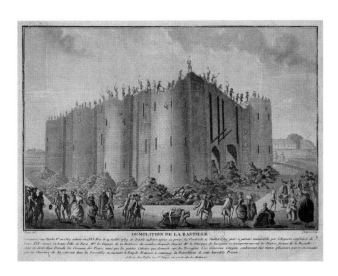

Joseph-Alexandre Le Campion after François Martin Testard, *Demolition of the Bastille,* color engraving, 1789

destruction, and to the threshold's potential ritual function in social practice more broadly defined. What can be suggested with the help of Lefebvre's architectural model of mediation is that such an image presents us with a series of thresholds (of windows as passageways) whose ultimate semantic effect inserts itself into an ever more far-reaching mode of collective response to the urban surround. The spatial metonymy of dispersion is everywhere to be found in revolutionary images of destruction. Another anonymous version of the same event published in the *Révolutions de Paris* and titled "the irritated people" includes throwing objects from windows as part of a public spectacle. Jean-Louis Prieur's depiction of the *Pillage de la Maison Saint-Lazare* takes that same spectacle to the streets. And in Joseph Alexandre Le Campion's colored engraving of the demolition of the Bastille (after a drawing by François Martin Testard), the piles of debris encircling the building's foundation perceptibly metamorphose, with each stone cast from above, into uniformly pyramidal—and entirely monumental—shapes.[21] These are all trenchant recapitulations of particular events, but they are also general blueprints for the changing symbolic relation between a certain class of people and certain spaces in the city. By laying bare the mechanisms of propulsion and dispersion, of repetitious collective gestures and the activation of the threshold, these examples attest to the formation of a central visual trope in the representation of destruction—a trope finding monumental expression in pyramids of debris.

Hence, with the second case in point, the monument's capacity to transform destruction into a kind of revolutionary rite of passage, one calling forth its very own commemorative procedures as the following eyewitness account makes clear:

> The monument was erected at the entrance of Franciade, formerly Saint-Denis, in the middle of the square. Each patriot was a worker. They made a verdant mountain or triumphant allegory to the *mountain* party of the Assembly. Cypresses, pines, lilies, firs, and grass were planted there. The heart of this mountain offers a grotto made from the debris of the tombs of the kings of France. The marbles, which had once decorated these sepulchers, were brought in great number to form vaults and pillars of this patriotic grotto. I saw several sandstone figures of kings placed across pillars to serve as a pediment. The most beautiful materials of this kind were used artlessly by free hands. This bizarre monument erected to liberty is perhaps the most philosophical lesson of its kind.[22]

We owe this narrative of iconoclasm's final outcome to an official who, in mid-November 1793, went to Saint Denis to draw up an inventory of works left behind by the Commission des Monuments in the wake of the dismantling of the royal necropolis' tombs. An ink wash drawing possibly by architect Charles Percier, found in one of the large drawing albums of the archaeologist and museum founder Alexandre Lenoir, gives a sense of the result: a grass tumulus with an entrance to a grotto framed by three royal *gisants*; four cypresses planted at the base of its left flank on the right; a bust bears an inscription dedicated to Jean-Jacques Rousseau. The drawing adds an additional explanatory note: "View of the Mountain made with the statues of the Kings in 1793."[23]

This emblematic mountain—this revolutionary counter-monument—was erected in honor of recently martyred revolutionaries Jean-Paul Marat and Louis Michel Le Peletier de Saint-Fargeau. On the last day of *Brumaire* in the year II (November 9, 1793), it served as the first "station" in a festival to martyrs and great men (whose international roster included Benjamin Franklin and William Tell), which had been conceived and sponsored by the Republican Society of Franciade (formerly Saint Denis). The published account of the original festival not only names the author of the counter-monument—a certain *citoyen* Haquin, who received for his efforts entry to the Society's deliberations—but also gives a description of its meaning and ephemeral context.[24]

As for the "philosophical lesson" such a "bizarre monument erected to liberty" might have taught, it was David who had the most to learn from artless hands and the mountain they erected with fragments. The lesson was this: that the remnants of pillage might, after all, be brought into the realm of the public sphere. Small wonder that when he was commissioned to erect a statue of the people, his allegorical image of Hercules was destined to stand on "truncated debris of [royal] statues ... confusingly piled up." "Such monuments are worthy of us," David proclaimed, because "the people who have adored liberty have always erected them."[25]

What astonishes most, in the end, is that the dialectical position of the revolutionary monument could have expressed itself so vividly in formal terms. The juxtaposition of these two undertakings—the temple and the mound—highlights both a break from the past and the continuation of earlier models, prompting central questions about the transformations of public art in the age of revolution: How did official and popular conceptions of public art collide and coalesce? How did iconoclastic destruction coincide with new possibilities for the civic monument? And finally what did it mean, in ideological terms as much as representational ones, to replace the image of the king with that of the people?

1 A.-F. Artaud de Montor, ed., *Encyclopédie des gens du monde* (Paris: Treuttel et Würtz, 1836), vol. 7, 752. Unless otherwise indicated the translations are mine.

2 Alexis de Tocqueville, *De la démocratie en Amérique* (Brussels: Hauman et Cie, 1840), pt. 2, vol. I, chap. xvi, 132–33.

3 Jean-François Marmontel, "Allégorie," *Elémens de littérature* (Paris: Chez Née de la Rochelle, 1787), vol. 5, 131.

4 See esp. Mona Ozouf, "Le Panthéon: L'École normale des mort," in Pierre Nora, ed., *Les lieux de mémoire. T. I. La République* (Paris: Gallimard, 1984), 139–66; Mark Deming, "Le Panthéon révolutionnaire," *Le Panthéon, symbole des révolutions* (Montreal: CCA, 1989), 97–151; Erika Naginski, *Sculpture and Enlightenment* (Los Angeles: Getty Research Institute, 2009), 217–286.

5 The term was coined by James E. Young, "The Counter-Monument: Memory Against Itself in Germany Today," *Critical Inquiry* 18/2 (Winter 1992): 267–96; see also his entry, "Monument/Memory" in Robert S. Nelson, Richard Shiff, eds., *Critical Terms for Art History* (1996; Chicago: University of Chicago Press, 2003), 234–47.

6 *Historia naturalis*, bk. 35, chap. 36.

7 Antoine Chrysostome Quatremère de Quincy, "Sur le Démos de Parrhasius," in *Archives littéraires de l'europe* (Paris: Heinrich, 1805), 259–61.

8 Lynn Hunt, *Politics, Culture, and Class in the French Revolution* (Berkeley: University of California Press, 1984), 87.

9 Emmanuel-Joseph Sieyès, *Qu'est-ce que le Tiers-État?* (1789), 3.

10 See David D. Dowd, *Pageant Master of the Republic: Jacques-Louis David and the French Revolution* (Lincoln: University of Nebraska Press, 1948); Robert L. Herbert, *David, Voltaire, "Brutus," and the French Revolution: An Essay in Art and Politics* (London: Allen Lane, 1972); Warren Roberts, *Jacques-Louis David, Revolutionary Artist: Art, Politics, and the French Revolution* (Chapel Hill: University of North Carolina Press, 1989); and Ewa Lajer-Burcharth, *Necklines: The Art of Jacques-Louis David after the Terror* (New Haven: Yale University Press, 1999).

11 Antoine Chrysostome Quatremère de Quincy, *Rapport fait au Directoire du département de Paris sur les travaux entrepris, continués ou achevés au Panthéon français…* (Paris: Ballard, 1793), 73.

12 Antoine Chrysostome Quatremère de Quincy, "Projet de groupe à exécuter au fond du Panthéon français,"

c. 1792. Paris, Bibliothèque nationale de France, Département estampes et photographie, RESERVE QB-370 (44)-FT 4.

13 Ibid., 39.

14 Antoine de Baecque, "The Allegorical Image of France, 1750–1800: A Political Crisis of Representation," *Representations* 47 (1994): 137.

15 Quatremère de Quincy, *Rapport*, 74.

16 See Marc-René Jung, *Hercule dans la littérature française du XVIè siècle: De l'Hercule courtois à l'Hercule baroque* (Geneva: Droz, 1966), and Robert E. Hallowell, "Ronsard and the Gallic Hercules Myth," *Studies in the Renaissance* 9 (1962): 242–55. The iconographic tradition is studied by Leopold D. Etlinger, "Hercules Florentinus," *Mitteilungen des Kunsthistorischen Institutes in Florenz* 16, no. 2 (1972): 119–142. See also Theodore Reff, "Puget's *Gallic Hercules*," *Journal of the Warburg and Courtauld Institutes* 29 (1966): 250–263.

17 Jean-Jacques Lequeu, "La porte du Parisis qu'on peut appeler l'arc du peuple," 1794, plume, lavis, aquarelle. Bib. nat., départment estampes et photographie, ETS RESERVE HA-80 (2).

18 See Hunt, *Politics, Culture, and Class,* 87–119, and Judith E. Schlanger, "Le peuple au front gravé," in Jean Ehrard and Paul Viallaneix, eds., *Les fêtes de la révolution* (Paris: Société des études Robespierristes, 1977), 387–95.

19 *Revolutions de France et de Brabant* 52 (1790).

20 Henri Lefebvre, *La production de l'espace* (Paris: Éditions Anthropos, 2000), 242.

21 Bibliothèque nationale de France, Département estampes et photographie, RESERVE FOL-QB-201 (119).

22 "Surplus des objets d'art à conserver qui se trouvent dans la ci-devant abbaye de Saint-Denis…," in Louis Courajod, *Alexandre Lenoir, son journal et le muse des monuments français* (Paris: H. Champion, 1878), vol. 1, xci.

23 Anon. "Vue de la montagne de Saint-Denis," undated. Paris, Musée du Louvre, Département des arts graphiques, RF 5282.18, Recto.

24 H. Blanc, *Procès-verbal de la fête consacrée à l'inauguration des grands hommes, et des martyrs de la liberté, qui à eu lieu à Franciade … de la République française, une et indivisible* (Paris: Imp. de la Citoyenne Hérissant, 1793), 8–9.

25 Jacques-Louis David, *Discours pronouncé par le citoyen David, dans la séance du 17 brumaire, l'an IIè de la république* (Paris: Imp. nationale, 1793), 2–3.

The Sacred, the Quotidian, and the World Trade Center Memorial

Michael Arad

Truth exists as an emotional as well as a rational concept, but architects and planners rarely discuss emotion. Conversations about public space, cities, and citizenship often revolve around earnest discussions of meaning, politics, and identity, and as an architect I have understood them, internalized them, and believed in them; yet it was a cerebral and rational belief, while real belief is often based in the domain of the heart, not the mind.

I believe that had I not been in New York on September 11, 2001, and the days that followed, I would not have discovered for myself the emotional side of the truth that public spaces are the bedrock of a society—places where a notion of community, of assembly, of belonging, come into being—and without them that sense of being, and being connected, simply would not exist.

Having lived in New York for a couple of years before the attacks, I knew the place, but I was not of it. New York was a city of strangers, a place where one could disappear in the crowd. Yet afterward, it suddenly felt as if there were no strangers; we were all in it together. A moment that crystallized that personal transformation came a few nights after September 11, when I found myself, unable to sleep, making my way to Washington Square Park. There in the quiet and dark hours of the middle of the night I found a few people who also felt a need to be in the presence of others at this most trying time. No words were exchanged, no ceremony was conducted, and none was required. The city had provided us with all we needed: a place to stand together.

The quiet compassion, the stoicism, and the determination that I witnessed in everyday New Yorkers impressed me greatly. I do not think that these qualities and attributes came into being out of thin air. I believe that public spaces—humble street corners and grand squares—were the seedbed that cultivated this sense of measured defiance. New Yorkers literally came together, and in doing so found strength in each other, and a way to respond united in hope and in sadness to the unimaginable, rather than being divided by fear.

In the aftermath of the destruction at the World Trade Center site, some people were able to consider rebuilding within a few days or weeks, and by late 2001 an exhibition of proposals was presented at the Max Protetch Gallery in Chelsea. I myself could not think at the time about what rebuilding might mean. It felt too soon and like too raw a wound to touch. But I did feel the need to respond in some way that would give voice to my feelings—to design, to imagine, to commemorate. And if not at the World Trade Center, where bodies were being pulled out of the smoldering debris, then nearby, by the shore of the Hudson River—another place that felt like a threshold between the city and a world beyond.

I imagined the surface of the river torn open, forming two square voids, with water cascading into these inexplicable empty spaces and failing to fill them up. It was a surreal image that seized my attention and demanded that I find a way of making what seemed physically impossible. I spent close to a year sketching and modeling in my free time. At the conclusion of a year's work, a self-directed cathartic exercise, I built a small sculpture with a concealed water pump: a simple black cube of Plexiglas, its top a square of water that had two square voids breaking its surface. I took this shimmering and softly gurgling piece to the rooftop of my East Village apartment building— where I had witnessed the burning towers—and photographed it against the Manhattan skyline. I could see the absence of the twin towers in the skyline mirrored and reflected in the two voids in the foreground, a view that captured for me a sense of bewilderment, loss, and ongoing absence—the emptiness that a viewer standing at the edge of the Hudson River might experience.

Having completed this personal journey, I set the model on a high shelf and forget about it until about a year later. In the interim, New York City responded to the task of rebuilding the World Trade Center (WTC) site

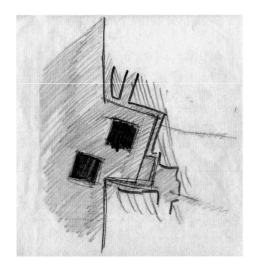

Sketch of twin voids in the Hudson River, 2001

with unprecedented public engagement. Public forums took place to debate how the city should rebuild the site and Lower Manhattan, and people who had rarely given thought to how our built environment is constructed became passionately engaged in this discussion. What emerged from that process was an amalgam of democracy and backroom deals by politicians and developers, and led to the selection of a master plan by Daniel Libeskind that returned all 10 million square feet of office space to the WTC site.

The plan, christened Memory Foundations, restored some of the streets that had been "erased" by the creation of the WTC in the 1960s. It subdivided the 16-acre WTC superblock into four unequal quadrants by bringing Greenwich and Fulton Streets back to the site; the largest resultant quadrant, bounded by West Street, Liberty Street, Fulton Street, and Greenwich Street, contained the footprints of the former twin towers and was set aside as a site for memorial and cultural use, while the remaining three quadrants, as well as the site of the Deutsche Bank building to the south of the site, were reserved for five new office towers. The commercial restoration of the site was driving the redevelopment.

Following the selection of this master plan, a competition was announced for the design of a memorial. Unlike the master plan competition, this would be open to anyone, and many people from around the world responded; by the end of June 2003, 5,201 entries had been submitted.

The master plan had prescribed tightly defined boundaries for the memorial, setting it within a constellation of built elements that concealed it from the north and east, through the placement of large buildings dedicated to unspecified cultural uses, and severed the memorial site from the city to

Photograph of river voids model against Manhattan skyline, 2002

the west and south by depressing the site 60 feet below adjacent streets and sidewalks. The footprints of the twin towers were delineated with buildings that would come up against them or bridge over them.

As I looked at the competition brief, I thought of my own experiences in New York City in the aftermath of the attacks, and I reflected on the important role public space played in my understanding of the events and the city's response to them. The master plan seemed to sever the site of the memorial from the city, when the opposite was called for, to my mind. This was somewhat of a paradox because the master plan in its entirety was in fact successful in weaving the 16-acre site back into the urban fabric of the city through its reintroduction of significant elements of the old street grid—Fulton Street and Greenwich Street—and by relying on individually delineated buildings that conformed to former street walls elsewhere in the development of the overall site. Yet when it came to the memorial itself, the master plan suggested a withdrawal from the everyday fabric of the city, a detachment that I am sure arose from positive intentions, yet I felt it was mistaken. I believe that public space is highly resilient in functioning in varied ways at different times without losing a sense of identity or composure. The site of a mournful vigil one day can at other times accommodate political dissent, a school field trip, or an afternoon of social recreation. I saw that resiliency in the public spaces of New York in the aftermath of September 11, as sites such as Union Square turned from farmers market to something altogether different and profound, and then returned again to everyday use. The sacred and the quotidian could exist together and in fact reinforce one another with layers of meaning and memory.

I was also personally ready to begin the process of designing, though I felt that the site's history was so powerful that any design should be deferential, letting history speak for itself without the need for dramatic embellishment. Design flourishes that imprinted the individual, idiosyncratic, and personal stamp of a designer felt solipsistic. The history of this site had to be engaged on clear terms that let the past violence manifest itself unmistakably, but not in a way that fetishized or erased it; it should be neither amplified nor reduced.

As I began to think about the design of a memorial on this site, I returned to my earlier investigation of the voids in the Hudson River and asked myself whether I could bring these voids to the site, not as an echo of what happened elsewhere but as a trace of what happened here, using absence to make the past present, visible, and tangible. Doing so would require a completely different strategy for this site than the one the master plan was prescribing, but that did not deter me, as I had no expectations that my design proposal would be selected. Like a reader sending a letter to the editor of a newspaper, I saw this as an opportunity to express my view and share it with others, to challenge the accepted path, but with little hope of changing the direction of the project.

By choosing to ignore the competition guidelines, I was freed of the multiple constraints they imposed on the site and was able to focus on what I thought was important: making absence present and creating an urban public space, a civic plaza that would connect this site to the rest of Lower Manhattan. Through a long and difficult process, the design remained about those two simple ideas.

The process we went through—and it quickly became a large and at times unwieldy "we" once the project was selected in January 2004—was extremely challenging, with political and emotional currents pulling the project in different directions at times. Everybody was a stakeholder, but some more so than others. I believed that I should hear out anybody who cared deeply about this project, but I knew that it would be impossible to develop a design that would address every request and concern, many in opposition. If I could better understand the root cause of an expressed concern, I thought, then perhaps I could mitigate it, even if in a way unimagined by the person who was offering a sweeping change to the design I had proposed and was trying to get built.

One of the first areas of design development was the waterfalls. Working with Dan Euser, our fountain consultant who constructed a full-scale mockup of a corner of one of the memorial pools in his backyard outside of Toronto, we strove to create a strong visual effect with a minimal amount of water. Dan designed and constructed a series of different serrated edges for the angled weir that serves as the launching point for the waterfall, with an eye toward both beauty (clearly separated and visually distinct individual streams) as well as utility (feathered edges that would not snag fallen leaves). The process of refining the design of the waterfall, clearly central to the overall design but drawn in broad strokes for the competition submission, was a process of discovery and development. To me it is critical to understand design in these terms. Design is a process guided by clear direction, but open to change and discovery. I could not have imagined how beautifully evocative the sight of individual strands of waters would be, weaving

Waterfall at south pool, 2015

TIME AND MEMORY

Thirteen years after the September 11th attacks in New York City, the Tribute in Light memorial
was raised to honor and remember the victims of 9/11. The memorial, created by artists and architects
from New York, consists of two blue beams of light, made from 88 bulbs, 8,000 watts each.

TIME AND MEMORY

In 2014, marking the 25th anniversary of the fall of the Berlin Wall, 8,000 glowing orbs lined eight miles of where the wall had been. Orbs were released into the air to Beethoven's *Ode to Joy*. Installation designers, Marc and Christopher Bauder noted the importance of lightness and light in remembrance.

TIME AND MEMORY

Between May and October 2015, artist Janet Echelman's installation "As If It Were Already Here" was suspended above Boston's Rose Kennedy Greenway. The installation acted to sew the city back together, lines recalling memory of the raised highway that once was there.

Streets in Bahrain are filled with Shia Muslims for the Ashura religious festival commemorating Imam Hussein's martyrdom in 680 AD. Processions move throughout the streets during the day and night, showing how collective urban memory can be maintained and cultivated. Where are the people?

Artist Ralf Witthaus and his team use lawnmowers and brush cutters to provoke reflection on space, memory, and the "lost and forgotten." Above, the church square in Stühlinger, Freiburg im Breisgau contains twenty strips mowed into the lawn: as the grass grows back, the space is temporally transformed—a memory of the space lives on.

themselves into a billowing curtain of water where that individuality is lost and subsumed gradually over a 30-foot fall. Yet months of designing and testing different weir and serration profiles led to an outcome that wordlessly and powerfully expressed the inherent ideas of individual and communal loss that I had sought to represent all along. I write this to dispel the popular notion that designers somehow have a fully formed design in their heads, and all that is needed is for a builder to bring it into being. Instead, it is a drawn-out process, a process that enriches and develops a design. It is through interactions between different experts and a series of constraints that a design becomes more complex and is finally realized.

One of the most challenging moments in this process came in 2006, when the Memorial Galleries—spaces sacred yet secular that for me had been at the heart of the experience of visiting the memorial—were eliminated for reasons of cost, security, and concerns expressed by some families of the dead about descending below the memorial plaza, as well as competition between design teams for the memorial and the museum. It was a terrible blow, delivered on the most public stage, and I was unsure how I could respond to maintain the essential qualities of the memorial. At some juncture, the design team for the museum tried to preserve one of the four sides of the galleries that surrounded each pool like a cloister, essentially annexing the space into the volume of the museum and making it a place of spectacle, where the waterfalls were observed in an enclosed and glazed space. This ran counter to my understanding of the area as outdoor space, exposed to the elements and traveled through in a processional experience that culminated at the nadir of a descent and arrival at the edge of the void and pool, where

View of south pool, 2012

one encountered the names. This proposed measure, possibly intended to demonstrate appreciation of the architectural qualities of this vertically attenuated and elongated space, to my mind added insult to injury. Without the names of the dead, there was no purpose to these galleries, and to preserve a portion of them as a place of architectural wonderment betrayed a lack of understanding of their essential function as a space where life and death came together to share a common threshold, one that visitors, like Orpheus, could not cross but could linger at.

Eventually, after two years of developing dozens of design options that would display the names of the deceased at plaza level instead of in the Memorial Galleries, we settled on a design that kept the stoicism and compassion that had been part of the spirit of the memorial all along. An 8-foot-wide and 2-foot-high water table that delineated the voids and marked the tower footprints served as the source for the waterfalls and the basin for the names panels. The panels themselves took the form of an angular bronze winglike element, composed of darkly patinated inch-thick plates of bronze incised with names, which appear as shadows during the day and as light at night.

The new design emerged from an exhaustive process that sometimes felt directionless and driven by committee. It was acrimonious at times, as disagreements surfaced among the many designers involved in the project; the project would have taken a different path were it not for the leadership of people such as Amanda Burden, New York City's City Planning Commissioner, and Kate Levin, the City's Cultural Commissioner. These two, along with Deputy Mayor Patricia Harris, one of the jury members who selected the design, served as Mayor Michael Bloomberg's eyes and ears. They offered encouragement when the situation became difficult, critically evaluated the many design proposals, and most important, provided us with time to develop the design carefully and thoroughly despite growing public sentiment that the process was taking too long (it was). Mayor Bloomberg became chairman of the 9/11 Memorial Foundation in 2006 when New York Governor George Pataki, who had been leading the process, left office. At that point the design and construction process became much more focused, and fundraising for the memorial began in earnest and successfully. The mayor was intent on resolving controversial issues, such as the names arrangement, and moving forward with a clear schedule dictated by a desire to dedicate the site as we marked the passing of a decade.

One of the many parties that shared concerns with the memorial design team was the Mayor's Office for People with Disabilities (MOPD). There are of course many types of disabilities, but the leading directive from the MOPD was improved visual sightlines for people seated in wheelchairs. The name panels were accessible to sight and touch, and to my mind, these panels were the most significant element in the memorial design, but the MOPD was concerned that the void at the center of each pool, where water appeared to cascade down into an infinite abyss, was a critical part of experiencing the memorial that should be visible to all visitors, whether seated or standing. This requirement became a significant challenge to completing the project, having manifested itself late in the process, with the 2011 completion deadline already firmly set. At moments like this, a lot of bad suggestions typically are made that would allow a project to comply with new restrictions and move forward—and the same thing happened here. Suggestions were made for glass windows positioned between some of the names panels or operable scissor lifts that would elevate portions of the memorial plaza for those seated in wheelchairs. All of these ideas looked like last-minute add-ons that violated the spirit of the memorial and created a new vocabulary at odds with the existing design. Had it not been for the opportunity to study this new requirement carefully and thoughtfully, one of these proposals would have been incorporated into the design, seriously undermining it. Because we were given the time to resolve this demand in a way that was synthetic to the design of the memorial, the design improved as a result of this "constraint." Design is always about dealing with constraints creatively; design without constraints is pointless, though design with nothing but constraints is impossible. We were able to resolve this issue by chamfering the corners of the pools in a way that unintentionally but appropriately harkened back to the geometry of the destroyed towers and allowed us to carry the names around each void in a continuous ribbon, instead of four discrete lengths. This change poetically enriched the design, and the beautiful sculptural resolution of the corners as cantilevered elements, like the prow of a ship, permitted those seated in wheelchairs to have a view of the secondary voids equal to that of standing visitors. I think this turn of events illustrates that design is a process as much as an outcome, and that it is a process that must be engaged with clear direction and intention. The design of the memorial changed over an eight-year process in ways big and small, but the nature and the intentions of the design remained true to the original conception of the project.

A similar process of design and discovery took place when it came to the arrangement of the names of the deceased on the panels that surround the memorial. I had only the broadest sense of how the names should be arranged, but I knew that I wanted to give each name the opportunity to be placed in an individually expressive and distinct manner, emphasizing the particular and the universal, the private and the communal losses that were suffered. Graphically it would be easy enough to accomplish this by avoiding the conventional placement of names in stacked columns, but I felt that the logic behind the arrangement had to go further than that: each name should have a place, a physical place, on the memorial that was unique to it and belonged to that person and their family. I suggested a system of "meaningful adjacencies," whereby the next of kin of close to 3,000 dead would be asked if there were names of other victims next to which they would like to see the name of their loved one placed. My hope was that we could reflect on the rich and intricate complexity that wove these names together in both life and death. Friends, colleagues, and family members would be listed alongside each other, adjacent to one another, in an arrangement that fulfilled these requests, embedding in the memorial a hidden web of connections, readily understood by some, open to sharing and explanation with others. This idea was rejected as being too complex to implement by the Lower Manhattan Development Corporation, the agency that oversaw the design process until the Memorial Foundation took over that responsibility in 2006.

Absent another equitable way to arrange the names, I suggested that the names be placed in no order whatsoever. I made that suggestion with a heavy heart, because even the simplest way of arranging the names, in alphabetical order, unintentionally separated family members with different surnames. The proposal for a random arrangement of names angered many who lost relatives and created a firestorm of acrimony over the entire project, bringing fundraising to a standstill. It wasn't until 2006, some two years later, that a new course was set for the names arrangement under the guidance of Mayor Bloomberg, who insisted that the issue be resolved for the project to move forward. In discussing the names arrangement with the mayor, I asked him to consider my earlier proposal for meaningful adjacencies;

View of bronze panels at north pool, 2012

to my surprise, he accepted this idea despite the uncertainties involved in its implementation and its potential to upset family members if we failed to meet their specific requests.

The solution that emerged was to arrange the names based on where people were that day in September: the four planes, the two towers, the Pentagon, and the first responders, whose names are clustered by firehouse or police precinct (a ninth group, the victims of the February 1993 WTC bombing, appears as well, at the north tower footprint, close to where that attack occurred). Within these categories, what is a seemingly random arrangement is in fact a carefully composed order, the fruit of many months of painstaking and emotionally demanding labor.

The names arrangement is such an important part of the design of the memorial because every visitor can relate to individual stories on a personal level. "Close to 3,000 dead" can become an abstraction, something that visitors might fail to connect with, but when hearing the particulars of one story, as reflected in the names arrangement, a visitor finds a way into the moving narratives of that day. The Memorial Foundation has already made some of these stories available to visitors through a project that links oral histories collected by StoryCorps with a smartphone application for locating names on the memorial. Over time, additional means will emerge to enable visitors to understand the requests that drove the hidden logic of the arrangement, based on personal and individual stories of loss. They are not the single vision or voice of a privileged designer; they are the multiple voices of people most affected by the events of that terrible day.

A visitor and the memorial, 2011

Art, Trauma, and *Parrhesia*

Krzysztof Wodiczko

> *"The majority may prove to be wrong,*
> *but not the public space."*
> —Claude Lefort[1]

The democratic process depends on the vitality of public space. Public space is the space of rights.

Claude Lefort writes of public space, "This space which is always indeterminate, has the virtue of belonging to no one, of being large enough to accommodate only those who recognize one another within it and who give it meaning, and of allowing the questioning of right to spread."

The democratic principles that are constitutive of public space cannot be sustained if we do not provide the *cultural, psychological, techno-logical,* and *aesthetic* conditions for the inclusion (and acknowledgment) of voices that are economically, culturally, and socially marginalized and estranged—the voices of those who are perceived, treated, and at best tolerated as strangers, those who are labeled as "poorly adjusted" or "not integrated."

The well-being of the democratic process is connected to these people's capacity for speech and expression, as well as their emotional and mental health. Unfortunately, many of those who have a great deal to say are often so emotionally overwhelmed by what they have experienced that they remain silent. They are locked in a traumatic state of communicative incapacitation, a "freezing of the failure situation," to quote D.W. Winnicott.

Visibility and public testimony are closely linked to recovery from traumatic experiences. According to trauma theorist and clinician Judith Herman and many others who work with trauma, the struggle for recovery from trauma—finding a narrative voice through testimony—has a greater chance of success when performed as a public speech act, even more so when directed as a social utterance to and on behalf of others. Thus truth-telling and testimony have a restorative power. Psychologist Pierre Janet termed this act "presentification."[2]

Media art and performative public art can play a role in recovering—or "unfreezing"—the capacity to speak by creating situations in which marginalized or traumatized people might insert their experience into public discourse.

The key task of critical art and design in public space is to develop projects collaboratively with these emergent democratic agents. Rather than speaking for them, we—artists, theorists, designers, researchers, curators, educators, and so forth—can help these citizens and residents develop their own capacity to open up, speak openly, and become heard and visible. We must at the same time help create the conditions for what they say to be heard by others whose perspectives might be altered by these new democratic agents, a group comprised of "strangers" and the estranged.

There is a significant population of homeless New Yorkers who work day and night collecting bottles and cans on the city's streets. My *Homeless Vehicle* project sought to act as a shock-absorbing mechanism between the homeless population who inhabit the city's streets and the many others for whom the streets serve as a mere passageway. It seemed to me that the purportedly "illegitimate" occupation of the streets by the city's homeless was reflected by the "illegitimate" tools—such as borrowed shopping carts—that they used to collect bottles. I thought that the creation of a tool designed with and for the bottle collectors would not only aid in their day-to-day activities but also symbolically mark their right to occupy public space. The Homeless Vehicle can be used both for personal shelter and the storage of cans and bottles.

It became clear to me that the vehicle operated in a more complex way than intended. It was used not only as an object that articulated conditions of life but also as the communicative instrument for the user to help him or her to open and share their lived experience—their techniques of survival, witness, and critical vision. Further, it was used by the street audience as a lure and an "excuse" to come closer to the homeless operator, ask questions, and listen.

The user-operators of the vehicle began to act as presenters, narrators, performers, and storytellers. They testified as existential and political witnesses to a city undergoing rapid transformation. Communicating their often traumatic pasts and present ways of life was ordinarily a challenging task; however, the vehicles acted as a catalyst for speech.

Through its design, a "scandalizing functionalism," the Homeless Vehicle communicated a great deal of the conditions and techniques of homeless survival.[3] Its successful symbolic and functional operation began demanding new equipmental capacities to meet its emerging communicative role. The vehicle's user, no longer perceived as a faceless urban character, became a real person and an actor, a performer-presenter, conscious of his and her entertaining and instructing role.

However, the vehicle's communicative potential was as evident as its communicative insufficiency. While in many ways its symbolic function helped users to speak more openly about their experiences, it also lacked communicational equipment specifically used to aid and amplify this process.

The year 1990, when I completed the *Homeless Vehicle* project, marked a turning point in my work; the project took on an unforeseen communicative role that exceeded its already complex functional program. Upon a critical reevaluation of the Homeless Vehicle's shortcomings, my projects began using video technology and participatory and narrative strategies to reinforce their communicative objectives. The projections (video-based participatory monument animations) and instruments (specially designed performative communication equipment) were my first works to address these issues through the medium of public art.

Both the projections and the instruments provide participants with the psychological, cultural, technical, and aesthetic means for entering the public space as capable communicative agents who, with preparation, can master the art of speaking in public. Step by step, they recall, articulate, and share formerly overwhelming life experiences. Armed with psycho-cultural prosthetics, and empowered by the monumental scale of civic edifices, they become—to borrow a term from Foucault—"fearless speakers." The aim of both the projections and the instruments is to inspire and assist the users (whom I call the "operators" or "animators") in developing and "projecting" their voices and gestures in public space. The projects are designed as a psychological, aesthetic, and political passage that assist these incipient democratic agents so that they can move from private confession

to public testimony, toward transformative action in public social life. The process of creation begins with a "preparatory" video recording that is integral to the project's development. This entails repeatedly recording, erasing, and re-recording testimonies; the process aids participants in developing their thoughts. Gradually they become psychologically and politically empowered, and come to see themselves as artistic creators in their own right. This first step is crucial because it is the moment when participants reflect on their personal experiences—which is often emotionally and politically fraught—and develop the capacity to present themselves and their stories to the public. Editing the recorded material and projecting it in public, also crucial stages in the process, come after this initial step.

Projections "animate," in real time, the façades of public buildings. Maarten Hajer and Arnold Reijndorp suggest that the social and cultural aspects of public space "should be based on open conditions for developing and holding to one's own opinion and capacity for judgment through the processes of symbolic communication, confrontation, and exchange with others."[4] My work seeks to create such conditions by using architectural and spatial forms as dynamic screens onto which meaning can be inscribed and reinscribed, and thus exchanged.

In the Kunstmuseum Basel projection *Sans-Papiers* (2006), four immigrants agreed to talk about their experience living in Switzerland. Due to their legal status, these stories had formerly been "unspeakable." The speakers' bodies were projected onto the museum, which was chosen because of its perceived social value. The monumental scale and visibility of the projection were significant, as they presented purportedly "illegitimate"

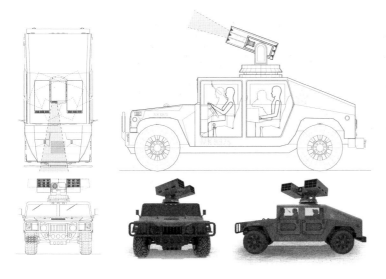

individuals as legitimate through their appearance on the Kunstmuseum, one of the most prominent cultural institutions in Basel. The night projection brought these *sans-papiers* from the margins of the city to full view—to the center of our political and cultural attention.

Their bodies were visible only from the waist down, and it seemed as though they were sitting on top of the building. One was confronted with the experience *looking up* at the immigrants. This configuration evoked the experience of looking up at a parent or teacher as a small child—of listening to stories and lessons someone more experienced and wiser than oneself. The point of this dynamic was not only to see the immigrants as larger than us, but also to make ourselves feel smaller than them.

The monumental scale of the projected bodies made the large building seem, by comparison, about three meters high. The public listened to immigrants' stories while watching their hands gesticulate and their legs casually kick against the building. Though the stories were often painful, there were also moments of humor.

While they are much smaller in scale, the wearable instruments that I have developed share many psychological and political objectives with the monumental projections. *Dis-Armor* (1999–2000) was a set of armor enhanced by media components that was designed to help shield its wearer from the anxieties of face-to-face communication. The design was inspired by action figure toys that were popular at the time. The instrument was designed specifically for Japanese students and "school refusers" (a group of mostly junior high school students who refused to accept the state of the school system and thus did not attend; in this way, they differ significantly

from drop-outs). These students are often survivors of school bullying and of domestic conflicts—parental abuse and violence. They have critical opinions about parenting, families, schooling, methods of education, teachers, and Japanese culture, but do not speak much. Even when they do, they are often not listened to under normal circumstances. These psychologically vulnerable young people have difficulty with speech and facial expression; they need extraordinary means to offer unsolicited communication. The design of *Dis-Armor,* developed in consultation with these students as well as a school psychiatrist and a psychoanalyst specializing in school refusers, was a response to such a need.

The helmet contains two video cameras, a microphone, a transmitter, and a rearview mirror. The backplate holds two LCD screens, which relay images of the user's eyes in real time, and a speaker, which relays the user's voice. The screens and speakers face backward, so that the user can communicate with their back to their addressees in an indirect, mediated, or mediatized "safe" way without appearing to be rude or revealing unease or lack of confidence. Their presence was amplified by the increased size of their eyes, which appeared to bring them closer to their interlocutors while preserving a comfortable distance. The Dis-Armor was designed to allow for both real-time and prerecorded communication, enabling the user to freely switch from one mode to another. Thus the instrument used media technology to transform an individual incapable of successful public speaking into someone symbolically and functionally "wired" and empowered for communication.

Since the development of the projections and wearable instruments, my work has engaged not only with themes of intervention and public

space, but also with testimony, monument, trauma, healing, and the stranger. The development of my work has been influenced by Chantal Mouffe's notion of agonistic democracy and Michel Foucault's concept of fearless speech, or *parrhesia*.

In her writing, Mouffe suggests that a vital democracy is characterized by agonistic debate, which takes place between adversaries or rivals on shared symbolic terrain (as opposed to Carl Schmitt's formulation of an antagonistic political relationship, which occurs between "enemies" with no shared symbolic terrain).

For Mouffe, agonism is to be distinguished from rational reasoned argument, or deliberate communicative action (both in its Habermasian variant, in which debate is regulated by rules, and the variant derived form Hannah Arendt, in which disputes are resolved through persuasion). "While for Habermas consensus emerges through what Kant calls *disputieren*, an exchange of arguments constrained by logical rules, for Arendt it is a question of *streiten*, where agreement is produced through persuasion, not irrefutable proofs," Mouffe writes. She criticizes the Arendtian understanding of agonism for being an "agonism without antagonism," and argues instead for a passionate, adversarial exchange of opinions.

"According to the agonistic approach, critical art is art that foments dissensus, that makes visible what the dominant consensus tends to obscure and obliterate," she writes. "It is constituted by a manifold of artistic practices aiming at giving a voice to all those who are silenced within the framework of the existing hegemony."[5] This act of giving voice to the silenced is precisely what I seek through these instruments and projections.

Mouffe's concept of agonism doesn't determine what kinds of political statements are correct, right, just, or true; rather, it addresses the social processes
that allow one to speak politically. This characterization is shared by Foucault's concept of fearless speech, or *parrhesia*.

The word *parrhesia*, normally translated as "free speech," appears
for the first time in Greek literature in the 5th century BCE and was in use
until the early Christian era. The task of the *parrhesiastes* (or fearless speaker) was to be articulate, publicly open, and able to speak out honestly, based
on his own experience, while offering an unsolicited and brave public criticism aimed toward positive change.

In ancient Greece, *parrhesia*—the Athenian right and duty (and
later, even art) of "free speaking," of outspokenness, was the very core of the
democratic process and the life of public space. However, this "fearless and
free speaking" required special political and ethical qualifications.

There is a fundamental difference between the profoundly exclusive form of Athenian democracy, in which the concept of *parrhesia* originated, and the constitutionally inclusive form of democracy of our time. Greek
democracy recognized only a small group of male property owners as citizens
of the polis, while excluding women, slaves, and foreigners. In its present
form, modern democracy promises—at least in principle—the fundamental
right of participation to every citizen and resident, regardless of circumstance. This includes the right to communicate in public—to speak and listen
fearlessly. This extends even to strangers among strangers: immigrants *sans
papiers*, "undocumented aliens," the homeless, soldiers returning from war,
and many other "others." They too have potential rights, the "right to rights,"

the right to assert these rights, and the right to access them through the democratic struggle in the cultural and political sphere.

The potential fearless speaker needed to perfect him- or herself (in Athenian democracy, the speaking subject was, unfortunately, restricted to *him*self). Foucault's interest in *parrhesia* stems from his interest in the ancient notion of "care for the self." *Parrhesia* is a technique not only for public speaking, like rhetoric, but also for speaking the truth about oneself requiring (and contributing to) the care for the self.

This concept of "care for oneself" is crucial to my work. Without perfecting ones own psychological, emotional, and mental state, one is not equipped for public communication, let alone parrhesiastic speech in public space. Parrhesia, like public space itself, is both a clinical and critical matter. What is needed is not a Deleuzian symptomatology, but rather a developmental expressive therapy geared toward emotionally charged and articulate public communication. Public space is not only a stage for democracy but also a healing environment for free and open speaking. Art and design have a crucial role to play in contributing to its development as such.

In studying *parrhesia,* Foucault is less concerned with the truth itself than with the *practices* of "truth-telling" and the role of the agent who enacts them. This leads to a set of questions with lasting resonance. Foucault asks:

> Who is able to tell the truth? What are the moral, the ethical, and the spiritual conditions which entitle someone to present himself as, and to be considered as, a truth-teller?

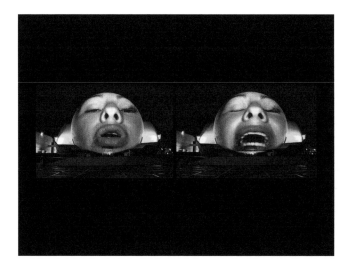

> About what topics is it important to tell the truth? (About
> the world? About nature? About the city? About behavior?
> About man?) What are the consequences of telling the
> truth? What are its anticipated positive effects for the city,
> for the city's rulers, for the individual, etc.? And finally:
> what is the relation between truth-telling and the exercise
> of power, or should these activities be completely inde-
> pendent and kept separate? Are they separable, or do they
> require one another?[6]

Truth-telling in the *parrhesia* mode raises questions about who is able to tell
the truth, what truth can be spoken, what the consequences of truth-telling
are, and what the relation is between truth-telling and power. Foucault says
that *parrhesia* is "a kind of verbal activity where the speaker has a certain
relation to truth through frankness, a certain relationship to his own life
through danger, a certain type of relationship to himself or other people
through criticism, and a specific relation to moral law through freedom and
duty."[7] While the importance of the political and ethical qualifications of the
parrhesiates were strongly emphasized by Foucault in his lectures of 1983,
his lectures the following year emphasized with the equal importance the
capacity and ability of the interlocutor to *listen*.[8] Here, Foucault stressed that

the participant in Socratic dialogues also had to enter into a *parrhesia*stic pact in which they agreed not only to speak but also to listen to the truth spoken about themselves by others. Foucault suggests, therefore, that "*parrhesia* is the courage of truth in the person who speak and who, regardless of everything, takes the risk of telling the whole truth that he thinks, but it is also *the interlocutor's courage in agreeing to accept the hurtful truth that he hears.*"[9] Those who come forward with unsolicited and often unspeakable truth need interlocutors who can open themselves up to listen fearlessly. Therefore the truth in every genuine speech act lays not so much in content but in the emotional charge of both speaking and listening.

Foucault argues that the truth-telling act in ancient Greece required a field of mutual protection, trust, and courage.[10] In an attempt to create a "zone of truth-telling," my work seeks to create intermediate, transitory, and transitional artifices, situations, and events that facilitate the development of both fearless speaking and fearless listening through the exchange of memories, experiences, and critical visions. In particular, the *Homeless Vehicle* project (1988–89), *Tijuana Projection* (2001), and the *War Veteran Vehicle project* (2008) illustrate the relationship between art, trauma, and *parrhesia* in my work. I strongly believe that artistic projects that facilitate fearless speech can contribute to the development of a dynamic, agonistic public sphere that runs counter to the pain and silence that often follow trauma, and actively speaks out against the perpetuation of violence and bloodshed.

As described above, the Homeless Vehicle combines both communication and transport; it articulates the real conditions of work and life

SPIRITUAL SPACES

Varanasi is a sacred Hindu city located on the banks of the Ganges River. Miles of steps–known as ghats–lead down to the waterfront where cremations and religious bathing occur. Schools and temples fill the city where sacred cows walk freely. Many millions of pilgrims visit Varanasi annually.

Spiritual spaces have the power to bring people together. Millions of Muslims from around the world take pilgrimage to Mecca, fulfilling one of the five pillars of Islam. How and by whom are such sacred sites constructed, maintained, and expanded upon, especially with swelling numbers of pilgrims?

In 2011–2012, the Occupy London movement encamped in front of St Paul's Cathedral. Calling for global democracy, the movement surrounded the 1712 statue of Queen Anne. Prompting the temporary closure of the cathedral and subsequent resignations of clergy, there are often more to spaces of the political than we can at first see.

Often seen as a sign of purity and love, the white dove has symbolic meanings across religions and societies. White doves are released after a wedding in Palermo, a moment of great joy, while life goes on in the background.

SPIRITUAL SPACES

How is spirituality etched into the physical, material, and ephemeral pulse of a city? A person's shadow is cast against a mural painted on the side of a building lining a street in Athens. The street is empty during the financial crisis of 2015.

Handmade baskets of rice, flowers, holy water, incense, and food, called *canang sari,* line streets in Bali as daily offerings to Hindu gods. Families pass down this tradition in the home while the offerings are placed in the public domain. Do notions of private and public shape spaces of the spiritual?

for this group. In this sense, the Homeless Vehicle is both a practical piece of design for the daily needs of the homeless as well as a device for the homeless person to become a *parrhesiastes*—a speaker of uncomfortable truths.

The purpose of the *Tijuana Project* was to use technological tools to give voice and visibility to the women who work in the *maquiladora* industry in Tijuana. Those who participated in the project wore a special headset (comprised of a camera and a microphone) while giving testimonies on a variety of issues, including work-related abuse, sexual abuse, family disintegration, alcoholism, and domestic violence. These problems were shared with an audience of more than 1,500 as the women's voices were broadcast via loudspeaker and their faces were projected on the 60-foot facade of the Omnimax Theater at the Centro Cultural Tijuana. This project was part of InSITE2000, a binational contemporary art project based on artistic investigation and activation of urban space in San Diego and Tijuana.

...*Out of Here* is a projection-based installation that focuses the experience of war veterans engaged in active combat in Iraq as well as Iraqi civilians. In the installation, sounds of everyday life are interrupted by the noise of destruction and chaos, which seems to be unfolding outside the walls of the gallery. This immersive projection was based on work undertaken with medics, soldiers, and refugees affected by the conflict in Iraq. They shared their wartime experiences through video and audio reenactments, which were then projected onto the gallery walls. The projected stories reflect the physical and psychological environment of combat, as well as the fragmented nature of memories of distressing or uncertain situations.

In the same vein, the *War Veteran Vehicle* project seeks to offer a tool for those who have experienced war firsthand to share their experiences with others. Military vehicles such as the Humvee (United States), Land Rover (United Kingdom), and Hunker (Poland) were equipped with special rotating projection units sound and video "battle stations" that replace canons and rocket launchers—projectiles—with projectors. The vehicles facilitate the recording of testimonies, which can then be projected onto blank walls, monuments, and other sites in public space, resulting in a powerful visual and acoustic resonance. Their aim is to arm war veterans for a new battle, this time against misinformation that circulates about war through the reinscription of city monuments with previously silenced voices, witnesses to a new history of war and suffering. In doing so, they hope that this history will not repeat itself.

Tragically, those who should be the first to testify as *parrhesiastes* are often discouraged and even incapacitated by the very experience they should be publicly protesting, announcing, and denouncing. As a result of traumatic life events, their ability to openly share their suffering through testimony has been shattered. They may suffer a loss of motivation, expression, and even of memory. Thus they keep silent. Even when given a political and technical opportunity to speak, they are often not able to speak fearlessly. In other words, the mere act of offering a podium, a lectern, a microphone, a megaphone, or a cultural and political stage does not necessarily mean that these individuals will speak fearlessly, or be heard.

I believe that experimental tools such as the *Homeless Vehicle*, the *Tijuana Projection*, and the *War Veterans Vehicle* can act as psychological, cultural, and political aids for those who are unable to open up and communicate in the open. Through their use, they might help these incipient *parrhesiastes* redevelop their ability to open up to themselves and others, while offering a platform for the transmission of their voices and images in public space. Ultimately, the communicative and performative properties of the tools inspire such developments, but the act of speech is ultimately undertaken by their users. It is their fearless speech—the art of public testimony and performance—that is the most important part of the project development.

To animate public space, one must animate oneself. Conversely, animating oneself helps to animate public space—politically, psychologically and artistically. Here, Mouffe's agonistic pluralism, Foucault's return to *parrhesia,* and Judith Herman's testimonial "Acts of Public Truth" merge in the development of one complex political psycho-social, techno-aesthetic, and cultural-communicative project that seeks to develop new platforms for critical memory, public testimony, and recovery from trauma.

1 An earlier version of this essay appeared in *Art & the Public Sphere*, 1, no. 3 (December 2011).
Claude Lefort, "Human Rights and the Welfare State," in *Democracy and Political Theory* (Minneapolis: University of Minnesota Press), 41.
2 Pierre Janet, *The Mental State of Hystericals: A Study of Mental Stigmata and Mental Accidents* (New York: Putnam, 1901).
3 While pragmatically responding to the needs of the homeless, the appearance and function of the the Homeless Vehicle aim at focusing public attention on the unacceptability of such needs and in this way further scandalize the scandal of homelessness. The vehicle's design is responding to needs that should not exist in a civilized world, but which unfortunately do exist. The "utopia" of the vehicle is based on the assumption that its articulating function and scandalizing presence will contribute to better public consciousness (regarding

the unacceptable homeless situation), toward political and social change and a new situation in which the homeless will no longer exist and there would be no longer a need for the homeless vehicle and its design.
4 Maarten Hajer and Arnold Reijndorp, *In Search of a New Public Domain: Analysis and Strategy* (Rotterdam: NAI Publishers, 2001).
5 Chantal Mouffe, "Artistic Agonism and Public Spaces," *Art & Research* 1, no. 2 (Summer 2007). http://www.artandresearch.org.uk/v1n2/mouffe.html
6 Michel Foucault, *Fearless Speech* (Los Angeles: Semiotext[e], 2001), 169.
7 Ibid., 19–20.
8 Michel Foucault, *The Courage of Truth*, trans. Graham Burchell (London: Palgrave Macmillan, 2011).
9 Ibid., 13.
10 Ibid., 130.

German Visions of Marseille (1926–1943): Modern Stage or Place of Perdition?

Jean-Louis Cohen
Translation by Peter Sealy

Marseille, 1943

Paris was not the only field in which Franco-German interference took place.[1] Cities such as Frankfurt, Hamburg, Cologne, Munich, on the one hand, and Strasbourg and Metz (obviously), but also Lyon, Lille, or Marseille have been engaged in complex relationships. Marseille had been attentively observed and heavily visited by Germans since the 18th century. The young Arthur Schopenhauer noted for instance in his journal in 1804: "I am convinced that Marseille is the most beautiful city in France."[2] The present argument will dwell upon a particularly tense encounter between Germany and Marseille, a turbulent Mediterranean metropolis.[3]

Two months after the November 1942 Axis invasion of France's "unoccupied" zone, the daily *Marseille-Matin* published the following release from the regional prefecture:

The old harbor of Marseille, c. 1930

> For military reasons and in order to guarantee the security of the population, the German military authorities have notified the French administration of the order to proceed immediately with the evacuation of the area north of the Old Port, between the quai du Maréchal-Pétain, la Tourette, the rue Caisserie and the rue Chevalier-Roze. For its part, the French administration decided to launch a vast police action for reasons of internal security, in order to remove from the city of Marseille certain elements whose activities caused a grave risk for the entire population. The French administration strove to make sure that these two operations were not to be confused.[4]

After the evacuation of some 11 hectares, German Army sappers dynamited 1,482 houses within this area and 20,000 persons were rounded up and first sent to the Royallieu internment and deportation camp in Compiègne, and from there to various concentration camps in Germany.[5] For many reasons, this episode is unique in the history of the Nazi occupation of France. With the exception of zones damaged by combat, no other urban area was subjected to such destruction by occupiers. The exact conditions of the operation are precisely known, as are the tortuous circumstances of the neighborhood's reconstruction after the Liberation, which led, among other things, to the building of Fernand Pouillon's famous housing scheme.[6]

The question that I would like to ask is how this unique episode can be understood and linked to the bundle of representations of Marseille that developed in Germany from the onset of the 1920s. The operation undertaken by the Nazis with the assistance of the Vichy police lies at the intersection of a decades-old policy of urban renewal and a series of literary, photographic,

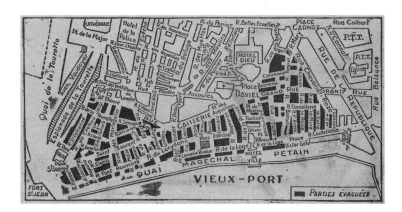

Old Port District, Marseille, 1943, plan of "evacuated areas"

and cinematographic representations of a neighborhood and a city that were in many ways overexposed.

A century after Arthur Schopenhauer's declaration, numerous German and Austrian artists and intellectuals converged on the Mediterranean city in the 1920s. They were interested in the juxtaposition of the colorful city and a fascinating technical object: the *pont transbordeur* built by the engineer Ferdinand Arnodin in 1905. A sort of southern analogue to the Eiffel Tower, it became a notable object of fixation for German photographers and artists.[7] Herbert Bayer and Germaine Krull photographed the bridge. It starred in László Moholy-Nagy's 1929 film *Impressions of the Old Port of Marseilles,* in which he strove to develop his "new vision" of the city, previously shaped from the top of the radio tower in Berlin. But Moholy-Nagy was not captivated solely by Arnodin's bridge. Marseille's urban ambiances also caught his attention:

> It is so hot that one has the impression that even the roads will melt. But the throngs never cease on the large avenue de la Canebière. The tramways ring out, the cars accumulate; in the middle, a funeral procession descends slowly toward the Old Port. Six women carry the coffin.

August Sander, photograph of the Transborder Bridge

> Artificial flowers and sacred objects decorate the funerary
> convoy. Only in the countryside can we still see such scenes
> at home, during communions or the feasts of the Virgin.
> Dressed in black attire, the mourners make their way
> through the dense traffic under the burning sun.[8]

Next to the transporter bridge, Moholy-Nagy focused his attention not on the Canebière, but rather, for supposedly practical reasons, on the neighboring blocks:

> I had at my disposition a fixed length of film (300m) and
> I thought that it was best not to present the whole of a large
> city on so little film. So I chose a neighborhood of the
> larger city, the Old Port, an area little known to the public
> because of its unhappy social situation, its misery and
> its insecurity. I did not want to make a purely impressionist
> reportage, but finally I had to settle for a sketch of the
> situation. I was not even able to take high angle shots to
> better grasp the whole. When, in shadowy blocks, I finally
> managed to penetrate into an upper-floor apartment,
> I was received with such hostility that I had to flee rapidly,
> and, in the street, I was often seriously threatened.[9]

A kind of double synecdoche of the city is thereby put in place. The first makes the transporter bridge the index of the city's industrial modernity. The second makes the Old Port the index of the whole of working-class Marseille. But this clear duality presented in Moholy-Nagy's film fades in the stories of other observers and writers, and it is this multiple Marseille that dominated.

The Austrian novelist Joseph Roth portrayed Marseille around 1925 in a series of brief texts on "white cities," noting, "Marseille is New York and Singapore, Hamburg and Calcutta, Alexandria and Port Arthur, San Francisco and Odessa.... It is no longer France. It is Europe, Asia, Africa, America. It is white, black, red and yellow: each drags his own country on the soles of his shoes and transports it thus to Marseille."[10] Writing for the *Frankfurter Zeitung,* Roth clarified this vision of humanity gathered on the docks of Marseille:

> Here come horsemen from Turkestan, in wide trousers
> gathered at the ankles, swathing their bandy legs. Then
> little Chinese sailors in snow white uniforms, like boys in
> Sunday suits; the great merchants from Smyrna and
> Constantinople, so powerful, it's as though they dealt in

kingdoms, not carpets; the Greek traders, who never
their deals inside four walls but only ever in the open,
perhaps in order to provoke God the more; the little ships'
cooks from Indochina, whisking lightfootedly through
the evening, swift and silent like nocturnal animals; Greek
monks, with long hempen beards; native priests, carrying
their own bulk in front of them like someone else's load;
dark nuns in colorful throng, each one an element from
a funeral procession.[11]

This representation of the crucible of nationalities embodied by Marseille
was not the one highlighted by Walter Benjamin, who discovered the city in
the following year, meeting Siegfried Kracauer for the first time in the process.[12] Without delay he shared with Gershom Scholem his affection for this
"sleeping city of unspeakable beauty."[13] Benjamin's famous text "Hashish in
Marseille" put forward his hallucinatory vision of the city. But in an article
published by the *Neue Schweizer Rundschau* in 1929, Benjamin lingers on
Marseille's borders, the limits between the city's sprawl and the hills surrounding its northern districts:

These, when they were my first steps in this city, had to
follow one of my old rules for travelling: this was, unlike
most foreigners who, once disembarked, inconveniently
cram themselves into the city center, I first explore
the periphery, the outskirts. I soon began to appreciate
how much this principle—uniquely here—was needed.
Never had a first hour of *flânerie* brought me so much than
the one I passed between the basins and the docks, the
warehouses, in the miserable quarters, the scattered
asylums of distress. The suburbs are the city in a state of
emergency, the terrain upon which the decisive combat
between city and country takes place in perpetuity.
Nowhere is this battle fiercer than between Marseille and
the Provençal countryside. It is the hand-to-hand combat
of telegraph poles against agave plants, barbed iron
wire against the barbs of palm trees, the gas clouds of the
stinking corridors against the humid shadow of the plane
trees, the breathless stoops against the mighty hills.
The interminable rue de Lyon is the mine that Marseille has
dug under the landscape so as to explode it at Saint-Lazare,
Saint-Antoine, Arenc and Septèmes, and then to bury it

> under the fragments from this grenade of all the languages
> of geography and commerce: Alimentation moderne, rue
> de la Jamaïque, Comptoir de la Limite, Savon Abat-Jour,
> Minoterie de la Campagne, bar du Gaz, bar Facultatif.
> Atop all of this a fine dust made of sea salt, lime and mica
> accumulates.[14]

This dust enveloping Marseille is also palpable in the city center, around the Old Port:

> My footsteps bring me next to the most far-flung docks,
> reserved for the great transatlantic liners, under the
> sharp rays of a sun setting lower and lower, between the
> foundation walls of the old city on my left and arid hills
> or the quarries to my right, in the direction of the high
> transporter bridge which closes this magical quadrilateral
> carved by the Phoeniciens as a vast square facing the
> sea: the Old Port.[15]

Benjamin's direct experience of the transporter bridge led him to be particularly sensitive to Sigfried Giedion's evocation of this structure, Giedion having also visited Marseille as he prepared his book *Building in France, Building in Iron, Building in Ferro-concrete*. Giedion's often-quoted claim that the "basic aesthetic experience of today's building," is that in which "things," seen from the Eiffel Tower or Marseille's transporter bridge, stream "through the delicate iron net suspended in midair" so that "as one descends, they circle into each other and intermingle simultaneously" is doubtlessly more informed by his experience of the bridge than the tower.[16] Benjamin's love for Marseille was intense. In 1928, he wrote to Walter Cohn: "I know now that it is more difficult to write three pages on Marseille than a book about Florence."[17] The following year, he wrote to Hugo von Hofmannsthal that his texts on this "marvelous city" reflected "without doubt his weakness for a city he loved for the most humble reasons, and with which he grappled like none other. To describe it in one sentence is more difficult than to describe Rome in a book."[18] His interest in Marseille's urbanism was particularly strong, as he told Jean Ballard, publisher and editor of the *Cahiers du Sud,* who published his "Hashish in Marseille," affirming himself "happy to be able to know [his] ideas on urbanism as they related to Marseille": "Maybe you have already understood how much I love your city. My love would profit greatly from being enlightened by your book which is founded, I am certain, on knowledge that an outsider, while strolling, could never acquire."[19]

Joseph Roth also perceived the vitality of the port of Marseille in 1925. Roth was struck by the "chaos of this vast order," and also a dust, this time coal dust:

> "Is it here, the immense door through which we go to
> the immense seas of the world? No, it is instead the
> huge store for common consumer goods from across the
> European continent. Here are barrels, cases, beams,
> wheels, levers, tanks, ladders, tongs, hammers, sacks,
> sheets, tents, vehicles, horses, motors, autos, tyres. Here
> is the intoxicating and cosmopolitan scent that rises
> when a hundred hectoliters of turpentine are warehoused
> next to a hundred quintals of herring, when petroleum,
> pepper, tomatoes, vinegar, sardines, Russian leather, gutta-
> percha, onions, saltpeter, alcohol, sacks, soles, canvas,
> the royal tiger, hyenas, goats, angora cats, cattle and carpets
> from Smyrna exhale their hot vapors; and when to finish
> the greasy and heavy coal smoke envelops the living and
> the dead, uniting all the odours, penetrating all the pores,
> saturates the air, veils the stones and shows itself in the
> long run to be so strong that it filters the sounds as, for so
> long, it has filtered the light."[20]

As for Kracauer, he evoked an "apparition on the Canebière" in his 1928 novel *Ginster*.[21] The vision he conjured in 1926 in an article in the *Frankfurter Zeitung* is that of "two planes," that of the port, a "liquid place," and that of the square, probably la Plaine, whose walls "[seal] off the labyrinth." He is struck by the "distress of the warehouses' naked walls" and that which borders them:

> In the spongy depths of the harbor quarter the fauna of
> humanity is teeming, and in the puddles the sky is pristine.
> Outdated palaces are converted into brothels that outlive
> every ancestral portrait gallery. The mass of humanity
> in which the peoples of different nations blend together is
> flushed through avenues and bazaar streets. These define
> the borders of the districts into which the human tide
> disperses. In the shell-like windings of one of those districts
> rages the eternal mass of small-time tradespeople.[22]

In fragmentary notes, Benjamin also considers the elements of Marseille's urban landscape, sometimes finding echoes of Paris and attaching himself, like Kracauer, to places like "die Karree"—once again, probably la Plaine, the prostitutes' neighborhoods and the historic monuments, of which he gives a particularly piercing view, as with the case of Léon Vaudoyer's cathedral, the Major, which he calls "Marseille's train station of religion": "At the time of the mass, trains of sleeping cars are assembled here for eternity."[23] Benjamin has harsh words for the population of this "yellowed set of teeth, through which the saltwater escapes": "The people of the port are a bacillus; the porters and prostitutes embody human decomposition."[24]

Space does not permit a complete survey of the most striking reports from the many journalists or writers who passed through Marseille in the 1920s and 1930s: the reporter Egon Erwin Kisch, Erika and Klaus Mann, or Kurt Tucholsky, who compared the form of the port to that of the "Alster at Hamburg" and noted "this frightening profusion of houses that rise around a large basin of water, straight houses, crammed together, almost menacing, always one row atop another, invading the hillside, they encircle the old port."[25]

While Marcel Pagnol's populist films reinforced the images of old Marseille's iconic characters in the eyes of the French public, the image of the city constructed by conservative forces was profoundly negative, of a sort of Mediterranean Chicago. The adventures of the gangsters Carbone and Spirito were folded without difficulty into those of their American colleagues. For far-right critics, the port through which the foreigners menacing the French race disembarked made Marseille into a symbol of the invasion of

the "*métèques*." In 1937, *Le Matin* evoked "this foreign scum in the dumping ground of France, who 'come as they please.'[26] Certain authors contributed to the construction of this Chicago-esque representation. In *L'homme foudroyé,* Blaise Cendrars called Marseille "the only capital of antiquity that does not crush us with the monuments of its past." "Marseille seems well behaved and jocular," but "it is dirty and distorted" and above all "one of the most mysterious and hard to decipher cities in the world."[27]

A veteran of the French Foreign Legion like Cendrars, Ernst Jünger recalls one of Marseille's "shady neighborhoods" in his 1936 *Afrikanische Spiele (African Diversions)*, published in French in 1944: "The air was full of foreign odors from the great warehouses and marine detritus, from this breath of commercial anarchy which impregnates and animates all maritime cities."[28] In their 1933 *Notre Provence*, the nationalist writers Charles Maurras and Léon Daudet described a "living and swarming repertory," "this giant shell where all the languages rustle," with its "picturesque streets neighboring the port, which smell of oil, garlic, and a worse odor."[29] Of all the senses, Marseille brings smell to the forefront. Even the art historian and member of the Académie française Louis Gillet repeated this same tenor, writing in the official magazine of the municipality *Marseille* of 21 October 1942:

> On the Accoules hillside, between the city hall and
> the Major, resides an obscene Suburra [the brothel district
> in ancient Rome—ed.], one of the most impure cesspools
> in Marseille's sad glory, where the froth of the Mediter-
> ranean gathers with a level of decrepitude and a degree of

ILL. 18. — VUE AÉRIENNE DU QUARTIER DE LA CATHÉDRALE
APRÈS AMÉNAGEMENT DES ACCÈS AU PORT

Jacques Gréber, *Development Plan for the Extension and Beautification of Marseille,*
1933, view of the Cathedral and Panier district after transformation

rottenness which, without having seen it, we would find difficult to imagine. It seems that venality and leprosy spread their corruption to its very stones. This worm-eaten hell, this sort of decomposing mass grave, is one of the places where tuberculosis wreaks the most havoc in the world. It is the empire of sin and of death. How can the pus be drained from these once patrician neighborhoods, now abandoned to the blackguards, to misery and to shame, so that they may be regenerated? The best we can do is to find in this bilge the few elements worthy of conservation, to organize a rescue and to treat this part of Marseille as a museum where the visitor will seek grounds for reverie.[30]

This diatribe can be linked to the stigmatizations of the "accursed neighborhoods" of Paris and other French cities. Such an image associating delinquency and bastardization drifted across France's borders, notably to Germany.

Alongside these circulating representations, Marseille modernized itself during the interwar period. The most fruitful proposal was that of Jacques Gréber, an architect and urban planner familiar with American cities. He created a regional plan in which the city's overall zoning was redefined. While motorways were planned for the periphery, the center was to be the subject of a modernization project, in which the districts between the Old Port and la Joliette were to be replaced by an airier fabric. Following France's capitulation in 1940, Eugène Beaudouin was tasked in 1941 with

Cité de l'architecture et du patrimoine, newspaper coverage of the Plan Beaudoin

continuing Gréber's project, notably by producing more detailed plans for the reorganization of the existing city.

The occupation marks a threshold in the conception of urban renewal, notably with the project for the îlot *insalubre* (diseased zone) in Paris's Marais district, the object of a violent polemic in 1941. Jean-Charles Moreux and others raised the notion of the *quartier-musée*, which would be mentioned in passing by Gillet. Meanwhile, the Marseille municipality led a parallel study on its slums and the historical buildings to be preserved and enhanced.[31]

However, the case of Marseille is unique in its radicalism. Between 1940 and 1943 the Phocaean city became a hub for refugees and fugitives seeking passage to the Americas. In her novel *Transit,* Anna Seghers vividly describes the flow of humanity leading to the Old Port:

> The last few months I'd been wondering where all this
> was going to end up—the trickles, the streams of people
> from the camps, the dispersed soldiers, the army
> mercenaries, the defilers of all races, the deserters from
> all nations. This, then, was where the detritus was flowing,
> along this channel, this gutter, the Canebière, and via
> this gutter into the sea, where there would at last be room
> for all, and peace.[32]

Kracauer, his American visa in his pocket, met Walter Benjamin for the last time on the road to Port-Bou, which was to be the latter's tragic final

View of the destruction of Marseille's Old Port

destination. Numerous other Germans and Austrians were incarcerated at the Les Milles internment camp, having first made Marseille into the capital of surrealism, if only for awhile. One of them was the writer Lion Feuchtwanger, who published *The Devil in France* during the war, a book that echoes Friedrich Sieburg's best-seller *Dieu est-il français*, but whose chapter on Marseille is sadly only skeletal.[33]

      Although Beaudouin developed his work under the authority of the Vichy government, the destruction of the port area was not undertaken in January 1943 to accelerate his urban renewal operations. Instead, the Germans' pretext for demolition was an attack by the Resistance. The chain of decisions can be described as follows: With the arrival of the Wehrmacht on November 12, 1942, an order was given to the occupiers to "avoid, as strictly as possible, all contact between the population and the German divisions stationed inside the old city and the port. As a port city, Marseille is known for being a reservoir of criminal elements and a dangerous hotbed of contagion."[34] In fact this "hard to decipher" city, to use Cendrars' term, was—exceptionally within occupied France—placed under the direct control of the SS. Heinrich Himmler therefore oversaw operations in Marseille; his orders were executed by the chief of the SS and of the Gestapo in France, Karl Oberg, assisted by the secretary general of the French police, René Bousquet. In response to an attack against a brothel frequented by Germans, Himmler moved to directly carry out Hitler's personal instructions to "raze" a city that

The Maison Diamantée, c. 1930

had "forever" been "a bandit's den."[35] On January 18, 1943, he ordered Oberg to produce "a radical and complete solution for the purification of Marseille." This involved a "total dynamiting of the criminals' neighborhood." Himmler notably ordered the destruction of the (largely mythical) "subterranean passages" and "caverns" that formed Marseille's *Unterstadt,* a term that can be translated in many ways—as the "lower city," but also as the city of the *Untermenschen,* or subhumans. He considered Marseille to be a "pigsty" (*Saustall*). And since "Marseille's pigsty is France's pigsty," he ordered Oberg to make sure the French police participated "to the widest extent" in the operation.[36]

It is noteworthy that the prefect designated as Marseille's administrator, Pierre Barraud, declared several days later to the German consul that "the Old Port owes its destruction to its bad reputation: it was known everywhere as the world's most dangerous criminal center," while "in reality, it is inhabited for the most part by fishers, artisans, and peaceful folk."[37] To carry out the operation, the Germans worked closely with Bousquet, while the Inspector of Historic Monuments Jules Formigé tried somehow to save the most the most remarkable buildings—the city hall, the Maison Diamantée, the hôtel de Cabre, and the hôtel du Chevalier Magrin. A communiqué dated February 1 finally announced: "The municipal administration wants to reassure the city's population about the fate of those buildings of historical, archeological, or aesthetic interest. Since January 24, the city's urban planner has been tasked with identifying these buildings, as well as the architectural components worthy of preservation.[38] In fact, only a few *hôtels particuliers* escaped destruction. The destruction—which was considered to be exemplary—was meticulously documented by the *Propagandakompanien*'s photog-

View of the destruction of Marseille's Old Port

raphers and journalists like the "correspondent" Walther Kiaulehn, who led a successful postwar career as a best-selling author. While originally sympathetic to the left, Kiaulehn was recruited and supported by Joseph Goebbels. During the war, he became a theater actor, all the while publishing books on Berlin and editing the *Münchner Merkur*'s literary gazette.

In a special issue of the German Army's propaganda magazine, *Signal*, Kiaulehn reported that, while positioned atop the transporter bridge, he had read Gillet's text, which he cited at length to justify the Nazi intervention. Strangely, the issue of *Marseille* magazine containing Gillet's article is missing from the bound volume conserved by the French national library in Paris. The district's destruction is presented by Kiaulehn as a kind of positive contribution on behalf of the occupier toward the completion of French projects. He noted that "the cesspool has been purified" in this "rare instance of a war measure coinciding with projects adopted long before by the municipality and the government": in this case, Beaudouin's plan. Supporting this justification, *Signal* itself published a perspective view presented as being "made following the French architects' plans," but which was in fact a graphic interpretation of them.[39] Several months after the German operation, the municipal magazine *Marseille* affirmed that the "new situation, while completely unpredictable, had profoundly modified the conditions of the problem under consideration" and justified the full resumption of the project, then awaiting final approval. The "demolition of the Old Port" was only a "coincidence," or the result of a "fluke."[40]

View of the destruction of Marseille's Old Port

While Kiaulehn changed his mind and pleaded for its preservation, the transporter bridge survived only eighteen months longer in the area it once dominated. Criticized since its erection by lovers of old Marseille, it had been largely unused since the 1930s. Its dismantlement was ordered by the Vichy government, justified by the need to recover metal; it contained over 1,180 tons of steel. The Germans destroyed it on August 22, 1944, only three days before the city's eventual liberation, in order to prevent allied ships from entering the Old Port.[41]

The history of the area's reconstruction is too long and complex to be recounted here. Judged by public opinion in Marseille to be at least indirectly responsible for its destruction, Beaudouin was relieved of his duties, and replaced first by Roger-Henri Expert, then André Leconte, and finally Auguste Perret, who supported Fernard Pouillon's plan. While debate raged before construction finally got under way, the press returned to the events of 1943. A conspiracy by the Banque de Paris et des Pays-Bas was unearthed, for it had agreed in 1942 to the formation of a joint development company with the city, the Régie foncière et immobilière de la Ville de Marseille, to carry out part of Beaudouin's project. The general council of the Bouches-du-Rhône demanded an investigation in 1946.[42] The operation undertaken on the fortifications of Paris came evidently to mind as a precedent. It was even suggested in the left-wing press that Beaudouin had personally acquired lots in the district.[43]

The episodes of January 1943 became the stuff of fiction. Hugo Fregonese's 1957 *Seven Thunders (or The Beasts of Marseille)* recounts the adventures of two escaped British soldiers hiding in the port area. A French paperback version published the following year showed the dust cloud from the explosions rising in front of the silhouette of Marseille on its cover.[44]

Would the destruction of the Old Port area have been averted had its interwar representations been different? Nothing supports this affirmation, and it is possible that Gréber and Beaudouin's cleansing project would have been undertaken in any case, leading to the conservation of a greater number of historical buildings. The fact remains that the aggressiveness with which Himmler and Oberg operated cannot be dissociated from the images they and Hitler had endorsed. In parallel with the representations made by intellectuals attentive to the colorful scene of the docks and to the poetry of the popular quarters, these images, along with the many tropes propagated by French and German xenophobes, had murderous effects: an "urbicide" in the context of genocide.

This text originally appeared as: "Visions allemandes de Marseille (1926–1943): scène moderne ou lieu de perdition," in *Metropolen 1850–1950: Mythen–Bilder–Entwürfe*, Cohen and Helmuth Frank, eds. (Berlin: Deutscher Kunstverlag, 2013), 351–67.

1 On the notion of interference, see Jean-Louis Cohen and Hartmut Frank, eds. *Interférences/Interferenzen: Architecture, Allemagne, France, 1800–2000* (Strasbourg, 2013).

2 Arthur Schopenhauer, *Journal de voyage* (Paris, 1989), 143, quoted by Heinke Wunderlich, *Marseille vue par les écrivains de langue allemande* (Paris, 2000).

3 We may also note Marseille's unfortunate appearance in urban planning treatises, for in his *City-Planning According to Artistic Principles*, published in 1889, Camillo Sitte inadvertently situated the Place St-Michel, called in Marseille the "Plain" ("*la Plaine*"), in Nîmes. The Viennese architect notes pertinently that it consists of a "square cut through the heart of a maze of winding streets." Camillo Sitte, *Der Städtebau nach seinen* künstlerischen *Grundsätzen* (Vienna: Graeser, 1889), 105.

4 *Marseille-Matin* (January 28, 1943).

5 Christian Oppetit, ed., *Marseille, Vichy et les nazis: le temps des rafles, la déportation des juifs* (Marseille, 1993), and Ahlrich Meyer, ed., *Der Blick des Besatzers. Propagandaphotographie der Wehrmacht aus Marseille 1942–1944* (Bremen, 1999).

6 On the reconstruction of Marseille, see Sheila Crane, *Mediterranean Crossroads: Marseille and Modern Architecture* (Minneapolis: University of Minnesota Press, 2011); Jean-Lucien Bonillo, *Reconstruction à Marseille: architectures et projets urbains, 1940–1960* (Marseille, 2008); Danièle Voldman, *Fernand Pouillon, architecte* (Paris, 2006).

7 See Bernard Millet, ed., *Le pont transbordeur et la vision moderniste* (Marseille, 1991).

8 László Moholy-Nagy, quoted by Krisztina Passuth, "Moholy-Nagy Marseille, Vieux-Port–1929," in Bernard Millet, ed., *Le pont transbordeur et la vision moderniste* (Marseille, 1991), 68.

9 László Moholy-Nagy, quoted by Passuth, ibid., 69.

10 Joseph Roth, "Marseilles Revisited," in *Report from a Parisian Paradise: Essays from France, 1925–1939* (New York: W. W. Norton, 2004), 130.

11 Joseph Roth, "In the French Midi," *Report from a Parisian Paradise*, 56–57.

12 Klaus Michael, "Vor dem Café. Walter Benjamin und Siegfried Kracauer in Marseille," in Michael Opitz and Erdmut Wizisla, eds., *Aber ein Sturm weht vom Paradiese her: Texte zu Walter Benjamin* (Leipzig, 1992), 203–16.

13 Walter Benjamin, letter to Gershom Sholem, September 18, 1926, Archives Benjamin, Akademie der Künste, Berlin.

14 Walter Benjamin "Myslowice–Braunschweig–Marseille: Une histoire de haschich," in *Rastelli raconte... et autres récits*, trans. by Philippe Jaccottet (Paris, 1987), 41–42.

15 Ibid, 42.

16 Sigfried Giedion, *Building in France, Building in Iron, Building in Ferroconcrete*, trans. J. Duncan Berry (Santa Monica, CA: Getty Center for the History of Art and the Humanities, 1995), 91. Translation of *Bauen in Frankreich, Bauen in Eisen, Bauen in Eisenbeton* [1925].

17 Walter Benjamin, letter to Alfred Cohn, October 22, 1928, Archives Benjamin, Akademie der Künste, Berlin.

18 Walter Benjamin, letter to Hugo von Hofmannsthal, Berlin, June 26, 1929, in Walter Benjamin, *Gesammelte Briefe*, 6 vol., vol. 3, 1925–1930, Christoph Gödde and Henri Lonitz, eds. (Frankfurt, 1997), 472. Benjamin uses the expression "wundervolle Stadt" in another letter to Hugo von Hofmannsthal, dated October 30, 1926.

19 Walter Benjamin, letter to Jean Ballard, San Remo, February 2, 1935, in Walter Benjamin, *Gesammelte Briefe*, 6 vol., vol. 5, 1935–1937, Christoph Gödde and Henri Lonitz, eds. (Frankfurt, 1999), 31.

20 Joseph Roth, "Marseilles Revisited," in *Report from a Parisian Paradise*.

21 Siegfried Kracauer, "Apparition sur la Canebière," in *Rues de Berlin et d'ailleurs* (Paris, 1995), 172–73; first published in *Ginster* (Berlin, 1928).

22 Siegfried Kracauer, "Two Planes in The Mass Ornament: Weimar Essay (Cambridge, MA: Harvard University Press, 1995), 50.

23 Walter Benjamin, "Cathédrale," *Images de pensée* (Paris, 1998), 107.

24 Walter Benjamin, "Marseille," *Images de pensée,* 103.

25 Kurt Tucholsky, "Marseille," in *Gesammelte Werke* (Reinbeck, 1960), 1138, quoted in Heinke Wunderlich, *Marseille vue par les* écrivains *de langue allemande* (Paris, 2000), 125.

26 *Le Matin*, September 29, 1937.

27 Blaise Cendrars, *L'homme foudroyé*, quoted in Julie Agostini and Yannick Forno, eds., *Les écrivains et Marseille, anthologie commentée de textes littéraires sur Marseille du ve siècle avant J.-C. à nos jours* (Marseille, 1997), 284–85.

28 Ernst Jünger, *Jeux africains*, quoted in Agostini and Forno, eds., 299.

29 Charles Maurras et Léon Daudet, *Notre Provence* (Paris: Flammarion, 1933), quoted in Agostini and Forno, eds., 274–75.

30 Louis Gillet, *Marseille* 21 (October 1942), quoted in Walther Kiaulehn, "Marseille," *Signal* 7 (April 1943).

31 Raoul Busquet, "Les origines de la maison Diamantée," *Marseille* 18 (June 1941): 2–10; Pierre Barraud, "La lutte contre les taudis dans les programmes des grands travaux," *Marseille* 19 (August–October 1941): 2–8; Henri Ripert, "Les taudis," *Marseille* 19: 9–15.

32 Anna Seghers, *Transit*, trans. Margot Bettauer Dembo, (New York: New York Review of Books, 2013), 35. First published in 1944 (Boston: Little Brown).

33 Lion Feuchtwanger, *The Devil in France: My Encounter with Him in the Summer of 1940,* reprint (Los Angeles: USC Libraries, Figueroa Press, 2010). First published in 1941 (New York: Viking Press).

34 335th Infantry Division, Division Order 60 (December 15, 1943), in Meyer, ed., 162.

35 Adolf Hitler, as told by Robert Aron, *Histoire de Vichy* (Paris, 1954), 616.

36 Heinrich Himmler, letter to Karl Oberg, 18 January 1943, in Meyer, ed., 171.

37 Consulate General of Germany in Marseille, letter to German Embassy in Paris, February 8, 1943, in Meyer, ed., 173.

38 Communiqué for "all newspapers" (February 1, 1943), Archives départementales des Bouches-du-Rhône, box 76 W 104.

39 Kiaulehn, 1943.

40 "L'urbanisme à Marseille en 1943; le dernier état du plan d'aménagement et d'extension de Marseille," *Marseille* 23 (August 1943): 19–23.

41 Marcel de Renzis, "Marseille mutilée," *Marseille* 25 (May 1945): 44–46.

42 Conseil général des Bouches-du-Rhône, motion of 3 July 1946, Archives départementales des Bouches-du-Rhône, box 12 O130.

43 Jean-René Laplayne, "L'architecte Beaudouin proposait déjà en 1942 un 'curetage' du Vieux Marseille. Aujourd'hui il est chargé de la reconstruction de Strasbourg," *La Marseillaise* (January 1952).

44 Rupert Croft-Cooke, *Les sept tonnerres* (Paris, 1958).

Neighborhoods and Neighborliness

Urban Protest and the Built Environmental Foundations of Insurgency and Citizenship

Diane E. Davis

The large number of political protests that swept through the cities of Tunisia, Egypt, Libya, and other parts of North Africa and the Middle East in the aftermath of the Arab Spring captured world imagination not just because of their momentous historical import, but also because they literally showed the enactment of democratic sentiments in the form of bustling bodies physically clamoring for rights and recognition in the face of dictatorial power.[1] Without news cameras, however, such insurgent urbanism would neither have been accessible to the world nor understood as violently disrupting the status quo. Even a tweet could not have rendered legible the same intensity of emotions conveyed by images of people physically encamped at the seats of political and economic power, or angry mobs marching toward a phalanx of armed police. In this regard, the global media has taken a cue from the playbook of urban design, recognizing that visualization is not just central to the task of understanding but holds the potential to inspire better futures yet to be built. Even so, it is not merely the pictures of amassed bodies that force recognition of a collective challenge to the status quo. The physical location of these acts also matters. In many of these protests, public squares served as the proverbial "center stages" upon which collective action against societal injustices became both possible and symbolically meaningful.[2] Much like Tiananmen Square, the mere mention of Tahrir Square, Pearl Square, Green Square, and even Zuccotti Park evokes images of people whose power to confront an autocratic system needs only the proper physical venue.

The Semiotics of Public Squares

When they enact and voice their rights as citizens in highly symbolic spatial locations, people have the collective capacity to speak truth to power. Yet for precisely this reason, regimes have long sought heavy-handed and subtle measures to control or limit congregation. Even in the United States, most major cities require a public permit to hold a demonstration. In nondemocratic settings, a much wider array of tactics is used to curtail public gatherings, ranging from military containment of public sites to the proactive monitoring and strategic interception of communications used to plan mobilization.

The grand redesign of Paris boulevards by the renowned Baron Haussmann was crafted with an eye to thwarting mass urban rebellions associated with the 1848 uprising. In the contemporary era, states continue their efforts to control mobility and seal off open spaces as a central response to the challenges imposed by collective action. This means that public space's starring role in social protest and democratic struggle is not merely physical. Urban spaces become "public" not merely because they are materially constructed as such but because they are forcefully appropriated by citizens for public purposes ranging from complaining to claim-making to insurgency in the face of state domination or injustice.[3]

In many nations, state power was built on elite efforts to control vibrant cities and their hinterlands, as well as to monopolize the markets, governing institutions, and symbols of their predecessors. Most capital cities hold one or two monumental public squares that serve as symbolic sites for the principal institutions of power, whether political, religious, or cultural. It thus is no surprise that these same locations draw the critical or dissatisfied masses, whose very presence in and appropriation of symbolic spaces makes a statement that a country's governing institutions must be opened to include the very people whose bodies inhabit that space. These collective actions give life to French urban philosopher Henri Lefebvre's "right to the city" oratory as a plea for more general societal inclusion.[4] They make visible and public the question of to whom a city belongs, in terms of space and socioeconomic benefits, and they suggest that a physical "retaking" of certain spatial sites might become the first step in a protest or insurgency challenging the larger social and political order.[5] In light of such logic, it is not so surprising that in March of 2013 the Iranian government banned the traditional fire festivals (*Chaharshanbe-Suri*) from public spaces for fear that such gatherings would enable clashes, disturbances, or other forms of anti-government protest.

Even so, the more autocratic the regime and the more forceful or violent the protest, the less an identifiable public square or clearly defined public space is actually needed to challenge the status quo. In such instances, unrest is more likely to spill beyond the familiar or easily managed spatial bounds of the public square. And when public squares are *not* routinely occupied, we also know something about citizenship. Either the status quo is not under fundamental challenge, whether literally or figuratively; or conversely, the depth, critique, and extent of citizen dissatisfaction with existing power structures is so great that congregating in public space is either futile or potentially reckless. In the latter settings, citizens will turn not to public squares but to more clandestine venues like the streets or the underground. The point here is that both citizenship and insurgency have a physicality, even though they may not share the same spatiality. Demands for citizenship rights are more likely to be enacted in public squares and other iconic sites that are recognized and monitored by states as appropriate venues for claim-making, while insurgency flowers in interstitial, marginal, peripheral, dispersed, and less readily controllable spaces where the state's power and authority is less easily wielded. Likewise, the occupation of public squares or other urban spaces as a means of enacting citizenship will both reflect the depth of dissatisfaction and serve as the catalyst for social and political negotiations between citizens and the state, with the hope that the latter will ultimately accommodate or respond to physically expressed dissatisfaction. When such accommodation is unlikely, citizen protests may gravitate to other sites or take on more insurgent forms.

Spaces of Citizenship

The Occupy protests in the United States, many of which focused on dismantling a fundamentally unequal economic system, are good examples of vibrant citizenship being conventionally displayed through the occupation of parks and other public spaces, only some of which were iconic public squares.[6] The desired permanence of these protests through the erection of fixed encampments near financial districts (and in some places, via the establishment of insurgent infrastructure such as toilets and wooden shelters at those sites) was intended not just as a visual and conceptual juxtaposition to the Wall Street-type buildings that often surround these open locations. Protesters also aimed to celebrate and institutionalize the use of public spaces as essential sites of citizen dissent, calling attention to economic power as much as to the state. But in light of the ways that the American legal system both enables and constrains the physicality of citizenship in urban space by empowering local authorities to control urban property, in most American cities the Occupy strategists were prevented from making public sites their own autonomous urban villages. Although the target of protests may have been banks, protesters were forced to retreat—or their tents were forcibly removed—when the courts and the police ruled against their right to remain on the streets. And paradoxically, some of the movement's larger failures to institutionalize their presence in American politics owed to the pure physicality of their claims as well as the fact that many of the Occupy protesters both derived and found their political agenda within the physical act of occupying public space. For example, in contrast to the protests in Tahrir Square, where the motivation for opposition to the regime of President Hosni Mubarak and the ouster of his successor, President Mohammed Morsi, were built on a sustained political critique that permeated all aspects of life, not just the right of citizens to gather publicly, many of the Occupy protestors saw the taking of public space as the primary object of political deliberation and opposition.

Few would deny that the Occupy movements evolved a new form of articulating citizenship by strategically deploying public spaces in the construction of a larger movement for democratic citizenship. But the movement's preoccupation with the physical sites of the protest was so great that at times it inadvertently served to sideline some of the larger social and political injustices that inspired indignation in the first place. Many of the more fundamental political goals of large-scale societal transformation fell to the wayside in the struggle to remain physically ensconced in the formally designated Occupy spaces. Such strategies can be further contrasted with those deployed in the Egyptian case, where Tahrir Square initially became the physical platform for a variety of political claims from various competing groups, all sharing a desire for large-scale political change but not agreeing on its components. Whether from anti-Mubarak, anti-Morsi, anti-military, pro-Islamic, or pro-democratic forces, all Egyptians appear to have agreed that being in Tahrir Square would symbolize the necessity of a fundamental sociopolitical transformation in forms of governance in Egypt, thus explaining why small groups of protesters grew into a mass mobilization, energizing thousands in a short amount of time and keeping them committed for days on end. In this sense, it stands almost as the obverse of the Occupy movement, where there may have been unity of purpose among those initially visiting or camping at Occupy sites, but greater disunity over time as questions emerged about whether and how the symbolic appropriation of the site should be linked to a larger national movement for change.

Part of the difference here rests in the divergent political contexts. In Egypt the "physicality of citizenship," as enacted through protests in an iconic public space associated with government power, can be understood as a call for recognition of the rights of citizenship in an urban and national context in which such forms of claim-making have been controlled, monitored, or repressed by the state for decades. In such an environment, any actions to lay claim to public space will be seen as a direct challenge to the power and legitimacy of the government. In the Occupy movement in the United States, protest is a relatively routine form of enacting citizenship, and it unfolds in a political and spatial environment where such actions are legally sanctioned or tolerated (it may be worth noting that Zuccotti Park was designed as a privately owned public space in order to offer tax advantages to real-estate developers). Public spaces in American cities may offer a physical venue for voices not readily heard within the halls of legislative power, but as a platform for dissent they often fail to fundamentally challenge the status quo, serving instead as a format for giving voice to those who seek

HOUSE AND HOME

After World War II, many Sicilians moved from their homes in Agrigento to the Lea Valley in England. Generations of families organized meetings, celebrations, and meals such as the one pictured in the home above. What makes a home? How does a sense of home change between generations and countries?

A woman sits in the shade of a tree in Xiamen, China. Tree roots grow around foundations of buildings, anchoring in the soil and reaching toward sunlight. How does house and home play into the psychology of the city?

In cities across the world, artist Tadashi Kawamata has created temporary installations, such as above in Paris in 2008, that collectively form the exhibition *Tree Hut*. Who has what view of the city? Where is home?

HOUSE AND HOME

Robin Hood Gardens, designed by Alison and Peter Smithson, was built in 1972 as a social housing
unit for Tower Hamlets in East London. Some cherish the space as historical while others call for
its demolition. Who is heard in this debate over housing and ownership of space, place, and memory?
What is social? What is housing?

What makes a home in a city? What makes a city a home? Since the Rose Revolution in 2003, the city of Tbilisi has changed significantly while delicately balancing the preservation of historic sites.

The Sicilian capital and port city of Palermo has experienced corruption by the mafia and neglect in post-War years, however citizens have built homes and homes have built neighborhoods. How do feelings of home and homelessness shape the streets of the urban?

RECYCLING

Nicknamed "Smokey Mountain," the Stung Meanchey Municipal Waste Dump in Phnom Penh, Cambodia, was around 100 acres large before government officials moved it farther from the city in 2009. The dump moved, but where did the people go? What is the cost of capitalism?

RECYCLING

At Phnom Penh's Stung Meanchey Municipal Waste Dump, around 2,000 people, including approximately 600 children, work sorting waste to sell for recycling. People live in makeshift huts around the dump. This happens all around the world. Who really pays?

The New York City Department of Sanitation (DSNY), the largest in the world, reports 13,000 tons of garbage produced daily by businesses (and collected by private companies). DSNY collects 1,760 tons of recyclables daily. In Times Square, a woman sells sorted recyclable waste. How are cities consumed? How do cities consume? Who practices sustainability?

to join, reform, or redirect—rather than overturn—the existent structures of politics. This surely is citizenship, but citizenship in a democracy is relatively stabilizing, whereas citizenship marshaled in the call for revolutionary transformation, as occurred with the Tahrir Square protests in Egypt, is a more destabilizing form of political insurgency. In the latter conditions, public squares and concrete spaces for physical protest are absolutely necessary precisely because the ballot boxes as sites of change are likely to be closed off.

Infrastructures of Insurgency
The distinction between citizenship and insurgency is relevant not just for political theorists but also for those who seek to understand geographies of protest and whether there are established spatialities associated with particular forms of collective action or opposition politics. One way to pursue this line of thought is to contrast the forms, meaning, and strategies of protest deployed in public squares with those that unfold in other types of urban spaces. How do the physical attributes of built environmental space mold citizen mobilization? Can spatial forms or modes of territorial connection be seen as a relatively autonomous element in the construction and study of urban protest and its impacts on citizenship and insurgency?

As discussed earlier, protest in a public square conjures up images of democracy at work—concerned and proactive citizens gathering together peacefully to voice their opinions to a benevolent government. Public squares and central plazas are usually cavernous sites that concentrate large numbers of people in a single location, providing collective interaction that in its form will reflect a mass rather than class or hierarchically stratified society. Yet because there is often a state logic involved in the construction of public squares, or even a market logic involved in the creation of central plazas, these spaces are usually monitored by the state and others in power to keep collective action in check. And when mass protest becomes so unwieldy that even armed police cannot control the tumultuous crowds, governing officials often seek other forms of spatial control or physical intervention to minimize the collective power emanating from these places. Among these techniques, the erection of walls and barricades is among the most common.

In Egypt, the resurgence of riots and protests centered in Tahrir Square, both after Mubarak's departure in 2011 and in citizen dissatisfaction with the Morsi government, brought out nascent tensions within and among divergent political forces competing to guide the country's political transition, thus motivating authorities to control public spaces and who could enter them. In the initial revolutionary upheaval in Egypt, the Mubarak regime placed heavy concrete blocks around key government buildings to

prevent protesters from reaching the Interior Ministry.[7] In the protests leading to the military coup that removed Morsi from power, concerted actions
were taken to prevent the deposed leader's sympathizers from occupying
Tahrir Square, even as pro-democracy demonstrators were allowed to congregate. With access to this iconic public venue blocked, Morsi supporters
marched through streets and claimed major intersections, using other sites
in the city to express their dissatisfaction in ways that physically divided
the city's territory along factional political lines. Such responses show both
the spatial possibilities and limits of enacting citizenship through collective
protest in a single public square; they also remind us that the types of protests emerging in streets and lateral spaces leading to and from public squares
may have an entirely different ethos and political logic than those focused
on public squares. For example, central plazas are often preferred sites
because of their closeness to the symbols of power, but roundabouts may
invite more insurgent politics and enable more disruptive and effective revolutionary action. Many so-called public squares are in fact traffic intersections masquerading as public spaces; and although they sometimes serve the
same function, traffic intersections are not as easily walled or controlled
without impeding the flows of citizens and goods that provide the economic
and social lifeblood of a city.

Likewise, there is much more at risk when authorities put key
transport nodes on lockdown, or when the city's transport grid comes to
a standstill in an effort to squelch political protest, than when masses camp
out in a highly monitored public square. The intersection of roads and different modes of transportation also facilitate the coming together of different

classes of people from all parts of the city. Because these intersections and roundabouts transform into sites of greater historical weight when they are used as dramatic stages to air public grievances, they remind us that both function and form define the proverbial public square and the spaces of citizenship.

So why is there so little emphasis on major confluences of transportation networks and their impacts on protests or the physicality of citizenship, and so much more attention focused on the romanticized notion of public squares? Is it merely sexier to see civic centers and public squares as emblematic democratic spaces? To a degree, yes, at least if one takes the perspective of those chronicling protest events. Media observers in the democratic West may target common spatial and political symbols such as public squares as they try to make sense of the mysterious or "exotic" foreign locales awash in protest, in part because this is easier and more visually expedient than linking mass mobilization in physical space to the complicated social, political, and economic dynamics that run beneath the surfaces of rebellion. The Sidi Bouzid protests in Tunisia sparked the greater North African and Middle Eastern revolution not just because of protest, but because the outrage was inspired by the political repression of an informal street vendor—a type of activity that relies on free movement in public space and is ubiquitous in the plazas and streets in cities in this and other regions of the world. Yet the everyday repression on the street that sparked the Tunisian uprising did not lend itself to permanent media coverage and was almost immediately overshadowed in the Western media by a focus on the monumentality of mobilizations in Cairo's Tahrir Square, Green Square, and

Zuccotti Park. To the extent that outside observers often equate a successful revolt with a concentration of violence in yet another iconic public square, such pictures became part of the Western media arsenal. But those with an appreciation of spatial practice and urban design must be prepared to move beyond such assumptions. They must ask whether and how urban infrastructures such as roads and bridges can provide a network for sustained social and spatial mobility and interaction in ways less likely to be controlled by the authorities, or to ascertain when the unencumbered free flow of people within and between public squares, roads, bridges, and other types of infrastructure might give rise to a full-blown insurgency, if not a revolution.

The 2010 clashes in central Bangkok between the Red Shirts and the Thai army highlight the importance of mobility in space—as opposed to the fixity associated with protest in public squares—and its significance for 21st-century urban insurgency. Two primary locations in Bangkok occupied by the Red Shirts included the Phan Fa bridge, a major intersection, and the Rajaprasong intersection at the heart of the city's commercial district.[8] Dominion over these key transportation nodes was critical because the Red Shirts arrived from outside Bangkok in buses, trucks, and boats. Claiming and monitoring important intersections in the city ensured that the protesters gained momentum as the crowds swelled, and facilitated the Red Shirts' abilities to attack and occupy politically significant buildings such as the Interior Ministry in their quest to overthrow Prime Minister Abhisit Vejjajiva. Controlling major intersections also meant shutting down access to large swathes of commercial activities—aggressive acts that intensified the pressure on the government. Bangkok's famously crowded streets were empty

Ratchaprasong Intersection, Bangkok, Thailand, 2010

during the clashes, a visible reminder of the Red Shirts' ability to disrupt economic, political, and social life if their demand for change was not met. The Red Shirts occupied no public squares or ordered civic spaces; rather, the streets functioned as the tool, symbol, and platform of protests.

Similarly, the street was a key unit of analysis in the revolution in Libya. Anti-government protesters were flooding urban roadways, alongside the police and the military, trying to take back Libya one street at a time, one city at a time. In spite of Muammar Qaddafi's brutal use of air strikes and imported mercenaries, in the initial months of the struggle protesters transformed the geography of Libya into a giant public square of sorts. Oddly enough, Green Square in Tripoli, a city almost entirely controlled by Qaddafi until his death, remained peaceful because tanks blocked the roads into the city and the army shot any protester attempting to move toward the square. Turning Green Square into the equivalent of Tahrir Square was the dream of Libyan protesters, but such objectives were continually thwarted by the authorities, who had programmed counter-uses of the space to undermine such a possibility. During much of the conflict, Green Square remained in the hands of Qaddafi, who used it to celebrate Jamahiriya Day with elaborate parades that manifested his iron grip on the city's streets and open spaces.[9] The Libyan example demonstrates the futility of public squares as driving forces of political change without a true public to articulate and physically access such spaces for their own democratic purposes. And precisely for this reason, the streets of towns such as Benghazi and Brega became the real sites of dissent, because they were not so easily colonized by the authorities.

Even in the case of Egypt, citizen access to Tahrir Square through existent roads and intersections has been as central to protest outcomes as were the wide-open spaces downtown that received the peripatetic masses. This was first well reflected in the initial revolutionary upheaval of 2012 by the circulation in the oppositional blogosphere of a map that laid out a physical plan for citizen movement, showing how residents of Cairo's urban periphery might best access the city's downtown streets, and pinpointing preferred routes for arrival at Tahrir Square. This map was accompanied by a script offering suggestions as to exactly where to start assembling, what to chant, whether to congregate on major streets—and which ones, and how to direct these activities toward the takeover of government buildings with maximum effect. Likewise, even in less revolutionary protests, free movement in urban space is both precondition for and object of struggle. This was clear in protests in India for gender rights, in reaction to a barrage of gang rapes. As citizens took to the streets in this democratic country's capital of Delhi, expressing their public contempt for the state, they faced numerous obstacles similar to those imposed in Egypt. As reported by the media: "Just to reach the protest sites, the crowds defied multiple government efforts to keep them away. Officials had shut down many central subway stations, curtailed bus service, diverted traffic, and even invoked a law making it illegal for more than a few people to gather."[10]

Socio-Spatial Distance and Urban Protest
Although increased mobility in space can enable acts of protest, just as public spaces can serve as symbolic sites for enacting citizenship, the question of

whether these and other built environmental factors will motivate—rather than just mediate—political dissatisfaction remains a central question. To what extent does the built environment itself generate protest or citizenship claims? Preliminary studies on social movements have shown that groups of citizens who feel most institutionally, culturally, politically, and geographically distant from governing institutions and/or the ruling classes tend to be a main source of rebellion, while those with social, spatial, and political proximity to sources of power and authority may be less likely to mobilize, rebel, or revolt.[11] Such findings help explain why the occupation of public spaces near centers of political and financial power can both symbolize and performatively bridge the distance between citizens and the government. This in essence is what protest is all about: reducing the gap between ruler and ruled, have and have not, rich and poor.

The concepts of *proximity* and *distance* do more than explain why we frequently see demonstrations of citizenship in locations closest to the physical institutions of the governing elite, or why citizens furthest from the halls of power might undertake such acts. They also make clear how and why the selection of certain sites for protest itself serves as a technique intended to bridge power distances—both literally and figuratively—by seeking new forms of social and spatial proximity.[12] To be sure, activists' strategies frequently take into account the fact that citizens in all locations of a city have a stake (and a potential role) in protest outcomes, not merely those with the physical access or geographic wherewithal to journey to public squares to speak truth to power. But this does not mean that all citizens will unite socially, politically, and spatially when they seek to enact their citizenship claims. Nowhere was this clearer than in Cairo during the troubled and violence-filled weeks of August 2013, following the counter-revolutionary military coup, when outraged supporters of the deposed President Morsi were denied access to Tahrir Square and faced military threats of forcible eviction from all city streets if they continued to protest. With such bans on the "physicality" of their citizenship, the pro-Morsi movement responded by capturing a key site in the city as their privileged territory and setting up a fortressed encampment—a "pop-up city" with pharmacies, shelter, electricity, and other critical urban services that symbolically and spatially identified the camp as a site of alternative sovereignty.[13]

The fragmentation of Cairo's urban spaces according to political loyalties reinforced divisions within civil society over the revolutionary transition, thus prolonging instability and keeping the city in a permanent state of contestation. Paradoxically, such developments often serve to strengthen the state's repressive hand as it seeks to restore urban order, further undermining citizens' capacity to mobilize around citizenship claims. Sometimes, however, the spatial distribution of protests will enable more insurgent outcomes. The simultaneous enactment of citizenship or insurgency across urban space may be all that is needed to call attention to the distance between the governed and the governing and to set the engines of change in motion, as was the case in Egypt in 2011. Igniting popular protest in a movement that spans urban space is no easy feat, to be sure, in part because the physical layout of cities usually reflects or reinforces social and class distinctions. In highly unequal societies with autocratic institutions, such patterns may be even more severe, just as the state's control over urban spaces is more airtight.

In Tripoli's Green Square, citizens mobilized from all parts of the city sought to oust the Qaddafi regime, yet they failed because the power of the state was stronger than that of the people, and because the Libyan government was able to use violent force to control both the streets and public squares of the capital city, effectively restricting mobility and fragmenting potential unity among citizens. Significantly, the state's control of the urban core helped energize violent struggle in the periphery of the country, ultimately leading to Qaddafi's defeat. Yet upon his death, the Libyan government lacked a central figure, and the involvement of foreign powers in the form of military and diplomatic occupation created further ambiguity about who was in control. Combined with the fracturing of the opposition movement across rural and urban lines, it remained unclear who represents the political core and who constitutes the periphery—or who is close to or far from power in social, spatial, or political terms. In such a transitional context, public protest and social mobilization declined and targeted acts of insurgency and terrorism increased, in ways that limited citizen willingness and capacity to mobilize in public spaces of the city.

The point here is that overall spatial conditions and whether they enable citizen unity in a city will factor into the nature of protest and its potential for success. While political change has continued to gather momentum in many cities of North Africa and the Middle East, what remains unclear is the extent to which the social fissures underlying initial political protests will limit ongoing citizen struggles to create a new future. To figure this out, the concepts of distance and proximity also provide clues. Indeed, the vast majority of protesters who originally stormed Tahrir Square in 2011 may have shared a common sense of political distance from the repressive state, but in social terms were far from united, with some sharing more proximity to the ruling elite in social outlook even if not in institutional terms. Since then, some protesters remained distanced from the halls of power, while others became connected to the political institutions and social organizations that governed Egyptian society. The resurgence of massive protests against President Morsi in July 2013 was fueled by demonstrations from citizens who had participated in the 2011 uprisings but found themselves dissatisfied with the political outcome, in part because they remained distanced from the new governing circles. That many of the same groups protesting the Mubarak administration in Tahrir Square returned to the same venue to protest their exclusion, and that these demonstrations return the military to power, has only served to complicate the path of reform and change. Not unlike many of the cities that participated in the Arab Spring, Cairo is a city of extremes, whether understood in terms of income, Westernization, ideology, or another fault line of cultural, social, religious, or political difference. In this setting, social tensions—or distances—among citizens and between them and the state are frequently the norm, and city spaces often become the territorial domain around which they unfold. If we want to understand the relationships between protest, citizenship, insurgency, space, and political change, particularly in the months and years to come, we must factor into our account a closer understanding of the spatial correlates of social distance and how they may produce identity conflicts that enable or constrain protest unity, or how these tensions themselves can be brought to the surface by changes in and struggles over the urban built environment, whether in public squares or elsewhere.

Such an approach also seems relevant for understanding a spate of protests in Istanbul, where multiple publics clashed over their rights to publicly assert their divergent social identities and political projects in the built environment of the city. The spring 2013 protests in Taksim Square erupted in opposition to the Turkish government's plans to build an upscale mall that citizens argued would destroy a cherished public park. When citizen occupation of public space was met by coercive backlash from the authorities, the exchange of violence delegitimized the Erdogan government before a court ruling put the project on hold. Yet this was far from the first time that an upscale redevelopment project would generate identity conflicts over the urban spaces of the city. Artist-led gentrification in the Istanbul suburb of Tophane several years earlier had pitted culturally conservative residents against the liberal art-loving crowds, with divergent views of secularism, nationalism, and fundamentalism weaving through the protests. During the Tophane Art Walk in September 2010, a mob of religiously conservative longtime residents attacked partygoers in the galleries, smashing windows and throwing rocks in indignation at the art gallery owners and their guests.[14] Art was not the issue so much as the artist-led gentrification in the neighborhood and the liberalization and secularization of culture that followed. Each side blamed the other for hostilities. Art gallery owners claimed that longstanding residents wanted them to leave so they can comfortably conduct their illicit activities in the shadows. Residents countered by arguing that higher rents resulting from the galleries' location in their neighborhood were undermining their quality of life; they also claimed that the new artist-residents were mocking their conservative culture while also displacing them.[15]

The conflicts in Tophane, as well as in Taksim Square to a great degree, raised the question of who has the right to urban space, and how citizenship rights should be defined at the level of the neighborhood when protesters and/or the state disagree over the character of the built environment. On one side of the controversy stood art gallery owners and their artist clients, who are contributing to the economic revival of the suburb; on the other side were longstanding residents, many of whom occupy houses formerly belonging to Greeks and Jews who left Turkey in prior conflicts over citizenship and nationality. In this sense, the Tophane case serves as a microcosm of the social distances among Istanbul's multicultural residents and their uneasy relationship to each other and to Turkey as a nation, raising such tough questions as whether Istanbul and its constituent urban spaces "belong" to the new cosmopolitan elite of the city, to its prior residents, or to all Turks? At minimum, it reminds us that socio-spatial conflict and protest may be inevitable when groups use control of the urban built environment to exclude "others" or to reinforce their own cultural or nationalist identities by laying competing claims to public spaces.[16]

The controversy over a proposed Islamic Center in New York City close to a decade after 9/11 demonstrated a similar complexity.[17] Plans to build an Islamic cultural center near the former World Trade Center generated vicious protests and a debate over the uses and abuses of urban space to symbolically empower certain cultural groups who were considered "national enemies" by a small but vocal extreme of the U.S. population. Proponents argued that the building would stand as a constant visual symbol of moderate Islam's presence in the city, helping observers distinguish between law-abiding Muslims and terrorists. Opponents claimed that the cultural center would serve as a provocative reminder of 9/11, inciting hatred and constant repudiation by those who would not care to make the distinction between al-Qaeda and Islam. Either way, the controversy may have been less about architectural representation, land use, urban design principles, or the urban planning process (given the fact that the zoning board had approved the project months before the controversy) and more about how citizenship and identity conflicts play out in the urban built environment, as well as about who has a right to the city in either material or symbolic terms.

Crucially, some of the most violent and divisive protests came from far-flung places thousands of miles from New York, as perhaps best reflected in a Florida preacher's call for mass public burnings of the Qur'an, across the nation, to protest the building of the Islamic center in far-off Manhattan.

Historically, questions about who has the right to the city and the legitimacy to determine its built environment have remained at the local scale, close to the site. But as the world becomes more global, and as major cities like New York have increased their presence in the national and global imagination, concepts of distance and proximity are in flux. The question of who should be involved in urban decision making for these cities is now under challenge. This is precisely what ties the example of the Tophane art attacks to the controversy over the Islamic center in Manhattan, and which raises new questions about who has "rights" to a city and whether virtual and real geographies of distance and proximity are equally relevant. National protests over the cultural center in Manhattan owed not just to anti-Islamic sentiment but also to the unspoken sense that land-use decisions in New York City were of national importance, suggesting a new way of linking the urban built environment to protest and insurgency, even as it calls for further reflection on the most appropriate scale for understanding such interactions.

Urban Design and the "Physicality of Citizenship"
In the contemporary era where scales and venues for the enactment of citizenship are shifting, we must ask whether and how urban design can enable democracy and/or citizenship, insurgent or otherwise. To be sure, a prior question might be: Have planners and urban designers been involved in the construction of protest landscapes that enable citizenship in the first place? The history of Tahrir Square shows that it was precisely the failure of urban planning that led to the unintended construction of the public square, which eventually became the physical launching pad and international symbol of Arab Spring.[18] That is, it was the protesting citizens who most clearly articulated Cairo's central city plaza as a site for citizenship claims, thus elevating it to the status of a "public square." Similarly, the case of Bangkok highlights how demonstrators recast the use of an expertly engineered system of roads and bridges to capture political visibility, while the Occupy movements in the United States sought to turn professionally designed urban parks into insurgent spaces by voicing their claims. In all of these examples, protest spaces were not formally designed so much as constructed, articulated, and created by citizens.

When considering citizens' potential to design or socially construct the spaces of political change, special attention must be paid to the use of Internet technology in mounting protest demonstrations and inspiring dissent.[19] Technology too has the potential to undermine the traditional uses of physical space and the built environment, perhaps even turning well-planned and expertly designed spaces into something altogether different than originally intended. Of course, whether technology will make the Hyde Parks of the world disappear, and the extent to which parks, streets, sidewalks, and public squares will be replaced by the Internet as the preferred site for mobilization, still remains to be seen. Perhaps the blackout of popular websites like Wikipedia and Google during the SOPA/PIPA protests gives a sense of the limited future of virtual citizenship, thus reinforcing the importance of physical citizenship and the role of professional urban designers in ensuring that such spaces continue to exist in cities of the future.

If Tahrir Square had been intentionally constructed as a protest landscape by urban planners, would Egypt's democratic revolution have been more or less successful? Likewise, did the plebian design and construction of camps for pro-Morsi loyalists in Cairo make this insurrection more likely to challenge the status quo and politically transform Egyptian society, even if it did so by inspiring a military counter-response? It is impossible to know the answers to these questions. But rather than trying to attribute citizenship claims and losses to either the designers or users of public space, it may be more useful to recognize that the sheer act of challenging the gap between "design from above" and "citizen claims from below" is the most effective strategy for fomenting revolt, a sort of "insurgent design" that builds on the formal properties of place but creates something new in the process. Whether cast from above or below, or enacted by citizens or state, urban design is political, as are the planning decisions that give life to design projects, particularly when they empower citizens to make public their sentiments. The design of space must be considered central to the struggle to create a new social order. But even so, urban design is only one element in the construction of a democratically inclusive public sphere. Public squares will remain empty and the streets silent if the public itself is not on the move. So what can we conclude about the role of formal urban design in creating democracy, whether in terms of spatial integration, political inclusion, or other common manifestations of such ideals? If any urban artery and clearing can be used for demonstrations, are well-designed public squares as sites of protests actually necessary? If people wishing to exercise their physical and political citizenship become accidental insurgent designers, is the role of professional urban design redundant, at least in the creation of public spaces? And if so, what then are the roles of urban design and planning in the creation of socially just cities and in enabling urban citizenship?

Perhaps the value of design professionals lies not just in the explicit construction of protest landscapes but in the response to and recording of physical claims to citizenship in the already built environment. After the rebels took Tripoli, they renamed Green Square as Martyrs' Square, as a symbol of respect to those who had lost their lives in the fight to reclaim Libya from Qaddafi and his forces. The streets and corridors in the insurgent camps in Cairo were named after martyrs as well, in commemoration to those who fought against the military to keep Morsi in power. Among other things, then, urban design—whether formal or informal—can preserve the spatial history and locations of citizen struggles by memorializing sites of insurgency and protest or constructing monuments and iconic architectural forms that will reflect the symbolism of the square and the importance of urban spaces in a country's history. Urban designers both plebian and professional can well serve the city and democratic ideals by becoming urban spatial scribes, using their skills and creative vision to make public the battles both won and lost in the hard-fought struggle to make the world a better place.

1 This essay deepens and extends a set of preliminary ideas prepared for a special journal issue on Revolution, edited by Ana Maria Leon Crespo of MIT's Architecture Department. See *Thresholds* 41 (Spring 2012).

2 For a focused discussion on public squares and their role in political claim-making, see Setha M. Low, *On the Plaza: The Politics of Public Space and Culture* (Austin: University of Texas Press, 2000).

3 For a more nuanced discussion of how residents use urban space to make citizenship claims, see James Holston's writings, particularly his chapter on "Spaces of Insurgent Citizenship," in *Cities and Citizenship* (Durham, NC: Duke University Press, 1999); James Holston and Arjun Appadurai, "Cities and Citizenship," *Public Culture* 8 (Summer 1996): 187–204; and Saskia Sassen, "The Repositioning of Citizenship: Emergent Subjects and Spaces for Politics," *Berkeley Journal of Sociology* 46 (2002): 4–25.

4 The now iconic concept of the "right to the city" was first proposed by Henri Lefebvre in *Le Droit à la ville* (Paris: Economica Anthropos, 1968). For a more recent theorization, see David Harvey, *Spaces of Hope* (Berkeley and Los Angeles: University of California Press, 2000).

5 Such claims are not always benign, however, and they may reinforce rather than liberate citizens from the power of the state, as made clear in Tali Hatuka's *Violent Acts and Urban Space in Contemporary Tel Aviv: Revisioning Moments* (Austin: University of Texas Press, 2010).

6 Many scholars have sought to analyze the successes and failures of the Occupy movement in the United States. Among those who take a particularly spatial perspective and who identify the role of public-private space in framing movement dynamics are Jerold Kayden, in "Meet Me at the Plaza," *New York Times*, October 26, 2011, and Judy Lubin, "The 'Occupy' Movement: Emerging Protest Forms and Contested Urban Spaces," *Berkeley Planning Journal* 25 (Winter 2012): 92–111.

7 The ways the Egyptian government sought to limit the mobility of Tahrir Square protesters is documented by David Kirkpatrick in his "Walls Prove No Barrier to Clashes on Streets of Cairo," *New York Times*, February 5, 2012, http://www.nytimes.com/2012/02/06/world/middleeast/egyptian-forces-appear-to-end-siege-of-ministry.html]. For further information on the spatiality of the Egyptian protests, see "A Closer Look at Tahrir Square," *Globe and Mail*, January 30, 2011, http://www.theglobeandmail.com/news/world/crisis-in-egypt/a-closer-look-at-tahrir-square/article1888147/.

8 BBC, "Thailand PM Abhisit in Pledge to End Bangkok Protest," May 15, 2010, http://news.bbc.co.uk/2/hi/8684363.stm.

9 Given the difficulty of verifying conditions on the ground during the revolt against Qaddafi, it is hard to do more than speculate about the spatiality of the conflict based on journalistic accounts. But considerable material on this theme is available from Ian Lee's account, "A Tale of Two Cities: Gaddafi's Tripoli," *Time*, March 3, 2010, http://www.time.com/time/world/article/0,8599,2056599,00.html, and from the *Huffington Post*, "Libya's 'Green Square' Changed to 'Martyrs' Square' on Google Maps," August 22, 2011, http://www.huffingtonpost.com/2011/08/22/libya-green-square-martyrs-square-google-maps_n_933565.html.

10 In response to the police's imposition of spatial barriers on protesters, citizen outrage was so explosive that "top government officials pleaded on national television for people to stay away." See Gardiner Harris and Heather Timmons, "Protests in India Intensify as Fury Grows over Handling of Rape Case," *New York Times*, December 24, 2012, section 1, A3.

11 For more on the relationships between proximity, distance, and challenges to state power, see Diane E. Davis, "The Power of Distance: Re-theorizing Social Movements in Latin America," *Theory and Society* 28 (Winter 1999): 585–638.

12 In this regard, protests that target borders are especially powerful in symbolic terms, holding the capacity to make routine dissent threatening to established territorial systems of control. For more on borders, see Tali Hatuka "Civilian Consciousness of the Mutable Nature of Power: Dissent Practices along a Fragmented Border in Israel/Palestine," *Political Geography* 31, no. 6 (2012): 347–57.

13 Ben Hubbard, "In Cairo Camps, Protesters Dig In and Live On," *New York Times,* August 10, 2013.

14 Violence between secular art gallery owners and religious residents in Istanbul is reported by Rosie Goldsmith, "Modern Art Boom Exposes Turkey's Tensions," *BBC News*, October 30, 2010, http://news.bbc.co.uk/2/hi/programmes/from_our_own_correspondent/9138192.stm. For more, see Borzou Daragahi, "Social, Religious Divide on Display in Attack on Turkish Art Walk," *Los Angeles Times*, September 26, 2010 http://www.latimes.com/news/nationworld/world/la-fg-0927-turkey-gallery-20100927,0,7529675.story.

15 For more on the Tophane controversy and its larger implications for citizenship and identity conflicts, see Jonathan Lewis, "Turkey: Istanbul Gentrification Opens Second Front in Culture War," *EurasiaNet,* January 3, 2011, http://www.eurasianet.org/node/62653 and Christopher Torchia, "Turkey: Gallery Attack Ignites Debate," *Business-week*, September 26, 2010, http://www.businessweek.com/ap/financialnews/D9IFGD2G0.html.

16 To get a sense of how identity politics in cities interfaces with nationalism in ways that can either drive political conflict or unity, see Diane E. Davis and Nora Libertun de Duren, *Cities and Sovereignty: Identity Politics in Urban Spaces* (South Bend: Indiana University Press, 2011).

17 For one interpretation of this conflict, particularly as seen from beyond New York, see Tina Susman, "Once-Controversial Islamic Center Opens in New York," *Los Angeles Times*, September 22, 2011, http://latimesblogs.latimes.com/nationnow/2011/09/once -controversial-islamic-center-opens-quietly-in-manhattan.html.

18 For more on the history of Tahrir Square, see Nasser Rabbat, "Circling the Square: On Architecture and Revolution," *Artforum*, April 1, 2011, and Nezar Al-Sayyad, *Cairo: Histories of a City* (Cambridge, MA: Harvard University Press, 2011).

19 Among leading urban scholars who investigate the relationships between Internet technology and urban protest, Saskia Sassen stands out in her willingness to introduce space into the mix. See her "Reading the City in a Global Digital Age: Between Topographic Power Representations and Spatialized Power Projects," *Revista* (Winter 2003): 12–17.

Urban Desolation and Symbolic Denigration in the Hyperghetto

Loïc Wacquant

Curtis insists on taking me to his neighborhood church for a visit with his pastor. As we hunker down inside his car, he puts on music by the rap group No More Colors at full volume, and the heavily distorted sound floods the cabin with its frenetic, pulsating rhythm. "It's my fav'rite song, 'cause it's *positive*: it tell d'kids enough killin's an' dope and shootin' an' stuff, don't do dat 'cause 'We're All Blacks, We're All in the Same Gang!'"—the song's inspiring if raucous chorus. He thumps on the dashboard to try to get the speaker on the driver's side to function and settles into his leather seat. And then the morbid spectacle of the corridor of dereliction that is Chicago's 63rd Street flashes by us as we rush toward Stony Island Avenue under the rusty elevated train line.

Curtis: At one time this neighbo'hood, you could get *anythin'* up and down this neighbo'hoo'—I mean, this was like d'*downtown* for the southeast side. I mean, (enthusiastic) you talkin' 'bout Buster Browns, uh McDonald's, Burger King, uh, Kenny Shoes, A&P's, I mean, I mean: *you name it,* you can get it up-n'-down here. Jus', I mean dis use to be a *hot spot* w back, back in the sixties, da late or early sixties. Yeah, dis used to be the spot right here.

Louie: What is it like today?

Today i's *down.* I mean, lotta thin's is changed. You can see fo' yo'self that everythin' is, (shaking his head) *half offa d'buildin's aroun' here is boarded up.*

What kindsa things go on in the street right here on 63rd Street?

Well, you have a lotta street walkers, you have yo' gang-bangers, you have o' *dope dealers,* yo' *dope users*—I mean [a tad defensive] that's in every neighbo'hoo', I'm not jus' sayin' this neighbo'hoo', I mean you have dat around here.

And it's *bad for the kids* that's comin' up in the neighbo'hoo' 'cause that's who they have to look up. They got people like *dese guys* [gesturing towards a cluster of men "shooting the breeze" by the entrance of a liquor store] tha's doin' *everythin' wrong* to look up to. I mean! Is that anythin' to try t'teach a kid, to be a dope dealer or a dope user, or to be a pimp?

You see like guys like this *hangin' out* up on d'street, *jus'* bein' aroun', *jus' hangin'* around bummin' for quarters 'n' dimes and stuff t'buy 'em wine [censoriously]. It's *bad* ya know, that dese guys, they messed up they lives and stuff, ya know, or they don't *care* too much about you know, how dey life gonna turn out to be. Ya know, half-a 'em is in they late forties, late thirties and jus' don't care anymore, but it's *bad* dat we got dese guys out here like this jus' for d'kids to look up to.

People that don't know nuttin' about the Southeast side, comin' 'roun' here and see this, and the first thin' they think about [mockingly, in an exaggeratedly scared voice] "*aw! I'm not getting' out ma car!* I'm not gon' leave ma car. I don't want ma kids to be 'round here or anythin'" ya know. *But,* it's somethin' for 'em to do [he honks at a blue Cadillac snailing along in front of us]. You see everythin' is boarded up. They tryin' to put a washer and dryer over here [he points to an abandoned building], a laundrymat over here. Now thata be good for the neighbo'hoo', for the community.

And look over here on the left …

It's a store that sell liquor, with another store that's boarded up that useta sell liquor an', you see people walkin' up an' down d'street with jus', they on a wish an' a prayer…

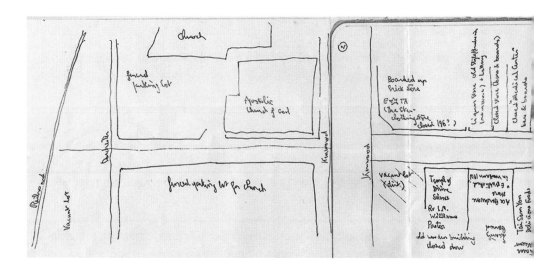

Ya know, *you can never say what's on dese guys min',* what's on d'peoples min' out dere, ya know: *they out here ta live, they live day-by-day.* And you know (raucous) *it's baaad,* jus'–jus' *imagine* you not havin' *a dream,* or anythin' that you tryin' *t'accomplish outa life* and [his pace accelerating] you *wake up,* an' you got yo' fingers crossed hopin' that one of yo' frien's, or somebody dat you know come in knock on yo' door an' you come outside and see 'em and they got a *scheme* up [in a passionate, revolted, voice]. I mean ya know you have ta *live like that everyday!* To hope that somebody come an' tell you dat they gotta, they got a *money idea* to make you, give ya a coupla dollars or som'thin' jus' go get drunk or le's go buy some dope and *get high?* I mean, ya know [his tone turning scared], I mean, could you *IMAGINE livin' a life like that?*

Now, I have seen a lotta ma frien's an' stuff, lotta guys that I be grew up with, a lotta guys that, ya know, tha's been, tha's been of age before I have, I see a lotta 'em *use drugs* n' *deal drugs* and did various thin's to, ya know, try ta fix they habit. Get theyself, you know, some dope, or put some money in they pocket ta try t'take care of theyself.

I know that's the life that they wanted to live but *I choose* the opposite [his delivery speeds up, as if he was scared again at the mere thought of the possibility]. I couldn't, ya know, it's a headache–I couldn't wake up, *I couldn't see myself wakin' up ev'ry day* an' stuff, wakin' up and *hopin'* that I find somebody ta, ya know, somebody tha's got a money idea ta help me get some money or put some money in ma pocket for me and my kids.

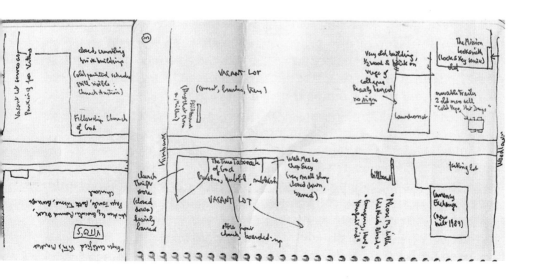

The guys that you grew up with, what've they become?

Ya know, my mom told me when I was of age an' stuff, I think aroun'
'bout fourteen or fifteen, she say it's gonna be a time when you gonna see
a lotta yo' frien's, some o'them gonna die an' some o' them gonna go to
jail. N' *sho' enough* I seen 'em, a lotta 'em, 'bout half o'them—well, not half,
that'd be stretchin' it a lil' bit too much, but a lotta ma friends has passed
away: *gang-bangin'* or a lotta 'em sellin' dope, I have a lotta frien's jus' *sellin'*,
jus' dealin' dope [his voice rising, not indignant but outraged], *strung out
on dope, sellin' cocaine* jus' to do another typa dope, uh—they call it Karachi
I think, tha's a downer.

[voice fading] N' a lotta my frien's is in jail. Some o'my frien's, I mean, I can
count d'friends on my own *one hand that did finish school* and ya know,
pursue they career in uh ya know, bus'ness career uh, ya know, tha's jus' tryin'
to make somethin' out theyself. I can count 'em on one hand. But I still see
'em, ya know, and speak to 'em ...

(Woodlawn field notebooks, October 17, 1990)

The urban desolation and social despair etched in this conversation and
exemplified along 63rd Street, one of the ghostly thoroughfares transsecting
Chicago's collapsing black ghetto at century's close, invites us to reflect on
the link between the built environment, social structure, and collective psychology. More precisely, it points to the need to elaborate theoretically and
empirically the connections between urban desolation and symbolic denigration in America's racialized urban core and assorted territories of relegation in the dualizing metropolis of the advanced societies (Wacquant 2008):
how the daily experience of material dilapidation, ethno-racial seclusion,
and socioeconomic marginality translates into the corrosion of the self, the
rasping of interpersonal ties, and the skewing of public policy through the
mediation of sulfurous cognition fastened onto a defamed place.

    The link between ecology, morphology, and representations was
a theme central to the Durkheimian school of sociology, as attested by
such tomes as Emile Durkheim's ([1912] 1993) celebrated analysis of "collective effervescence" in *The Elementary Forms of Religious Life*, Marcel
Mauss's bold investigation of *Seasonal Variations of the Eskimo* (Mauss
and Beuchat [1906] 1979), and Maurice Halbwachs's ([1942] 1958) probing
Psychology of Social Class. But it has rarely been addressed frontally by
students of urban inequality and poverty. From Robert Park and Ernest
Burgess to Louis Wirth on down to his postwar students, the Chicago School

did posit a correspondence between metropolitan morphology and psychology, with distinct "moral regions" corresponding roughly to the evolving ethnic and class quartering of space in the American city (Hannerz 1980). But its exponents were so intent on fighting the deep anti-urbanism of America's national culture and on elaborating the notion of (sub)cultural diversity that they devoted little attention to the negative synergy between material deterioration, institutional devolution, and the mental atmosphere of neighborhoods, in spite of the explosive racial tensions and conflictive class transformation roiling the metropolis before their eyes. More problematic still, they were oblivious to the role of the state as a stratifying and classifying agency that wields a dominant influence on the social and symbolic order of the city.

Likewise, the classic studies of the crisis of the dark ghetto during and after the upheavals of the 1960s addressed collective deprecation and depression, but they linked them primarily to pervasive unemployment and continued racial discrimination inflicted on lower-class blacks (Clark 1965, Liebow 1967, Rainwater 1970, Glasgow 1980, Wilson 1987), rather than to their proximate socio-spatial milieu and its distinctive ambiance and image. In this regard, they converged with the resurgent Marxist and political-economic approaches to urban disparity, which typically treated collective representations as secondary efflorescences or reflexes of material forces rooted in the realm of production and its disjuncture from the world of "community" (Katznelson 1982, Harvey 1989, Walton 1993). By the 1990s, the academic tale of the "underclass" took it as axiomatic that the inner-city poor were both destitute and dispirited—indeed, in the hegemonic accounts, the

moral degradation of this segment of the urban proletariat was not a consequence but the cause of their predicament. But it neither documented nor
related this state of mind to the physical and social state of the crumbling
ghetto and their structural determinants. With few partial and oblique excep-
tions (e.g., Bourdieu et al. [1993] 1999, Snow and Anderson 1993, Bourgois
1995, Young 2003, Gay 2005, Jamoulle 2009), then, observers of landscapes
of urban dereliction have paid little attention to the symbolic valence and
psychological tenor of entrapment at the bottom of the hierarchy of places
that make up the city. This essay is an invitation to fill this gap.

The neighborhood of Woodlawn is barely 200 yards from the University of Chicago Law School, yet worlds away. It is a few blocks east of the
boxing gym that served as hub for the ethnographic component of two nested
studies, the one a carnal anthropology of prizefighting as plebeian bodily
craft carried out in 1988–91, and the other a comparative sociology of the
dynamics and experience of urban marginality in the black American ghetto
and the urban periphery of Western Europe stretched over the ensuing
decade (Wacquant 2004, 2008). It gives a glimpse of the *physical dilapidation, social decay, and stunning depopulation* that were the first palpable
features of everyday life in the American hyperghetto at century's close.
Between 1950 and 1990, the ranks of Woodlawnites sank from 81,300 to
a mere 27,500 as their ethnic composition swung from 62 percent white to
98 percent black.[1] The number of housing units plummeted from 29,616
to 13,109, with fully one-fifth of the remaining structures left vacant and
widespread building abandonment, arson, and demolition. As the wage labor
market and the welfare state both retrenched from the area in the wake of

the riots of 1968 in response to the assassination of Martin Luther King, economic involution and organizational desertification set in. The decline and death of hundreds of commercial, social, and cultural establishments— from machine shops and barber shops to hotels, theaters, and restaurants, churches, banks, clothing outlets, and day-care centers—turned a vibrant neighborhood into an urban wasteland doubly segregated by race and class. The bustling commercial artery of 63rd Street mutated into a lugubrious strip dotted with the burnt-out carcasses of stores, boarded-up buildings (scavenged for metal, fixtures, and bricks), and vacant lots strewn with weeds, broken glass, and garbage.[2] Extending the thrust of the "new federalism" dictated by Washington after 1980, city policy shifted away from supporting lower-class residents and districts and toward attracting corporations and beefing up middle-class amenities. The ensuing breakdown of public services in the metropolitan core undermined the local institutions central to the strategies of preservation of the urban poor (Sánchez-Jankowski 2008), leaving them mired in rampant joblessness, crushing poverty, and escalating crime, as the predatory commerce of the street grew to fill the vacuum left by the ebbing of the formal economy.

How did the racially skewed economic, demographic, and political forces that combined to gut out the erstwhile proud "Black Metropolis" of Chicago (Drake and Cayton 1945, 1963), leaving it in a state of infrastructural and institutional abandonment unknown and unthinkable in Western European cities (see Kazepov 2005 for comparison), impress the consciousness of its residents? Curtis's depiction of 63rd Street indicates how urban desolation translates into *collective demoralization*, registered in feelings

of dejection, dread, and anger, as well as in the inordinately high rates of malnutrition and obesity, alcoholism and drug abuse, and depression and assorted other mental afflictions. The material crumbling of the neighborhood is but the physical manifestation of the sudden closure of the opportunity structure, incarnated by the social phantoms roving the street for whom existence is reduced to sheer subsistence *("they out here ta live, they live day-by-day")*. The amputation of objective life chances, in turn, collapses the social horizon of subjective expectations, leaving little room between utter despair *("jus' imagine you not havin' a dream")* and oneirism, represented, on the legal side, by massive participation in the Illinois state lottery and, on the illegal side, by narcotics distribution and consumption.

Anthropologists of place have taught us that public space is pregnant with civic meaning (Low and Smith 2005). In this regard, the physical disrepair and institutional dilapidation of the neighborhood cannot but generate an abiding *sense of social inferiority* by communicating to its residents that they are second- or third-class citizens undeserving of the attention of city officials and the care of its agencies. This message of social worthlessness is conveyed not only by the crumbling bridges, broken sidewalks, and leaking sewers, but also by the gradual replacement of the social welfare treatment of marginality by its punitive management through the aggressive rolling out of the police, the courts, and the prison, leading to astronomical rates of incarceration for lower-class blacks (Wacquant 2009).

The message of marginality is reinforced by the distinctive advertising imagery that visually dominates the streets. Billboards invite passersby to seek succor in the embrace of hard liquor ("Vampin' with the Brothers: Colt 45," "Misbehavin': Canadian Mist," "Be Cool: Smirnoff Vodka"); these ads remind them of their present economic quandary and the dreary fate awaiting their children ("Get A Job—Call Now—19 Dollars"; "No School, No Future"); and they invite them to resolve on their own festering problems that should be the responsibility of government ("Stop Black-on-Black Crime") or yet to collaborate with its repressive arm ("Save a Life: Tell On Your Neighborhood Drug Dealer").

The ominous placard blaring "Addiction is Slavery" over a black hand clutching pills reactivates the historic dishonor of servitude and links it syntagmatically with urban dispossession—except to suggest that today's inner-city derelicts are to blame for their predicament, insofar as their bondage is portrayed as the product not of subordination to a (white) master abetted by an indifferent political machinery but of a relation of self to self, in keeping with the neoliberal trope of individual responsibility that has percolated down to the rock bottom of the social order (as when Curtis seeks to establish his civic bona fides by exclaiming about the street zombies caught in the vortex of drugs and despair: "That's the life that they wanted to live, but *I choose* the opposite"). Indeed, both whites and the state are the absent presence that haunts the picture by their joint empirical invisibility and causal liability.

The decrepit physical setting, the unchecked institutional dysfunction, the grinding demoralization, and the pervasive aura of collective indignity suffusing the hyperghetto combine to tag its residents with an "undesired differentness" whose "discrediting effect is very extensive" (Goffman 1963: 5, 3), that is, a *stigma attached to territory* that becomes superimposed onto and redoubles the stigmata of race and poverty. People trapped in districts of social perdition widely perceived as nests of vice and violence, where only the discards of society would brook living, respond to the taint associated with dwelling in the *regio non grata* of their metropolis by deploying four strategies of symbolic self-protection.[3] The first is *mutual distancing and the elaboration of micro-differences:* they disavow knowing people around them and stress whatever minor personal property can establish separation from a population and a place they know to be defiled and defiling. The second strategy is *lateral denigration,* which consists in adopting the vituperative representations held by outsiders and in applying these to one's neighbors, effectively relaying and reverberating the scornful gaze society trains onto its urban outcasts. A third reaction to spatial vilification is to *retreat into the private sphere* and seek refuge in the restricted social and moral economy of the household, while a fourth is to *exit the neighborhood* as soon as one garners the resources needed to depart (as attested by the outmigration that cut the population of Woodlawn by 30 percent in the 1980s alone).[4]

Territorial degradation and defamation exercise a deleterious influence on the social structure of urban marginality through two routes. First, internally, stigmatization feeds back into demoralization, and the two converge to encourage residents of districts of dereliction to disassociate themselves from their neighbors, shrinking their networks and restricting their joint activities. This social withdrawal and symbolic disidentification, in turn, undermine local cohesion, hamper collective mobilization, and help generate the very atomism that the dominant discourse on zones of urban dispossession claims is one of their inherent features. Second, on the external front, spatial stigma alters the perception and skews the judgments and actions of the surrounding citizenry, commercial operators, and government officials.[5] Outsiders fear coming into the neighborhood and commonly impute a wide range of nefarious traits to its inhabitants. Businesses are reticent to open facilities or provide services for customers in "no-go areas." Employers hesitate to hire job applicants who, coming from them, are unreflectively suspected of having a lax work ethic and lower moral standards, leading to pervasive "address discrimination." Most decisively, when urban degradation and symbolic devaluation intensify to the point where neighborhoods of relegation appear to be beyond salvage, they provide political leaders and state bureaucrats with warrants for deploying aggressive policies of containment, discipline, and dispersal that further disorganize the urban poor under the pretext of improving their opportunities—as witnessed, for instance, with the campaign of "deconcentration" of public housing launched in the United States in the 1990s (Crump 2002) and the kindred policy of destruction of large clusters of low-income estates now under way across Western Europe (Musterd and Andersson 2005) that propose a false spatial solution to the real economic and political problems destabilizing lower-class districts.

This essay has proposed that the social psychology of place operates in the manner of a symbolic cog, latching the macro-determinants of urban political economy to the life options and strategies of the poor through negative collective representations of dispossessed districts that come to be shared by their inhabitants, by city dwellers around them, and by the political and administrative elites who design and run the range of public policies and services aimed at deprived populations. This points to the need for detailed field studies tracking how the stigma fastened on neighborhoods of relegation across advanced Western societies—the hyperghetto in the United States, the degraded working-class *banlieues* in France, the "sink estates" in the United Kingdom, the *krottenwijk* in the Netherlands, etc.—twists the nexus of urban ecology, morphology, and psychology and thereby skews the functioning of the institutions that shape the destiny of urban outcasts in the era of rising social insecurity.

The pictures and street diagram are taken from the author's field diaries and archives, 63rd Street in Woodlawn, South Side of Chicago, summer of 1989 and fall of 1991.

1 An earlier version of this essay appeared in *Sensing the City: A Companion to Urban Anthropology,* ed. Anja Schwanhäusser (Berlin, Boston: De Gruyter, 2016). All the figures in this section are culled and computed from various tables and appendices in Chicago Fact Book Consortium (1995), which itself relies on geo-coded tabulations of tract-level data from the 1990 Census.

2 This is not a Chicago particularity, as documented by Vergara's (2003) stunning photographic collage on the ghostly ruins of the inner cities of New York City, Newark and Camden (New Jersey), Philadelphia, Baltimore, Gary (Indiana), Detroit, and Los Angeles.

3 See Wacquant (2007) for a discussion of the specificities of territorial stigma – by contraposition to what Erving Goffman characterizes as physical, moral, and tribal stigmata – and of the thorny dilemmas it creates for collective claims-making and group formation among the urban precariat. For an elaboration on the varied strategies whereby residents cope with territorial taint on three continents and their determinants, see Wacquant, Slater, and Pereira 2014.

4 This is only a temporary or apparent solution: subproletarian families who leave their run-down districts in the American city do not go very far in social and physical space. They typically relocate in an adjacent area or in another tract sporting similar ecological, economic, and demographic properties (Sharkey 2008).

5 "We believe that the person with a stigma is not quite human. On this assumption, we exercise a variety of discriminations, through which we effectively, if often unthinkingly, reduce his life chances. We construct a stigma-theory, an ideology to explain his inferiority and to account for the danger he represents" (Goffman 1963: 5).

References:

Bourgois, Philippe. 1995. *In Search of Respect: Selling Crack in El Barrio*. New York: Cambridge University Press.

Bourdieu, Pierre et al. [1993] 1998. *The Weight of the World: Social Suffering in Contemporary Society*. Cambridge, UK: Polity Press.

Chicago Fact Book Consortium. 1995. *Local Community Fact Book, Chicago Metropolitan Area*. Chicago: Academy Chicago Publishers.

Clark, Kenneth B. 1965. *Dark Ghetto: Dilemmas of Social Power*. New York: Harper.

Crump, Jeff. 2002. "Deconcentration by Demolition: Public Housing, Poverty, and Urban Policy." *Environment and Planning D: Society and Space* 20, no. 5: 581–96.

Drake, St. Clair, and Horace Cayton. 1945, 1962. *Black Metropolis: A Study of Negro Life in a Northern City*. Chicago: University of Chicago Press, new ed. 1993.

Durkheim, Emile. [1912] 1995. *The Elementary Forms of Religious Life*. Trans. and with an introduction by Karen E. Fields. New York: Free Press.

Gay, Robert. 2005. *Lucia: Testimonies of a Brazilian Drug Dealer's Woman*. Philadelphia: Temple University Press.

Goffman, Erving. 1963. *Stigma: Notes on the Management of Spoiled Identity*. New York: Simon & Schuster.

Glasgow, Douglas G. 1980. *The Black Underclass: Poverty, Unemployment, and the Entrapment of Ghetto Youth*. New York: Vintage.

Jamoulle, Pascale. 2008. *Des hommes sur le fil. La construction de l'identité masculine en milieux précaires*. Paris: La Découverte.

Halbwachs, Maurice. [1942] 1958. *The Psychology of Social Class*. London: Heinemann.

Hannerz, Ulf. 1984. *Exploring the City: Inquiries Toward an Urban Anthropology*. New York: Columbia University Press.

Harvey, David. 1989. *The Urban Experience*. Baltimore, MD: Johns Hopkins University Press.

Kazepov, Yuri (ed.). 2005. *Cities of Europe: Changing Contexts, Local Arrangement and the Challenge to Urban Cohesion*. Cambridge, UK: Wiley-Blackwell.

Katznelson, Ira. 1981. *Urban Trenches: Urban Politics and the Patterning of Class in the United States*. New York: Pantheon.

Liebow, Elliot. 1967. *Tally's Corner: A Study of Negro Streetcorner Men*. Addison: Rowman & Littlefield, new ed. 2003.

Low, Setha, and Neil Smith (eds.). 2005. *The Politics of Public Space*. New York: Routledge.

Mauss, Marcel, and Henri Beuchat. [1906] 1979. *Seasonal Variations of the Eskimo: A Study in Social Morphology*. London: Routledge & Kegan Paul.

Musterd, Sako, and Roger Andersson. 2005. "Housing Mix, Social Mix, and Social Opportunities." *Urban Affairs Review* 40, no. 6: 761–90.

Rainwater, Lee. 1970. *Behind Ghetto Walls: Black Families in a Federal Slum*. New York: Aldine Publishing Company.

Sánchez-Jankowski, Martín. 2008. *Cracks in the Pavement: Social Change and Resilience in Poor Neighborhoods*. Berkeley: University of California Press.

Sharkey, Patrick. 2008. "The Intergenerational Transmission of Context." *American Journal of Sociology* 113, no. 4 (December): 931–69.

Snow, David A., and Leon Anderson. 1993. *Down on Their Luck: A Study of Homeless Street People*. Berkeley: University of California Press.

Vergara, Camilo. 2003. *American Ruins*. New York: Monacelli.

Wacquant. [2000] 2004. *Body and Soul: Notebooks of An Apprentice Boxer*. New York: Oxford University Press.

Wacquant. 2007. "Territorial Stigmatization in the Age of Advanced Marginality." *Thesis Eleven* 91 (November): 66–77.

Wacquant. 2008. *Urban Outcasts: A Comparative Sociology of Advanced Marginality*. Cambridge, UK: Polity Press.

Wacquant. 2009. *Punishing the Poor: The Neoliberal Government of Social Insecurity*. Durham, NC, and London: Duke University Press.

Wacquant, Tom Slater, and Virgílio Pereira. 2014. "Territorial Stigmatization in Action." *Environment & Planning A,* 46, June: 1270–80.

Wilson, William Julius. 1987. *The Truly Disadvantaged: The Inner City, the Underclass, and Public Policy*. Chicago: University of Chicago Press.

Walton, John. 1993. "Urban Sociology: The Contribution and Limits of Political Economy." *Annual Review of Sociology* 19: 301–20.

Young, Alford A., Jr. 2004. *The Minds of Marginalized Black Men: Making Sense of Mobility, Opportunity, and Future Life Chances*. Princeton, NJ: Princeton University Press.

Public Space and Public Sphere

Radical Politics as Counter-Hegemonic Intervention: The Role of Cultural Practices

Chantal Mouffe

Can artistic and cultural practices still play a critical role in societies in which every critical gesture is quickly recuperated and neutralized by the dominant powers? Such a question is increasingly raised, and there is no agreement about the answer. Many people argue that in our consumer societies, aesthetics has triumphed in all realms, and the effect of this triumph has been the creation of a hedonistic culture where there is no place for art to provide a truly subversive experience. The blurring of the lines between art and advertising is such that the idea of critical public spaces has lost its meaning: we are now living in societies where even the public has become privatized. Reflecting on the growth of the global culture industry, some theorists claim that Adorno's and Horkheimer's worst nightmares have become true. The production of symbols has become a central goal of capitalism, and through the development of the creative industries individuals are now totally subjugated to the control of capital. Not only consumers but cultural producers too are prisoners of the culture industry dominated by the media and entertainment corporations, and they have been transformed as passive functions of the capitalist system.

Fortunately this pessimistic diagnosis is not shared by everybody. For instance, there are theorists who claim that the analysis of Adorno and Horkheimer, based as it is on the Fordist model, no longer provides a useful guide to examine the new forms of production that have become dominant in the current post-Fordist mode of capitalist regulation. They see those new forms of production as allowing for new types of resistance, and they envisage the possibility of a revitalization of the emancipatory project to which artistic practices could make a decisive contribution. Such a view is supported by insights from André Gorz:

> When self-exploitation acquires a central role in the process
> of valorization, the production of subjectivity becomes
> a terrain of the central conflict ... social relations that elude
> the grasp of value, competitive individualism and market
> exchange make the latter appear by contrast in their political

> dimension, as extensions of the power of capital. A front
> of total resistance to this power is made possible which
> necessarily overflows the terrain of production of knowl-
> edge towards new practices of living, consuming and
> collective appropriation of common spaces and everyday
> culture."[1]

What is needed is widening the field of intervention of cultural and artistic practices by intervening directly in a multiplicity of social spaces to oppose the program of total social mobilization of capitalism. The objective should be to undermine the imaginary environment necessary for its reproduction.

I believe that important theoretical issues are at stake in this debate and that it is necessary to grasp them to fruitfully envisage how cultural practices could play a critical role and contribute to the struggle against capitalist domination. This requires, in my view, not only an adequate grasp of the nature of the transition undergone by advanced industrial societies since the last decades of the 20th century but also a proper understanding of the dynamic of democratic politics—an understanding that, I contend, can be obtained only by acknowledging its hegemonic character. I will examine those two questions in turn.

From Fordism to Post-Fordism

As far as the changes that have affected capitalist societies are concerned, various theories conceptualize them as either a transition from industrial to post-industrial society, a move from Fordism to post-Fordism, or a progression from a disciplinary society to a society of control. I will concentrate my attention on the first perspective and discuss it by examining the differences between the approaches influenced by the critical theory of Adorno and Horkheimer and those that are influenced by the Italian autonomist tradition. Their main disagreement concerns the role that the culture industry has played in the transformations of capitalism. It is well known that Adorno and Horkheimer saw the development of the culture industry as the moment when the Fordist mode of production finally managed to enter the field of culture. They present this evolution as a further stage in the process of com-modification and of subjugation of society to the requisites of capitalist pro-duction. For Paolo Virno and some other post-operaists, on the contrary, it is the culture industry that played an important role in the process of transition between Fordism and post-Fordism. According to them, it is in that field that new practices of production emerged, which led to the overcoming of Fordism. In his book *A Grammar of the Multitude,* Virno asserts that the space granted to the informal, the unexpected, and the unplanned, which for

Horkheimer and Adorno were non-influential remnants of the past, should be seen as anticipatory omens.[2] With the development of immaterial labor, they began to play an increasingly important role and opened the way for new forms of social relations. In advanced capitalism, says Virno, the labor process has become performative and mobilizes the most universal requisites of the species: perception, language, memory, and feelings. Contemporary production is "virtuosic" and productive labor in its totality appropriates the special characteristics of the performing artist. This is why he argues that the culture industry should be seen as the matrix of post-Fordism.

Theorists influenced by the autonomist tradition share the conviction that the transition from Fordism to post-Fordism has to be understood as dictated not by the logic of the development of capitalist forces of production but as reaction to the new practices of resistance of the workers. Disagreements exist, however, among them concerning the political consequences of this transition. Although many use the notion of "multitude" to refer to the new type of political agent characteristic of the current period, they do not envisage its role in the same way. Some like Michael Hardt and Antonio Negri celebrate in the "multitude" the emergence of a new revolutionary subject that will necessarily bring down the new form of domination embodied in empire.[3] Incorporating, although not always in a faithful way, the analyses of Foucault and Deleuze, Hardt and Negri claim that the end of the disciplinary regime that was exercised over bodies in enclosed spaces such as schools, factories, and asylums, and its replacement by the procedures of control linked to the growth of networks, is leading to a new type of governance that permits more autonomous and independent forms of subjectivity. With the expansion of new forms of cooperative communication and the invention of new communicative forms of life, those subjectivities can express themselves freely, and they will contribute to the formation of a new set of social relations that will finally replace the capitalist system.

While acknowledging the potential opened in the post-Fordist stage for new forms of life, other post-operaist theorists are not so sanguine about the future. For instance, Virno sees the growth of the multitude as an ambivalent phenomenon and acknowledges the new forms of subjection and precarization that are typical of the post-Fordist stage. It is true that people are not as passive as before, but it is because they have now become active actors of their own precarization. So instead of seeing in the generalization of immaterial labor a type of spontaneous communism like Hardt and Negri, Virno tends to see post-Fordism as a manifestation of the "communism of capital." This does not mean that he abandons every hope for emancipation, but it is in the refusal to work and the different forms of exodus and disobedience that he locates such hope.

I would certainly not deny the crucial transformations in the mode of regulation of capitalism represented by the transition to post-Fordism, but I believe that we should envisage this transition from the point of view of the theory of hegemony. I agree with those who insist on the importance of not seeing those transformations as the mere consequence of technological progress and of bringing to the fore their political dimension. They should indeed be understood as a move by capital to provide what was a fundamentally political answer to the crisis of governability of the 1970s. What I want to stress is that many factors have contributed to this transition and it is necessary to grasp the complexity of its dynamics.

A Hegemonic Approach

According to the approach that I am advocating and whose theoretical bases have been established in *Hegemony and Socialist Strategy: Towards a Radical Democratic Politics,* the two key concepts needed to address the question of the political are "antagonism" and "hegemony."[4] On the one hand, it is necessary to acknowledge the dimension of "the political" as the ever-present possibility of antagonism, and this requires, on the other hand, coming to terms with the lack of a final ground and the undecidability that pervades every order. This means recognizing the hegemonic nature of every kind of social order and envisaging every society as the product of a series of practices attempting to establish order in a context of contingency. Those practices of articulation through which a certain order is created and the meaning of social institutions fixed we call "hegemonic practices." According to such a view, every order is the temporary and precarious articulation of contingent practices. Things could always have been otherwise, and every order is therefore predicated on the exclusion of other possibilities. It is in that sense that it can be called "political," since it is the expression of a particular structure of power relations. What is at a given moment considered as the natural order, jointly with the common sense (Gramsci) that accompanies it, is the result of sedimented hegemonic practices; it is never the manifestation of a deeper objectivity exterior to the practices that bring it into being. Every hegemonic order is susceptible to being challenged by "counter-hegemonic" practices—that is, practices that attempt to disarticulate the existing order to install another form of hegemony.

I submit that it is necessary to introduce this hegemonic dimension when one envisages the transition from Fordism to post-Fordism. We can find interesting insights in the interpretation of that transition defended by Luc Boltanski and Eve Chiapello. In *The New Spirit of Capitalism,* they bring to light the role played by what they call "artistic critique" in the transformation undergone by capitalism in the last decades of the 20th century.[5]

RIGHT TO THE PUBLIC

Above, doors and windows open to the public. Air, light, sounds, and people flow through. As the city grows, how can the fundamental right to the public be ensured? What is the cost of losing this right?

In January 2016, two months after the terror attacks in Paris where 130 people were murdered, the Café Le Carillon reopened. While the attacks threatened the fundamental right to life and public enjoyment of this right, the café's reopening marks resiliency, bravery, and hope for cities across the world.

RIGHT TO THE PUBLIC

In 2012, the 355,000 square foot urban park called Superkilen was completed in Copenhagen, Denmark. Designed by Superflex, Bjarke Ingels Group, and Topotek 1 in collaboration with the local—largely immigrant—population. The project raises the question of how can design processes and outcomes be used to bring diverse communities and neighborhoods together?

Medellín's Mayor, Sergio Fajardo, alongside Alejandro Echeverri, Director of Urban Projects, worked with a local team creating public parks and buildings with the goal of uniting communities across Colombia. The Jardin Botanico-Orquideorama marks one of these spaces. How can design help ensure realization of the fundamental right to the public?

RIGHT TO THE PUBLIC

Located on 5 East 53rd Street in midtown Manhattan, Paley Park was created by Zion & Breen in 1967, and funded and developed by former chairman of CBS, William Paley. The 4,200 square foot space is privately owned yet public. Between buildings, the street level design provides a tranquil space.

How is the right to the public linked to the right to transportation and mobility? Designed by a multidisciplinary group, Team CS, the new Rotterdam Centraal Station was a cooperation between Benthem Crouwel Architects, MVSA Architects, and West 8. Each day, 110,000 passengers move through the station.

The public sphere is crucial for the distribution of news and gossip. Plazas and streets are lined with newspaper stalls; orators gather crowds discussing politics. How does the right to the public relate to the right to information? How does city design enable or disable the ability for citizens to bear witness, critique, and unite?

They indicate how the demands of autonomy of the new movements of the 1960s have been harnessed in the development of the post-Fordist networked economy and transformed into new forms of control. The aesthetic strategies of the counterculture—the search for authenticity, the ideal of self-management, the anti-hierarchical exigency—are now used to promote the conditions required by the current mode of capitalist regulation, replacing the disciplinary framework characteristic of the Fordist period. Today artistic and cultural production play a central role in the process of capital valorization, and through what they refer to as "neo-management," artistic critique has become an important element of capitalist productivity.

From my point of view, what is interesting in this approach is that it shows that an important dimension of the transition from Fordism to post-Fordism was a process of discursive rearticulation of a set of existing discourses and practices, and this allows us to apprehend this transition in terms of a hegemonic struggle. To be sure, Boltanski and Chiapello do not use this terminology, but theirs is a clear example of what Gramsci calls "hegemony through neutralization" or "passive revolution" to refer to the situation where, by satisfying them in a way that neutralizes their subversive potential, demands which challenge an established hegemonic order are recuperated by the existing system. To envisage the transition from Fordism to post-Fordism in such a way helps us to visualize it as a hegemonic move by capital to reestablish its leading role and restore its legitimacy.

By adding to the analysis offered by Boltanski and Chiapello the undeniable role played in this transition by workers' resistance, we can obtain a more complex understanding of the forces at play in the emergence of the current neoliberal hegemony. This hegemony is the result of a set of political interventions in a complex field of economic, legal, and ideological forces. It is a discursive construction that articulates in a very specific manner a manifold of practices, discourses, and languages—games of a very different nature. Through a process of sedimentation, the political origin of those contingent practices has been erased and they have become naturalized. Neoliberal practices and institutions therefore appear as the outcome of natural processes, and the forms of identification that they have produced have crystallized in identities that are taken for granted. This is how the "common sense" that constitutes the framework for what most people perceive as possible and desirable has been established. To challenge neoliberalism, it is therefore vital to transform this framework, and this is precisely what the hegemonic struggle should be about.

An Agonistic Politics

To envisage how to wage a successful counter-hegemonic struggle requires grasping what is really at stake in democratic politics. I have argued that, once the ineradicable dimension of antagonism is acknowledged, it becomes clear that one of the main tasks of democratic politics consists in defusing the potential antagonism that exists in social relations. This can be done by fostering an ensemble of institutions, practices, and language games that will make it possible for conflicts to take an "agonistic" form instead of an "antagonistic" one.[6] Let me briefly indicate what I mean here. While in an antagonistic type of political relation the conflicting parties perceive their opponents as "enemies" to be destroyed, in the agonistic one they treat them as "adversaries"—that is, they recognize the legitimacy of the claims of their opponents. This supposes that, although they are in conflict, they nevertheless see themselves as belonging to the same political association as their opponents, as sharing a common symbolic space within which their conflict takes place. What is at stake in the agonistic struggle is the very configuration of power relations around which a given society is structured. It is a struggle between hegemonic projects that cannot be reconciled rationally. The antagonistic dimension is therefore present and it is a real confrontation, but one that is played out under conditions regulated by a set of democratic procedures accepted by the adversaries. An agonistic conception of democracy acknowledges the contingent character of the hegemonic politico-economic articulations that determine the special configuration of society at a given moment. They are precarious and pragmatic constructions that can be disarticulated and transformed as the result of the agonistic struggle. Society, according to such a perspective, is not to be seen as the unfolding of a logic exterior to itself, whatever the source of this logic might be: forces of production, development of the spirit, law of history, etc. Society is always politically instituted, and the terrain in which hegemonic interventions take place is always the outcome of previous hegemonic practices; it is never neutral.

A central task of the agonistic hegemonic struggle has always been the production of new subjectivities, but in the present stage of capitalism such a terrain is more important than ever. Today's capitalism relies increasingly on semiotic techniques to create the modes of subjectification necessary for its reproduction. In modern production, the control of souls (Foucault) plays a strategic role in governing affects and passions. The forms of exploitation characteristic of the times when manual labor was dominant have been replaced by new ones that require constantly creating new needs and an incessant desire for the acquisition of goods. This is why in our consumer societies advertising plays such an important role. This role is not limited to promoting specific products but extends to producing fantasy worlds with which the consumers of goods will identify. Indeed, to buy something is to enter into a specific world, to become part of an imagined community. To maintain its hegemony, the current capitalist system needs to constantly mobilize people's desires and shape their identity, and it is the construction of the very identity of the buyer that is at stake in the techniques of advertising. A counter-hegemonic politics must therefore engage with this terrain to foster other forms of identification. This is why the cultural terrain occupies such a strategic place in politics today. To be sure, the realm of culture has always played an important role in hegemonic politics, but in the times of post-Fordist production this role has become absolutely crucial.

Agonistic Public Spaces

How can cultural and artistic practices contribute to the counter-hegemonic challenge to neoliberal hegemony? To tackle this issue we need to address the question of public space, and I will begin by indicating the consequences of the agonistic approach in this field. Its main contribution is to challenge the widespread conception that, albeit in different ways, informs most visions of public space conceived as the terrain where one should aim at creating consensus. According to the perspective that I am advocating, to the contrary, public spaces—which are always plural—constitute the battlegrounds where the different hegemonic projects are confronted, without any possibility of final reconciliation. My position is therefore very different from the one defended by Jürgen Habermas, who envisages what he calls the "public sphere" as the place where deliberation aiming at a rational consensus takes place. To be sure, Habermas accepts that it is improbable, given the limitations of social life, that such a consensus could effectively be reached and sees his "ideal situation of communication" as a "regulative idea." However, for the agonistic hegemonic approach, the impediments to the Habermasian ideal speech situation are not empirical but ontological. One of its main tenets is indeed that such a rational consensus is a conceptual impossibility because it posits the availability of a consensus without exclusion, which is precisely what such an approach reveals to be impossible.

Despite some similarities in terminology, my conception of agonistic public spaces also differs from the one of Hannah Arendt, which has become so popular recently. In my view the main problem with Arendt's understanding of "agonism" is, in a nutshell, that it is an "agonism without antagonism." What I mean is that, while Arendt puts great emphasis on plurality and insists that politics deals with the community and the reciprocity of human beings who are different, she never acknowledges that this plurality is at the origin of antagonistic conflicts. According to her, to think politically is to develop the ability to see things from a multiplicity of perspectives.

As her reference to Kant's idea of "enlarged thought" testifies, her pluralism is inscribed in the horizon of an intersubjective agreement. What she looks for in Kant's doctrine of aesthetic judgment is in fact a procedure for ascertaining intersubjective agreement in the public space. This is why, notwithstanding significant differences in their approaches, Arendt, like Habermas, ends up envisaging the public space in a consensual way.

To visualize public spaces in an agonistic way allows us to envisage how cultural and artistic practices can contribute to the hegemonic struggle. By bringing to the fore what the dominant consensus tends to obscure and obliterate, by making visible what neoliberal hegemony represses, critical cultural and artistic practices can play an important role in the creation of a multiplicity of sites where the dominant hegemony would be questioned. They should be seen as counter-hegemonic interventions that, by contributing to the construction of new practices and new subjectivities, aim at subverting the dominant hegemony. People working in the field of art and culture are indeed what Gramsci called "organic intellectuals."

I want to clarify that such interventions cannot be envisaged as having as objective to lift a supposedly false consciousness so as to reveal the "true reality." This would be completely at odds with the anti-essentialist premises of the theory of hegemony, which rejects the very idea of a "true consciousness." Identities are, according to this approach, always the result of a process of identification, and it is through insertion in a manifold of practices, discourses, and language games that specific forms of individualities are constructed. What is a stake in the transformation of political identities is not a rationalist appeal to the true interest of the subject but the inscription of the social agent in practices that will mobilize its affects in a way that disarticulates the framework in which the dominant process of identification is taking place, to bring about other forms of identification. This means that to construct oppositional identities, it is not enough to simply foster a process of "de-identification"; the second move, the moment of "re-identification," is crucial. To insist only on the first move is in fact to remain trapped in a problematic according to which the negative moment would be sufficient on its own to bring about something positive—as if new subjectivities were already there, ready to emerge once the weight of the dominant ideology was lifted. Such a view, which informs many forms of critical art, fails to come to terms with the nature of the hegemonic struggle and the complex process of construction of identities.

To envisage the role of critical artistic practices in terms of hegemonic struggle also means that the political strategy cannot be one of exodus. Such a view, advocated by a diversity of post-operaist theorists, comes in different versions, but they all imply that in the conditions characteristic of empire, the traditional structures of power organized around the national state and representative democracy have become irrelevant and will progressively disappear. Those who follow this approach believe that one can ignore the existing power structures in order to dedicate oneself to constructing alternative social forms outside the state power network. This is why they refuse any collaboration with the traditional channels of politics, such as parties and trade unions. They reject any majoritarian model of society, organized around a state, in favor of another model of organization of the multitude, which they present as more universal, a form of unity provided by common places of the mind, cognitive-linguistic habits, and the general intellect.

Conclusion

At this point I think it important to realize that the differences between the two approaches that I have presented cannot be understood simply in terms of different political strategies; we need to realize that they proceed from different ontologies. The strategy of exodus, based on an ontology of immanence, supposes the possibility of a redemptive leap into a society, beyond politics and sovereignty, where the Multitude would be able to immediately rule itself and act in concert without the need of law or the state, and where antagonism would have disappeared. The hegemonic strategy, in contrast, recognizes that antagonism is irreducible and social objectivity can never be fully constituted, and as a consequence, a fully inclusive consensus and an absolute democracy is never available. According to the immanentist view, the primary ontological terrain is one of multiplicity. In many cases, it also relies on a vitalist ontology according to which the physical and social world in its entirety is seen as the expression of some underlying life force. In all of its versions, the problem with this immanentist view is its incapacity to give account of the role of radical negativity—that is, antagonism. To be sure, negation is present in those theorists, and they even use the term antagonism, but this negation is not envisaged as radical negativity. It is either conceived in the mode of dialectical contradiction or simply as a real opposition. As we have shown in *Hegemony and Socialist Strategy,* to be able to envisage negation on the mode of antagonism requires a different ontological approach where the primary ontological terrain is one of division, of failed unity. Antagonism is not graspable in a problematic that sees the society as a homogeneous space, because this is incompatible with the recognition of radical negativity. The two poles of antagonism are linked by a nonrelational relation; they do not belong to the same space of representation and are essentially heterogeneous with each other. It is out of this irreducible heterogeneity that they emerge. To make room for radical negativity, we need to abandon the immanentist idea of a homogeneous saturated social space and acknowledge the role of heterogeneity. This requires relinquishing the idea of a society beyond division and power, without any need for law or the state and where in fact politics would have disappeared.

If our approach has been called "post-Marxist," it is precisely because we have challenged the type of ontology subjacent to such a conception. By bringing to the fore the dimension of negativity that impedes the totalization of society, we have put into question the very possibility of a fully reconciled society. To acknowledge the ineradicability of antagonism implies recognizing that every form of order is necessarily a hegemonic one and that heterogeneity cannot be eliminated; antagonistic heterogeneity points to the limits of constitution of social objectivity. As far as politics is concerned, this means that it should be envisaged it in terms of a hegemonic struggle between conflicting hegemonic projects attempting to incarnate the universal and to define the symbolic parameters of social life. Hegemony is obtained through the construction of nodal points that discursively fix the meaning of institutions and social practices and articulate the common sense through which a given conception of reality is established. Such a result will always be contingent and precarious and susceptible of being challenged by counter-hegemonic interventions. Politics always takes place in a field criss-crossed by antagonisms, and to envisage it simply as "acting in concert" leads to erasing the ontological dimension of antagonism (that I have proposed to call "the political") that provides its quasi-transcendental condition of possibility. A properly political intervention is always one that engages with a certain aspect of the existing hegemony to disarticulate/re-articulate its constitutive elements. It can never be merely oppositional or conceived as desertion because it aims at re-articulating the situation in a new configuration.

An important aspect of a hegemonic politics lies in establishing a "chain of equivalences" between various demands, so as to transform them into claims that will challenge the existing structure of power relations. It is clear that the ensemble of democratic demands that exist in our societies do not necessarily converge and can even be in conflict. This is why they need to be articulated politically. What is at stake is the creation of a common identity, a "we," and this requires the determination of a "they." As we have repeatedly emphasized, a relation of equivalence does not eliminate difference—that would be simply identity. It is only insofar as democratic differences are opposed to forces or discourses that negate all of them that these differences can be substituted for each other. This is why the construction of a collective will requires defining an adversary. Such an adversary cannot be defined in broad general terms like "Empire" or "Capitalism" but in terms of nodal points of power that need to be targeted and transformed to create the conditions for a new hegemony. It is a "war of position" (Gramsci) that has to be launched in a multiplicity of sites. This can only be done by establishing links between social movements, political parties, and trade unions, by a synergy between parliamentary and extra-parliamentary politics. To create, through the construction of a chain of equivalence, a collective will to engage with a wide range of institutions, with the aim of transforming them, is in my view the kind of critique that should inform radical politics.

No doubt, when we examine the future of radical politics through the hegemonic approach, we get a less optimistic view than the one put forward by Hardt and Negri, but a view that is clearly more optimistic than the one propagated by those who claim that there is no alternative to the existing order. Our societies are not necessarily moving toward an "absolute democracy of the multitude," but neoliberal globalization does not represent the end of history either. The configuration of power relations that has been articulated through hegemonic political interventions can always be disarticulated through counter-hegemonic ones. More democratic hegemonic forms of order can exist and we should fight to bring them about. What have to be abandoned are dreams of an absolute democracy, or messianic illusions à la Agamben, of a completely different kind of politics beyond law and violence. Such views lead to a dead end because they impede us from grasping the nature of politics and the necessity to engage with a multiplicity of agonistic democratic struggles.

1 Interview with André Gorz in *Multitudes*, no. 15 (2004): 209.

2 Paolo Virno, *A Grammar of the Multitude* (Los Angeles: Semiotext[e], 2004).

3 See for instance, their two jointly written books, *Empire* (Cambridge, MA: Harvard University Press, 2000) and *Multitude: War and Democracy in the Age of Empire* (New York: Penguin Press, 2004).

4 Ernesto Laclau and Chantal Mouffe, *Hegemony and Socialist Strategy: Towards a Radical Democratic Politics* (London, New York: Verso, 1985).

5 Luc Boltanski and Eve Chiapello, *The New Spirit of Capitalism* (London, New York: Verso, 2005).

6 I have developed this agonistic model in chapter 4 of my book *The Democratic Paradox* (Verso, 2000).

Matrix Space

Keller Easterling

Ethics travels along a Möbius strip of meaning. Sometimes it describes the maintenance of consensus around stated principles. Sometimes, in a partial inversion, it describes the maintenance of dissensus around a necessarily indeterminate struggle with circumstance and evidence. One notion of ethics operates in a declarative register and the other, in an active register. Each, even though traveling on opposite sites of the same surface and approaching from different directions, supports and challenges the other. Ethics is, at once, the solid stable state and the state of encounter. It is galvanizing and atomizing. The moment of certainty and the moment of uncertainty. The prescription and the epidemiology. The fix and the wager. The condition of "knowing that" and the evolving activities of "knowing how."

The ethics of the urban occupies the same Möbius, yet for architects and urbanists, designing urban declarations is more familiar than designing urban action. This is perhaps surprising since, in broader culture, urbanity is an important context for the active register of ethical endeavor—one generative of the very circumstances that challenge ethical consensus. The following contemplation offers no new declaration of ethical principles but rather explores approaches or techniques in an active register that expand a field of ethical endeavor in the city.

Declarations

In declarative ethics, theoretical constructs, master narratives, or shared cultural norms model society. These models (e.g., Christianity, capitalism, democracy, totalitarianism, human rights) become content in a story about good or bad acts. Arguing for the construct it deems to be superior, the discourse crafts ultimate tests (e.g., how does one treat "the other") as well as laws, norms, or behavioral precedent (e.g., how does one treat the other if the other is Hitler or a pedophile) against which to determine a good or bad action. This sort of ethical thinking may nourish activism that coalesces into a story with explicit principles—into a fight for the right. Strongly held, forthright beliefs offer techniques such as resistance and refusal to all that is not right. David must kill Goliath. An activist may fight and die for principles using techniques that have, at certain junctures in history, required enormous courage to enact.

Yet for many powerful players who survive on fluid, undeclared intentions, it is easy to toy with this declared content. When targeted, they wander away from the bull's-eye, or, switching the characters in the story, come costumed as resistance. Goliath finds a way to pose as David. In these situations, dissent is often then shaking its fist at an effigy. Activism that shows up at the barricade, the border crossing, and the battleground with familiar political scripts sometimes finds that the real fight or stealthier forms of violence are happening elsewhere. The binary of enemies and innocents, the epic heraldry and theme music of the righteous activist, may even play into the hands of a more slippery opposing power. The notion that there is an ethical consensus and proper realm of political negotiation even acts as the perfect camouflage for this elusive behavior.

When ethics can locate no technique beyond declaration, it has no choice but to cure its failures with another purification ritual, to tighten the content of the story or make of its opponent an even more mystical or vaporous ur-force, as Capital, Empire, or Neoliberalism frequently become. Still, any deviation from the proper techniques, even in an attempt to aid and broaden activism, may be interpreted as a betrayal of ethical principles. Manipulating the market is mistaken for collusion. Giving positive attention to agents of systemic change rather than opposition to a series of enemies is mistaken for an uncritical stance. Relinquishing the grip of resistance is mistaken for capitulation or ethical relativism. Answering duplicity with duplicity is mistaken for equivocation or lack of conviction rather than a technique to avoid disclosing a strategy. Righteous and combative narratives then exhaust themselves and escalate tensions. Dissent, in these instances, is inconsolable.

Like declarative ethics, the designs of architects and urbanists are often statements outlining a corrective program—a prescription for new volumes in new positions in the city. The most conventional urban plan is an object, a thing in which a precinct of the world is controlled with geometry. Like the manifestos of dissent, it has declared content. It can be represented in images. It replaces bad spatial arrangements with good spatial arrangements. In urban design and planning, these master plans have repeatedly confronted their own failures with yet another master plan—another declaration with a different design. Rule sets for urban design (e.g., CIAM, Team 10, Town Planning Associates), can also become declarative or corrective content offering, for instance, proper proportional dimensions or arrangements. Even when, moving away from the object or master plan, design has borrowed extradisciplinary techniques from, for example, social sciences, cybernetics, or mathematics, the desire has often still been to declare—to have data or equations that deliver the right answer. The fact that the world never seems to adopt the utopian schemes of planners can then be portrayed as a sad mistake, a lack of purity. If only the plans had been executed intact, their authors assert, they might have had a real chance of success. Only greater purity and adherence to the proposed scheme is the answer. Like the backlash against improper activist techniques, there is a backlash against straying from the core skills of the discipline. Sometimes, in these moments of purification, the purely rhetorical proposal is preferred over one that might risk an encounter with nonconforming or unsympathetic political or cultural circumstance. Like dissent, planning in these instances in inconsolable.

Actions

Declarative ethics perhaps conforms to a broader cultural habit that regards only statements of content as information. Goliath can come dressed as David because only name or identity matters. Any character can remain in disguise even if its activity is decoupled from its content—even if it is doing something different from what it says it is doing. Activity is often treated as only the background medium carrying the really consequential information of the story—the object with shape and outline that can be named.

We are perhaps less accustomed to the idea that activity is itself information, that, as Gregory Bateson famously wrote about a tree, a man, and an axe as an information system.[1] Yet the undeclared activities of an organization, especially when they are decoupled from the stated script, may be the most consequential information. In an organization that is saying something different from what it is doing, it is crucial to be able to register the information immanent in activity, even though that may be difficult to see. This activity, like the content of a cultural script, is material for ethical action.

Enacted ethics—ethics in an active register—is asking for the very degradation that declarative ethics denies itself. It is asking to be plunged into contradictory evidence. Activists, urbanists, or anyone in any discipline who is trying to operate within a master narrative is often asking for more actors, a more complex context—the abundance of messy evidence that provides more information for problem solving. Consider Bruno Latour and his call to strengthen studies of the social, or Esther Duflo and Abhijit Banerjee in their critique of economic theory, or human rights activists who find hidden dangers in universal notions of human rights. Perhaps most important to this contemplation, the messier, more robust context that these thinkers desire is often the urban context itself.

Matrix Space

Urban information is immanent in the activities and protocols of matrix space. This is arguably more and more apparent in contemporary global urbanism. We no longer build cities by accumulating masterpiece buildings. Buildings are not necessarily singularly crafted enclosures like statements or declarations, uniquely imagined by an architect. They are often reproducible products or nearly identical buildings made from formulas that travel around the world. As repeatable phenomena engineered around logistics and the bottom line, these formulas or spatial products constitute an infrastructural technology with elaborate routines and schedules for organizing consumption. This technology of matrix space is a medium of information, but the information resides in activity rather than object or text—invisible, powerful activity that determines how objects and content will be organized and circulated. Matrix space, with the power and currency of software, is an operating system for shaping the city.

In matrix space, the urban activist will have trouble locating this extra information within declaration. It is not there. When not only declaration but also activity can become information, the ethical endeavor has traveled to the flip side of the Möbius. It is transposed to another gear or another part of speech, as if from noun to verb. Ethical choices manifest not only in object forms or master plans but also in forms, like software, that operate in a different register.

Software

Matrix space, like software, makes certain things possible and certain things impossible. Like a software, it is not the declared content but the form that, extending into time, determines how content will play and what content will live or die. Matrix space is the generative medium or the protocols of interplay in the urban milieu. While we do not typically think of spaces as having agency, matrix space is *doing something*.

Still, how does one assess activity in static spatial arrangements? Spaces and urban organizations are usually treated not as actors but as collections of objects or volumes. Few would look at a concrete highway or an electrical grid and perceive agency in its static arrangement. Agency might be assigned only to the moving cars, the electrical current, or the inhabitants. We are less accustomed to the idea that physical objects in spatial arrangements, however static, possess agency that resides in relationship and relative position. We are also less accustomed to the idea that space, rather than code or text, can be a carrier of information.

Yet perhaps the idea is not so unfamiliar. Looking at a field of mass-produced suburban houses—a phenomenon common around the world—

the organization embodies a distinct activity that is very apparent. In the case of Levittown, for instance, the developer was not making 1,000 individual houses but a kind of agriculture of houses–1,000 slabs, 1,000 frames, 1,000 roofs, and so on. The site is like an assembly line that separates the tasks of building a house into smaller activities that are each applied across the entire population of houses, in sequence. Beyond the activity of humans within it, the arrangement itself renders some things significant and others insignificant. For instance, it is impossible to build an individual house that is different from the others. A protocol or a nondigital spatial software is *doing something* in the suburban field, and changes within the field constitute information—the changing relationship and consequence that is carried in space.

In this suburban field are object forms as well as active forms—forms that, like a software, organize the components of the field. The architect who has only been trained to make enclosures is prepared to redesign the single house or the object form within the field, while the active forms in the matrix space are less apparent. One active form within the field—one bit of code in its software—is the multiplier. One can see the house not just as an object but as a powerful multiplier of activities in a compound formula that works almost like a mathematical summation. Designing a single house gains little traction and is only swept up in the routines of this spatial software. Yet using the house as the multiplier of a new wrinkle or component of the process —allowing it to be the carrier of a new spatial germ—has the potential to alter a larger population of houses or recondition a larger suburban field. An active form, in this case a multiplier, engages or hacks into the software of matrix space and begins to register as information.

Active Forms

Active forms might describe the way that some alteration performs within a group, multiplies across a field, reconditions a population, or generates a network. They establish a set of parameters or capacities for what the organization will be doing over time. The designer of active forms is designing not the field in its entirety but rather the *delta* or the means by which the field changes—not only the shape or contour of the game piece but also a repertoire for how it plays. While engaged with material and geometry, active forms are inclusive of but not limited to enclosure or representation and may move beyond the conventional architectural site. These are forms that have time-released powers and cascading effects because they are able to introduce an unfolding relationship or a contagious component. Active form may partner with and propel object form, determining how it will align with power to travel through culture. The architectural object form may be an end in itself. Yet while still fulfilling all pleasures of object making, it may be used as an active form or an instrument of additional spatial change with additional powers and artistic pleasures. For active forms in infrastructure space, name or objecthood is less important than an ability to, for instance, inflect, ignite, propagate, or suppress. Designing the software rather than the singular prescription means designing an updating platform for shaping a stream of objects.

Matrix space is composed of repetitive components or multipliers—like the suburban house—that can be used as carriers or contagions in the network. Consider the way that elevators were a germ of urban morphology. Since matrix space is composed of interconnected populations of things, it also responds to active forms like switches or remote controls. Making adjustments to a choke point in a highway or telecommunications network is like tuning a switch that has ramifying and remote effects. We can evaluate the network topology or "wiring" of matrix space. Active forms can change this network architecture so that, for instance, an organization operates less like a hub-and-spoke and more like an all-access, linear, serial, or parallel network. An active form may also establish a relationship between interdependent variables, like a governor or a function in calculus.

Most designers are under-rehearsed in this register. If summoned to create something called active form, urban and architectural designers would naturally rely on what they are best trained to create—a formal object themed, choreographed, or dressed to represent action. A single enclosure would be crafted to *represent* a dynamic process. The program or use for the space (e.g., school or hospital) is treated as its activity. A more simple-minded confusion (made more powerful by being simple-minded) arises when action or activity is confused with movement or kineticism. The form might be considered to be active only if it is coated in digital sensors that respond to movement or touch. In grasping for apprehension of an evolving spatial field with changing components, the architect also might design the entire field of urban activity with a fixed architectural pattern, thus returning it to object form and the declarative "master plan."

Active forms, while sometimes elusive to designers, are quite ordinary and practical in many other disciplines. A geneticist cannot represent all of the gene sequences of DNA with an image of a double helix but can engage the ongoing development of an organism with an active form that alters one of those gene sequences. A computer scientist would never attempt to fully represent the Internet but would rather author active forms such as softwares or multipliers that ride the network with very explicit instructions. An environmentalist would not attempt to work on a forest by placing every bird in every tree or planting every sprig of undergrowth, but would rather send in instrumental players that inflect ecologies over time. Entrepreneurs design not only the product but also its passage through a market. They may use a mobile telephone network or a repetitive suburb to multiply products and desires. Economists and politicians introduce new forms of communication or transportation that recondition the city over time. In all of these examples, there is no desire for a singular, comprehensive, or utopian solution. Similarly, in the manipulation of matrix space, no universal system is declared, and it is not possible to control all outcomes—only modulate powerful spatial variables.

Disposition

Transposing to the flip side of the Möbius, active forms that break the code potentially extend the territory of ethical operations. Most of the highly optimized formulas for the spatial products of matrix space are written in the language of real estate operations or econometrics. The special softwares of the financial industry, for instance, have had enormous spatial impact even though spaces like suburbia are treated only as accidental by-products. Rather than merely entering content into default or de facto spatial formulas, design professions might author active forms and softwares that begin with spatial variables—variables that manage more palpable risks and rewards.

Yet if hacking into the world's dominant spatial softwares cannot be entirely controlled, how does one assess this stream of modulations? How does one make choices about how to inflect, propel, or arrest components of the organization? How does one assess not the declaration but the undeclared constitutions of the organization—what we might call its disposition?

Disposition, a familiar but nuanced word best understood by using it, usually describes an unfolding relationship between potentials. It describes a tendency, faculty, or property in either beings or objects—a propensity within a context. In philosopher François Jullien's simple example: a round ball on an inclined plane possesses disposition. The ball doesn't need to roll down the hill to posses that latent capacity, which is stored in relationship and geometry.[2] If we are going to consider active forms, we also need a way of assessing their ongoing effects in a spatial field. An architect might draw a plan, section, and elevation of an object or building as well as renderings that represent that object in situ. Disposition assesses the capacity or character of an organization that results from the circulation of active forms within it.

Network theorist Yochai Benkler deftly assembles reference to expressions for these special capacities in social media and the Internet commons. Rejecting technological determinism (such as that suggested by McLuhan), he refers to science/technology/society philosopher Langdon Winner's discussion of the "political properties" of technology and sociologist

Barry Wellman's reference to the "affordances" of technology. Benkler synthesizes: "Neither deterministic or wholly malleable, technology sets some parameters of individual and social action." When he writes that, "Different technologies make different kinds of human action and interaction easier or harder to perform," he precisely describes the capacity that we call disposition.[3]

For architecture and urbanism, as for many schools of thought, the distinction between understanding form as object and form as action is something like the philosopher Gilbert Ryle's distinction between "knowing that" and "knowing how." He provides a clown's performance as an example. "Knowing how," like knowing how to be funny, is not something that can be declared or named or reified as an object or event. It is for Ryle, "dispositional."[4] Ryle enjoys the ways in which dispositional expressions thrive in common parlance and are used as a way of describing an unfolding relationship of potential, relative position, tendency, temperament, or property in either beings or objects. Disposition is composed of sequential action. Ryle emphasizes the latency and indeterminacy of this dispositional action in both human and non-human subjects. A person has the capacity or tendency to sing or smoke. A dog can swim. Rubber loses its elasticity. Glass is brittle. A clown is funny. In this way, Ryle demonstrates that seemingly inert objects are actors possessing agency. They are doing something. He finds great sport in noting that while we work with dispositional expressions in everyday speech, in some logical systems this latent activity is treated as a fuzzy imponderable or an occult agency in "a sort of limbo world."[5] Again we treat activity as the mere background medium to the declaration that can be named or that can assure us of a correct answer.

Disposition allows us to see not only agency but also political temperament in organization. For instance, we can see the way in which simple topologies (e.g., binaries or arborescent, hub-and-spoke, or isomorphic organizations) are inherently more violent, weak, robust, or authoritarian simply by seeing the activities immanent in their arrangement—the activities they permit or deny. An urban enclave or a tightly optimized spatial product, like both a reentrant hub-and-spoke and a closed loop, is isomorphic in the sense that it only recirculates compatible information. It returns an organization to one thing rather than an arrangement of multiple things. The symmetrical face-off between two competing forces or the submission and conquest of one force over another are familiar binaries. While isomorphism and binary can embody a quotient of destabilizing violence or tension in their arrangement, they can also maintain stubborn forms of power even as they are clothed with scripts about freedom, openness, or brotherhood.

Dispositional expressions provide another way to make decisions and alterations in space. Designers can assess the object form that registers in plan, section, elevation, and model, but they can also assess the disposition of an organization with some of the same tools related to geometry, measure, time, program, and relative position. The aesthetic regimes that are about enacting rather than depicting are closer to the aesthetic regimes that attend performance. Most important, an unfolding performance provides further techniques for manipulating the invisible undeclared activities and political motives of matrix space—activities that often do not respond to our stiff prescriptions for change.

Political Arts

In the extended ethical territory of matrix space, the very things that make it powerful—its multipliers and its undeclared but consequential activities—are perhaps the same things that might be harnessed to empower new political arts for alternative political goals. These attributes are certainly what makes matrix space immune to righteous declaration and prescription. Matrix space—administered by mixtures of public and private cohorts and capable of outpacing law—constitutes a wilder mongrel than any familiar Leviathan for which we have a well-rehearsed political response. The matrix space that responds to form-making in another register—active forms or forms that operate like software—also responds to an enhanced repertoire of activism.

While in declarative ethics adherence to principles is cornerstone, for enacted ethics of matrix space, the markers are different. For instance, discrepancy rather than righteousness is instrumental. The discrepancy between content and activity, declaration and disposition—between what an organization is saying and what it is doing—is now important. The undeclared agency of active form itself offers a shrewder, cagier counter to the lubricated agility of most global powers. In matrix space, dispositional expressions also begin to garner more and more political power. Remaining undeclared or under the radar, the softwares of active forms can create unannounced and therefore more devastating groundswells and epidemics of change. They can expose the discrepancy between an organization's overt declarations and its latent character. They can rearrange the distributions of power and authority. They can influence temperament. They can tune up the organization to generate a sturdier, richer, more stabilized topology. With remote controls, they can invisibly and indirectly control the shape of matrix space.

If the world's most powerful players operate with proxies and disguises, perhaps righteous activism could use a secret partner. While binary opposition is sometimes warranted, and sometimes it is important to stand up and give a name to a cause, an auxiliary activist might more slyly shift

CHANGING CLIMATES

In June 2016, Paris witnessed torrential rain resulting in flooding across the city. The River Seine raised by 18 feet, which caused the city to close roads. President François Hollande linked the flooding with global warming. How can cities account for and help mitigate the affects of global warming climate change?

Air quality in Beijing has been declining due to a plethora of factors including coal burning. Above, people move through high levels of air pollution enveloping the Forbidden City. Experts have measured air pollution levels even 600 times higher than World Health Organization maximums.

Like many waterways around the world, the Gowanus Canal in Brooklyn was canalized for industrial growth. Consequently, high levels of pollution led to mandated site clean-ups. In 2011, The Canary Project documented how "climate change is likely to make the Gowanus Canal a flood zone." How can cities prepare?

CHANGING CLIMATES

In May 2015, over 1,100 deaths resulted from a heat wave across India where temperatures reached above 100°F. The temperatures in New Delhi caused asphalt to melt. Victims included many elderly, homeless, and construction workers. How can cities create solutions?

CHANGING CLIMATES

Hurricane Sandy hit New York City in October 2012, impacting hundreds of lives through death, displacement, and injury. Days after the hurricane, electrical lines were down throughout the city and streets were flooded. Above, the Flatiron building lights and streetlamps are completely off. What is a city without electricity?

PROTESTING POLITICS

In April 1981, Brixton police officers conducted Operation Swamp with the reported goal of decreasing street crime in the South London borough. Police were accused of racially targeting young black men through the 'sus' law that gave officers the power to stop and search anyone. Who creates the law and who enforces it? How do cities perpetuate violence? How can design perpetuate love?

During the Bloody Sunday shootings in Derry/Londonderry, Northern Ireland, in 1972, a local priest, Edward Daly, waved a bloodied white handkerchief as he tended to the dead and the dying. How can we bring moments of peace into violence?

Directed by Chris Marker and Pierre L'Homme, the film *Le Joli Mai* (or *The Lovely Month of May*)
documents Paris in May 1962. The image above, taken from the film, shows Parisian lives at a time
when France was not at war. How is art used to politically shape the urban?

The *dewanya* is an important gathering space in Kuwait where business and politics get discussed in an informal setting, mostly by men. Often associated with particular families, such as the Diwan al-Qaud in Mishrif, Kuwait (above), *diwaniyas* are generally visited in the evenings. How can we create urban hubs that are not only universally inclusive but also engender more public participation, more rigorous civic discourse?

On March 25, 1965, Dr. Martin Luther King Jr. lead a group of brave, passionate people from Selma
to Montgomery, Alabama, marching and calling for the right to equal voting access. The power
of uniting in the street, walking together in the public sphere, and using non-violent rallying methods
for political action, pushed political action onward.

the disposition of the matrix to relieve abuses and concentrations of power in a way that makes the righteous activist more effective. This auxiliary activist is something like a sneakier David in the David and Goliath story. A sneakier David would never go the trouble of killing Goliath if he could get the giant to do some of his work for him.

An expanded repertoire of political arts goes beyond resistance and refusal to entertain techniques that are less self-congratulatory, less transcendent, less automatically oppositional, more effective and sneakier—techniques like gossip, rumor, gifts, compliance, remote controls, meaninglessness, misdirection, distraction, comedy, or entrepreneurialism. These techniques are incarnations of the active forms discussed above, or they might be seen as the spin one puts on those active forms. Gossip and rumor are multipliers that can attend the multipliers of active form in infrastructure space. A gift or an award, like the pandas named "Unity" that China gave to Taiwan, can be an arm-twisting handshake that kills with kindness. Similarly exaggerated compliance is not collusion but a means to disarm and manipulate—to alter the disposition of authority or opposition and soften the ground for a change. Remote controls allow the activist to indirectly influence circumstances, often without being detected. Misdirections and distractions can lull and redirect the most intractable political situations. Comedy distracts and diffuses tension, but it also destabilizes both self-satisfied critique and hollow consensus. Entrepreneurs try to get the matrix to be a carrier of their ever-changing schemes. For them, there is no revolution, only revolutionizing. The techniques do not reference proper nouns or declarative political theories with capital letters. They cannot be pedantically defined. Not solutions, they are part of a dispositional process or exercise that politically instrumentalizes active forms. They are not taught but rather "picked up" as in the training of a hustler or a confidence man—preparation for a performance one can only know *how* to do. A rehearsal or exercise with active forms and dispositions in matrix space enhances the powers of object forms, supporting declarative ethics while offering a release into the enacted ethics of the urban.

1 Gregory Bateson, *Steps to an Ecology of Mind* (Chicago, IL: University of Chicago Press, 2000), 472.
2 François Jullien, *The Propensity of Things: Toward a History of Efficacy in China* (New York: Zone Books, 1995), 29.
3 Yochai Benkler, *The Wealth of Networks: How Social Production Transforms Markets and Freedom* (New Haven, CT: Yale University Press, 2006), 16–17.
4 Gilbert Ryle, *The Concept of Mind* (Chicago, IL: University of Chicago Press, 1949), 27–32, 43, 89, 116, 119–20.
5 Ibid., 119–20.

Borders and Boundaries

Edges: Self and City

Richard Sennett

Like many others, I have been thinking about how to give new life to the Left. Simply stirring up revolutionary zeal doesn't seem to get very far, since everyone—Right and Center as well as Left—is full of rage about something. More, there is the question about where struggle should occur, particularly in cities; we want to know where are the new political spaces. But I've had a particular concern about renewing politics on the Left, related to psychology. What kind of inner strength allows people to resist and combine with others? Is it simply a shared experience of oppression, or is it more subtle psychologically?

I would like to maintain that certain spaces in the city for politics intersect with certain psychological strengths—put simply, that where we are and what we feel combine. This potent combination occurs, I will argue, as an edge condition, in the city and within the self.

An old instance of this may make clear what I mean. Sephardic Jews were expelled from Spain in 1492; many wound up in the ghetto of Venice, an isolated space at the edge of the city—a space in which, however, the exiled Jews produced a distinctive set of religious practices and placed a new value on being Jewish. New experience as exiles literally on the edges of a strange city brought out a kind of psychological self-awareness and a certain flexibility that the Jews had not shown before inside Spain.

More generally we could say that an edge—as in the borders between two different ethnic communities in a city—is a zone of ambiguity; in learning to deal with the other across this uncertain, often tense divide, each group can become more socially skilled. The same is true psychologically; it is by learning to manage the uncertain borders of the self in relation to other selves that individuals develop what psychoanalysis calls "ego strength," the confidence to live in a complex world. In society, such strength can be put to political use; it can help people to resist injustice.

Edges in Time

A famous image from Freud's writings makes us think about the separations, the edges, of experiences over the course of time. He famously compared the human psyche to the city of Rome. Modern Romans tread over past scenes of love and lust literally buried beneath their feet in ages past; though a man or woman walking the streets today is unconscious of these hidden layers, the rubble built up by past habitation is the solid substance that supports his or her feet. The human psyche is, Freud argued, similarly layered; usually we are unaware of the depths below the surface, but this psychic rubble is the ground of our consciousness.

This is so seductive an analogy, but in one way so misleading. When people make the transition from one kind of experience to another, they often become aware of a dissonance or difference; this happens to children in the transition from dealing with parents to dealing with teachers; as adults, we feel the transit from an initial sexual encounter to a long-term love. The passage can excite or confuse us, but the important thing is that at the moment of transition itself we do not bury, forget, and go on; rather, we have instead a heightened awareness of the difference between past and present.

This is a kind of "transitional consciousness." Contrary to Freud, these particular moments are not psychic rubble; rather, they stay with us, helping us to distinguish one kind of experience from another, and so shape behavior. R.W. Winnicott first alerted psychologists to the importance of transitional moments that establish the borders between experience for children. Some recent studies of long-term memory complement this, pointing to the ability of elderly people to recall sharply moments of shift in their lives, even as the contents within each time layer have become fuzzy. Think, in a related vein, of the stimulations of shift, the provocations of transition, that occur in the poetry of Rimbaud or Rilke. The marker of value in all of these cases is a rupture, a tear in experience, rather than a smooth shift of scene, which creates that edge of experience.

But as we move from Freud's image of a time-edge as unconscious, buried psychic rubble to a more conscious idea, we need also to sharpen our spatial thinking about the edge.

Borders and Boundaries

In nature, edges come in two sorts; they appear either as borders or as boundaries. At the cellular level, the difference is between the cell membrane, which is a border, and the cell wall, which establishes a boundary. The cell wall holds as much material as possible within its confines; the cell membrane is more open to exchange with the outside. But not entirely so; a membrane is both porous and resistant—letting in nutrients, for instance, and expelling used material, yet trying to retain inside what is valuable to its ongoing functioning. Interestingly, the edge of a cell can switch between functioning as a wall or as a membrane. The pregnant fact for us, though, is the membrane condition: rather than simply an open door to the environment, this kind of edge is more complex. It is an ambiguous condition that has great consequences for more complex structures.

If we make a big mental leap from cells to natural ecologies, we find the difference between borders and boundaries to take on a new character. Now the boundary edge (as in the marking of territorial edges by tigers or bears) become zones of low interaction between species, whereas border edges (as in the meeting of water and land along the seashore) are high activity zones, places where creatures feed off other species and where the pace of evolution speeds up. The contrast between cell wall and cell membrane becomes, in natural ecologies, the difference between less intense and more intense life.

Let's make a further large leap. This ecological difference marks human communities too. Gated housing estates, isolated business campuses, and shopping malls are places surrounded by boundaries. These are in one way low-intensity habitats, because they are not much stimulated by difference. They have a single function and that's that. Left-wing planners such as myself are tempted simply to open them up, letting all sorts of "inappropriate" activities and people seep in, but it's not quite so simple. The model of the cell membrane cautions against taking sheer openness and lack of barriers as the corrective; there must be some combination of porosity and resistance, as in a mixed street of shops, flats, and small businesses, each distinct in purpose and activity within, yet contributing to the mix of people out on the street. We commonly say such compound places are "full of life" and that's more than a metaphor; it reflects a certain kind of edge.

Significant edges—which are membrane-like—do not just happen, nor are they easy to deal with. These edges require interpreting and a certain skill in navigating. If you think of a medieval urban wall like that surrounding Avignon, for instance, you might imagine from its stony bulk that this wall is an impenetrable barrier, a boundary of the most life-ending sort. You see it as inert and you don't much think about using it. In fact, Avignon's walls, far from the center, were places where Jews, prostitutes, and other outcasts tended to congregate, places as well where the unregulated black-market economy of the city flourished. Their inhabitants needed to know how to navigate these forbidden, complicated, often dangerous edges; more precisely, the inhabitants needed to become skilled in dealing with ambiguities of policing, black-market trading, and squatting at the wall. Knowing how to make the space work made the solid wall function as a membrane.

Like the anthropologist James Scott, I believe that this kind of seemingly apolitical experience in fact underlies the real experience of resistance in a wide variety of settings. For him, managing hostile, every-day realities is primarily something we do linguistically; for me, it is also something we do spatially. Poor people can learn to manipulate the physical environment when they have no chance of changing reigning discourses.

But there is a problem here.

The Threat of Boundaries

A big social fact today disarms people in using the environment so compe-tently: the dominance of boundaries over borders. Let's recur to Rome, though not Freud's time-layered Rome, but the Rome of today. It's now a city in which boundaries have replaced borders. If you walk an old area like the Piazza del Popolo, you see signs of gentrification on its side streets, the poor being pushed out as bourgeois bohemians move in; the big shopping streets are full of international chain stores; offices and workshops are moving out to faceless buildings on the periphery; tourists dominate the streets.

Most modern cities are becoming like this, outside of Europe as well as within it. Spatial segregation means that sites for mixture, for the experience of different peoples and different functions, are fading. Modern Beijing has been planned with a strict regime of spatial segregation, so has modern Mumbai. In the globalization of cities, the boundary is replacing the border; cities are ever less internally porous.

The political consequence of this replacement is that spaces where people can practice politics are disappearing. The unhappiness of the poor or of the immigrant is rendered invisible—invisible to privileged segments of the population. Calculative discourses—in zoning, "smart city" planning, and the like—push away unsettling forms of encounter. But the positive, mutually bonding aspect to practicing politics also disappears; the spaces poor people occupy become inward turning, and inward-turning spaces tend to shrink into smaller and smaller zones, people losing a sense of connection to comrades or fellow sufferers who are physically distant. As for resistance, so for cooperation; the places where people who differ might cooperate—in seemingly trivial activities such as managing a garden allotment or a playground—are shrinking as they become ever more subject to formalized rules.

Two Models of Political Space

The question then becomes: Where to resist boundary dominance? We have two models. One is to draw people out of their isolation into a central square or near a highly visible place like St. Paul's Cathedral. The spatial idea here is to create a vital center for political activity to counter the deadening effects of boundary-enclosure.

The other model of political space is to counter a bad edge with a good edge—against the boundary, the border. The streets of Mumbai's Dharavi slum, for example, function like Avignon's walls, as spaces full of amorphous, informal activity, both porous and resistant to the outside; an instance of the latter is that people have erected barriers to automobile traffic to keep the streets free for pedestrian commerce and a mixture of working and living space. More, Dharavi has taken in surrounding elements of people, economic activity, and even different religions; it is porous, as an Indian village will not be. Membranes of community such as Dharavi, if on a smaller scale, can be found in slums from Buenos Aires to Rangoon.

These two models of political space—the center or the membrane— serve different purposes. The center is a short-term space, the space of protest and demonstration, the space of visibility. The border is long-term space, a long term in which a single community becomes more complex, and communities seep into one another, a process that may be invisible initially. Another way to think of this is that the Occupy sort of space is about politics as an event, while the border is about politics as a process. For community organizers, I want to argue, the Occupy model is not the space we should aim at; we want to achieve more sustained goals in the border.

Just because the border is an ambiguous space, it is here that I would like to bring psychology into the picture. Certainly psychology provides no direct strategy for breaking the rule of the boundary, but it gives some insight into the kind of persons we need to be to practice membrane politics.

Strength

The membrane/border is important as a psychological concept: it locates where we develop inner strength, which writers like Heinz Hartmann and Erik Erikson call "ego strength." In a way, ego strength is a seemingly self-evident phenomenon: of course a strong self should be both porous and resistant; the individual should be able to retain what is valuable to him- or herself while being open to new influences. The bite in Erik Erikson's writings, however, was to emphasize just those disruptive time-edge experiences I alluded to before; unlike his contemporary Abraham Maslow, he conceived of human development as a succession of crises—a new love affair, a new job, promising pain or potential danger as much as pleasure. These crises must be interpreted, but usually they are incompletely resolved. Put another way, there is no one ideal equilibrium between porosity and resistance in the membrane of the self, no final right balance, only a continual effort to pay attention and to respond.

This insight is really important to us politically for two reasons: first, it tells us that strength is a matter of exploiting ambiguities rather than banishing them. The ego strength of some resisting injustice lies in focusing on what is unresolved or incomplete, exploiting that condition, finding, as it were, cracks in the wall. Second, this concept of ego strength cautions us against thinking of some fixed political property called "what I believe" or "my principles," because the self does not flourish by a rigid image. It cannot move forward and develop by hewing to fixed ideas of itself, and neither can politics.

Haunting though Freud's Rome is, this is why we would do better to compare the psyche to a city directly to horizontal space. We'd want to imagine the psychic center as a place of drives and instincts, to liken the center and periphery of a city to mental awareness of inner desire and outer necessity, and to see the urban/psychic membrane as the kind of edge where the activity of negotiating between inside and outside occurs, an ambiguous negotiation with no guarantee of agreement.

The membrane, that is, may be the most important space of the psyche. Here is the zone where interpreting uncertainty and ambiguity becomes more important than confessing feelings within. Its most challenging labor will be dealing with stimulation and experience that it cannot quite name or initially comprehend.

The human sciences have imagined strength and weakness in ways that ill serve our understanding of how people deal with injustice. This *deformation professionelle* appears in the metaphorical distinction between hard and soft. "Hard" deals in facts and structures, "soft" bathes in feelings and impressions. Twentieth-century social science privileged the hard over the soft as more compelling, more powerful, more political—with the result that the scope of human strength became narrowed; we could never truly understand "ego strength" or politically, the decision to seek alternatives to the hard facts on the ground, if we hewed to this way of thinking.

In terms of human cognition, the difference between hard and soft knowledge turns on whether we emphasize calculation or interpretation; the first is a matter of reckoning data, the second is a process of judging value. All human beings use both, as when in an argument we assemble information and then debate its merits. When pulled apart, each of these two forms of understanding regresses. Untamed, calculation can lead to closure—that is, to the desire for certainty and finality; closure sets up boundary conditions in the mind. Interpretation can become an endless stream of impressions, sentiments, and views, if open still unanchored; the mental risk is of a purely porous state to which the interpreting subject offers no resistance, no discipline.

A personal confidence—an ego strength—in one's ability to dwell in ambiguity is required to conduct a dialogue between calculation and interpretation. In this regard, we might imagine ego strength to be like a chemical reaction in which solids emerge from the swirling liquid mass of ingredients. Sociologists have long held that differentiation results from interaction—the truism applies to markets, for instance, in which traders gradually carve out distinctive niches for themselves; it applies to long-established cities whose streets have gradually taken on each a distinctive character. And it applies to the self, producing the paradox that there can be a correlation between ambiguity and concreteness: when something is perfectly clear, it belongs to a class of things; if something is obscure, it requires a more particular attention. It requires interpretation.

The social-science contrast between hard and soft has a practical social consequence. Oppressors deploy hardness—that is, closed discourses, final and certain in their terms—to shore up regimes; in the realm of capitalist labor, for instance, the ruler will deploy the certainties of "the market" to foreclose and fix obedience from hapless workers. Asking questions, introducing poisonous doubts, unsettling assumptions, are ways of resisting, through interpretation, this fixed, inert regime of power; we need supposedly soft, interpretative kind of thinking to challenge unjust social conditions. But the address must not become pure negation, an unending hermaneutic of suspicion. "Nothing good is possible" is the same as saying "I submit." I'm arguing, that is, for a kind of political discourse that comes out of a psychological conviction that one can manage ambiguity, that the possible resides in all the uncertainties and smudges of adult experience.

The Border Largely Conceived

A famous phrase of Seneca runs, "I need to be with others in order to know myself." For this to happen requires a certain kind of mental and physical space —an edge that functions as membrane, porous yet resistant, so that the self exchanges with others but does not meld in an oceanic way with them. Experience of a boundary is not likely to stimulate us; it's a dead edge. If you insist you are entirely different from me, there is no possibility of exchange. But also if you think your calculations about our relations are absolute and certain, then nothing much is going to happen between us. Whereas if our relations are more membrane-like, if we dwell in some mutual uncertainty and confusion, I am more likely to try to understand myself in relation to you, connected yet distinct.

The issue is not a matter of "mental space," which we might think of only as a metaphor; the border-membrane edge is also a physical place. To experience porosity in the psyche, it helps to be in a porous place rather than within a rigid boundary-land; people require a territory on the ground in which to learn how to take things into the self.

Politically, for the same reason, we should want to transform the boundaries of a regime into borders. When I marched and camped during the Occupy movements, I had the uncomfortable sensation that we should not be seeking a protected territory for ourselves, a territory that separated us from the ordinary life of London. Better to occupy space sporadically and unpredictably in the city, to conduct a more nomadic politics. This ambiguous use of space would have made Occupy a membrane politics, if you like, prompting both protesters and public to deal with one another in ordinary but anarchic circumstances. That kind of address to everyday uncertainty has equally to be the skill-set of the community organizer, who does not want just one-day strikes or one-month occupations but some more durable kind of political activity—which means, in a complex city like London, addressing the unresolved and unresolvable mixture of its population.

I would conclude simply by saying that both socially and psychologically, we need to strengthen borders and weaken boundaries. We need to do so for the sake of developing a more engaged social order, and for the sake of our own emotional development.

The Ethics of Charter Cities

Gerald Frug

Charter cities is an idea, organization, and website created by Paul Romer, an economics professor at New York University.[1] The basic idea of a charter city can be summarized in a few simple steps. First, one needs to find a developing country (Honduras? Mauritania?) that will cede to the charter city a large amount of its uninhabited land—enough land to enable up to 10 million people to live there. Next, the sponsors of the charter city need to write its charter, the document that specifies the basic rules that will govern the ceded territory. This document is the critical ingredient in the project. It is the charter that attracts investors, businesses, and residents to the venture. These people are attracted because the charter's rules protect investment, provide a business-friendly atmosphere, and ensure security for residents.

To be credible, the charter's rules need a guarantor—a country that will assure the investors, businesses, and residents that the charter's provisions will actually be followed. Most likely, this guarantor will be a developed country, one with an established and reliable rule of law (Norway? New Zealand?). With the land and the guaranteed rules in place, investors can begin to fund the city, businesses can begin to create jobs, and residents, from anywhere in the world, can come to live and work there if they choose. If residents become unhappy with their lives in the charter city, they are free to leave. This commitment to choice—to residents' freedom to come and go as they please—is another essential element of a charter city. It protects residents from abuse. Of course, while there, residents are subject to the charter city's rules. Moreover, no one will become a citizen of the country in which the land is located unless he or she is one already. Instead, residents retain citizenship in the country from which they moved. The territory will initially be governed by an executive committee. Later, an elected local government might be established (if the executive committee or charter authorizes it) as long as the charter itself is respected. Ultimately, if all goes well, the charter city will become a global city, a world-class business hub good for everyone—workers, employers, and investors alike.

There are many reactions one can have to this idea. The *Harvard Business Review* called it one of the 10 Breakthrough Ideas of 2010.[2] I am going to focus here on the ethical issues it raises, concentrating on the basic model sketched above. The charter city concept, however, is still in the idea-generating stage, and it is important to understand that modified versions are also being proposed.[3] At the moment, the furthest that a modified version has come to implementation is in Honduras. In early 2011, the Honduran Congress overwhelmingly approved a proposal, backed by the Honduran president, to create a charter city (they called it a special development region).[4] Major elements of the charter city proposal were included in the legislation—in particular, the almost complete severance of the charter city from Honduran control and the free right of entrance and exit of residents without regard to Honduran law. The legislation, however, sought to create more national control over the region than provided by the model outlined above. The initial governing board, called a transparency commission, was to be appointed by the president, as would the initial governor of the new city. (Afterward, the transparency commission was empowered to fill its own vacancies and appoint later governors.) Certain rights of residents (such as a minimum wage) were guaranteed by the legislation. And rather than being open to workers from the whole world, at least 90 percent of the employees of every enterprise had to be Honduran. Still, even with these provisions—indeed, even with a vague, albeit explicit, reservation of Honduran sovereignty over the territory—the Supreme Court of Honduras declared the legislation unconstitutional in October 2012. Such a delegation of authority over a portion of the country, the court ruled, was an unconstitutional abrogation of Honduran sovereignty.[5]

The model version of the charter city I have sketched is even more vulnerable to such an objection. And not just in Honduras. I am not going to discuss here, however, the reason for this vulnerability as a legal matter (the legal complexities differ from country to country). Instead, I intend to explore a more fundamental issue: the ethical problems that render the charter city project legally suspect. Law and morality are by no means synonymous, but a moral objection is a common way to buttress a legal argument. On the charter city website, the normative objection to its project is framed as guilt by association. It quotes an imagined opponent saying: "This sounds like colonialism. Colonialism was morally wrong. This must be morally wrong." The response the website gives to this objection is that the proposal offers people who now have limited options "the freedom to move to places that offer safety and opportunity ... Each year, millions of high income individuals move to countries where they can't vote because they want to pursue opportunities that they can't get at home. It is difficult to see how giving poor families a comparable choice can be viewed as morally wrong."[6]

Actually, it's not that difficult. Charter city proponents treat cities as objects of consumption. They portray potential residents as shopping for a city in which to live like they shop for any other consumer good. The only deviation from private market transactions they allow is that consumers make their choice not by handing over a credit card but by moving to town. By definition, this consumer-oriented vision equates the concept of freedom of choice with that of freedom of consumer choice. As a result, it radically limits the aspect of the self considered relevant in the design and implementation of city life. Consumption is an individual activity. Spurred by their own economic interest, people buy consumer goods one by one (or family by family) with little concern about the impact of their purchase on those living nearby. Values commonly associated with democracy—notions of equality, of the importance of collective deliberation and compromise, of the existence of a public interest not reducible to personal economic concerns—are of secondary concern, or no concern at all, to consumers. Yet it is widely recognized, in political theory as well as daily life, that reducing human experience to the act of consumption falsifies it. Worse still, the consumer-oriented vision of the city strengthens the consumptive aspect of the self over alternatives: consumer preferences help generate a social world that, in turn, shapes consumer preferences. By doing so, it narrows the aspects of human nature that cities have the potential of fostering.

One way to see this is by examining the conception of law that charter city proponents embrace. Law is absolutely central to their proposal. The reason that a charter city will work, proponents argue—in a way that Guatemala City or Nouakchott (the capital of Mauritania) currently do not—is that the right rules are set out in advance in the charter. But who writes these rules? The proposal is vague about this, but it seems likely that the initial developers will write them. Of necessity, they will be written without input from city residents (there aren't any yet) and, equally important, without approval from the country in which the city is located (the motivation for the idea is that that country's legal system doesn't meet the requisite standards). Once written, the proponents make the charter's rules very hard —virtually impossible—to change (as in Honduras). After all, if they could readily be changed, investors, business people, and residents could not rely on them. For the same reason, if a more democratic government is established, that government has to have limited power—it has to be required to abide by the rules that the charter has already set in place. The critical rules that structure city life are thus put into place without any public input—whether the public is defined in terms of democracy (the voice of residents) or of sovereignty (the national government). The guarantor country does not fill this gap. It enforces the charter's rules, but it doesn't write or modify them. The guarantor country's legal system is simply one more commodity that the charter city will purchase on the market (or get for free). The idea of law proposed for the charter city, in short, has been completely privatized—laws written by private individuals and enforced by people who, under contract, are not authorized to evaluate them. Potential residents, investors, and business people are presented with only two choices: opt in or opt out.

This consumer model removes—is designed to remove—the city and its legal system from politics, both national and local. Such a rejection of politics deprives the city's residents and the citizens of the larger nation in which it is located the ability to debate and revise the legal system that helps structure their lives. Charter city proponents respond to this objection by emphasizing residents' freedom of choice to move to or leave the city. This reliance on entrance and exit is an extension of the idea articulated in Charles Tiebout's article "A Pure Theory of Local Expenditures," written in the 1950s.[7] Tiebout focused on American suburbanization, which was at its height at the time he wrote. He sought to build an economic model of metropolitan suburbanization by seeing local "consumer-voters" (his term) choosing where to live in a metropolitan area by voting with their feet. To make the model work, he had to rely on a series of assumptions, including one that treats everyone in the metropolitan area as living on dividend income and one that posits that the system imposes no externalities on neighboring jurisdictions. The assumption about living on dividend income was necessary because, as a practical matter, poor people cannot afford to move wherever they like. This financial reality is exacerbated for charter city advocates, because potential poor residents have to be able to move not just to a nearby city but thousands of miles away and, if unhappy, able to move that far again. How any of this could be paid for is uncertain. (In Qatar, where more than 80 percent of the residents are not citizens, potential immigrants need to finance their trip through brokers or with an advance obtained from their Qatari employer, who becomes their local sponsor. There is no provision for financing the trip home.[8]) The problem of externalities is equally significant, both in the charter city context and for the suburbs. If charter cities were to become successful, they would drain resources from existing cities around the world. Rather than trying to induce investors and entrepreneurs to work on improving these cities, the charter city proposal is that they walk away from them and start afresh on uninhabited land.

The charter city's concept of law is not just privatized. It is also based on a misunderstanding of how law works. Proponents imagine that the right rules—rules that are not controversial and open to debate—can be adopted in advance and then be interpreted and enforced equally without

MOVING ABOUT

How do we move about the city? What signals do we learn to read in order to cross paths?
How does the weather influence movement? The above photo of a rain shower in Sydney, Australia,
reminds us of the perils, and joys, of walking in the rain.

Do roads act to unify or divide? How do highways change surrounding urban spaces? Above, a busy road in East London, adjacent to Robin Hood Gardens, is filled with cars, day and night, entering and exiting tunnels, producing sound and light.

275

MOVING ABOUT

How do people get to work? Who has access to what forms of mobility? Above, 32-year-old Colin Whitlow rides a Citi Bike (started by Citibank) across the Brooklyn Bridge twice daily between his work and home.

How can design influence how people move through a city?

Walking through the city, as countless people do daily, provides a tactile understanding and connection to urban space. Kūnmíng, China's parks, bridges, and pavilions designate spaces for leisurely walking, connected by networks of streets and sidewalks. When a pedestrian becomes the primary agent of a road or path, rather than a motorized vehicle, how does that affect the surrounding context as well as the design vocabulary of the city at large?

Tokyo's Shibuya Station represents one of the world's busiest crosswalks. Walking, biking, and driving through bustling city streets requires awareness and the negotiation of space. Although technology has increasingly enabled connection and mobility across cities, what is the cost on the experience of walking?

MOVING ABOUT

From 2008 to 2010, artist Chris Marker took over 200 photographs while riding the Paris Metro.
These images were featured in his exhibition *Passengers,* which question learned spatial segregation
and the definition of art, and celebrated the beauty of people during their daily commute.

Some trains in Pyongyang, North Korea, previously used by the German Democratic Republic, are now repurposed for public transportation. Only a few cars scatter the city, showing mobility as an indicator of status. Who has the freedom to move where and when? What is the cost of restriction?

Photojournalist Randy H. Goodman focuses her exhibition, IRAN: Women Only, on women, transportation, mobility, and rights in contemporary Iran. Above, a female taxi driver looks out the window of her cab in Tehran. Women's Taxi, a popular taxi company, is run by women, for women. Female drivers transport women throughout the capital and other cities.

controversy. No lawyer would think of law in this way. There are no "best practice" rules that can be adopted in advance in an apolitical manner. Presumably, a charter city's rules would be designed to reduce taxes and regulations. After all, that's the way to attract businesses and investors. But such a vision of the legal structure is a hotly debated topic in countries around the world. Besides, no matter what rules are adopted, the idea of a static law determined at the outset of an enterprise is unrealistic. Every legal system needs the ability to adapt and modify its rules as circumstances change. Legal systems struggle to find a balance that can accommodate a changing world while protecting the vested interests of investors, business people, and residents.

Who in the charter city model can seek to maintain such a balance? It cannot be the guarantor country. That country is not supposed to make law; it is supposed to enforce existing law. Indeed, simply giving it that role adds uncertainty rather than stability to the system. If (say) the law that a charter city adopts is Norwegian commercial law, its rules are now interpreted by Norwegian courts by placing them within the history and culture of Norway. The charter city proposal rips these parts of the legal system from this context. (Those aspects of Norwegian law that make it a high-tax, high-social-service country are likely to be dropped.) How is a Norwegian court going to interpret rules—even if they are copied from Norwegian law—when applied in a city, thousands of miles away, filled with people from all over the world (although, very likely, no one from Norway)? They might have no choice but to innovate, because there is no other dependable actor who can accommodate stability and change. Reliance on the city's executive committee would introduce its own form of unreliability: corruption. Put simply, the "rule of law" in the form that charter city proponents conceive of it—stable, technical, apolitical—does not exist. In the United States, "the dream of a mechanical justice is recognized for what it is—only a dream and not even a rosy and desirable one."[9]

Another way to appreciate the privatized nature of a charter city is to see it as proposing not the creation of a city but, instead, of a globalized version of a homeowners association. Homeowners associations are a form of collective living organized by the rules of private property. Some homeowners associations in the United States house a lot of people: Sun City, Arizona, has a population of more than 35,000. The rules of the association are established in advance by the developers—that is, before there are any residents and often before the construction of the development has begun. A board of directors is appointed by the developer to govern the territory. At first, the board is dominated by the developer; later it is elected by property owners (that is, the franchise is allocated not to residents but owners). The goal of the association is to provide a secure place for investment and living. As a result, the founding rules are made hard to change.[10]

Everyone recognizes that homeowners associations are not cities. They are private associations, not government organizations. The Constitution of the United States does not restrict their power, as it does for cities. A charter city is even less subject to domestic law than are homeowners associations. Homeowners associations are created and regulated by state law; state rules govern how they are managed. By contrast, the domestic law of the country in which the charter city is located does not apply to its territory (except in the limited way specified by the founding document). Moreover, the land in a charter city, like in a homeowners association, is to be held as private property. Indeed, unlike in a homeowners association, the city itself is envisioned as owning all of the land, not just the property held in common. Businesses and residents would lease the land.

Is a charter city too much like a homeowners association—too private—to be a city? Before answering this question, we need to recognize that charter cities are radically different from homeowners associations in two important respects. Residency would be open to people around the world, while homeowners associations embrace an exclusive idea of residency. And commercial life would vastly exceed that now found in any homeowners association. Does this openness to a multitude of residents and businesses transform a charter city into something more public than a homeowners association? The answer, I submit, is no. Even traditional cities, equally open to a wide variety of residents and commercial life, are becoming more privatized, albeit not to the extent of a charter city. It is important to understand the problematic assumptions that underlie this current trend toward privatization in traditional, public cities. The belief that charter cities offer a better hope than existing cities for people around the world rests on the same kinds of assumptions.

In theory at least, any governmental service can be delivered by a private business under a government contract. Garbage collection, ambulance services, and health care are familiar candidates for privatization, but there is no reason to stop there. Public schools could be replaced by private schools as long as students are given government-subsidized vouchers to pay for them. Police departments could be replaced by private security guards, judges could be replaced by professional arbitrators, and fire departments could be replaced by private emergency businesses. Some states have even transferred parts of their prison systems into private hands. Once you begin to take the idea of privatization seriously, you can quickly come to the view that government could be reduced to the performance of three tasks: the collection of revenue by taxation, the decision of which services this revenue should buy, and the negotiation and drafting (and, perhaps, the monitoring) of contracts with private businesses for the delivery of the chosen services. In fact, some of these jobs could be contracted out too. For example, government could hire a collection agency to enforce its laws, a private management consultant to determine what services to provide, and private lawyers to negotiate and draft its contracts. Taken to its limits, then, privatization could transform government simply into a revenue-generating mechanism run by a few people whose job would be to begin the process of contracting out, choosing the consultants and lawyers who, in turn, would continue the cycle of contracting and recontracting. As a means of employment and delivery of services, the state really could wither away.

Why would anyone *want* to go down this road to privatization? The usual answer people suggest is that private businesses are more efficient and better run than governments are. But what do the terms "efficient" and "better run" mean when they are invoked in this way? To some extent, private businesses are "efficient" because they do not have to comply with laws that routinely are applied to governments, ranging from civil service and competitive bidding requirements to the demands of the Bill of Rights. But if any of these laws serve a valuable purpose, one would think that they should be applied to the managers of publicly funded prisons, schools, and fire departments whoever they are; conversely, if these are not good ideas, they should not be applied to anyone. Why should "private" prisons, financed solely by tax dollars, be exempt from the constitutional requirement that prisoners be treated in accordance with the due process of law? Why should the constitutional restrictions on the arbitrary expulsion of students be applied only to schools labeled "public" and not those labeled "private," when both kinds of schools would be paid for by tax revenues and charged with the task of educating the locality's population? I think that the answer to these questions is that both kinds of institution should have to comply with the Bill of Rights. I also think that there is no more reason to fear corruption in a state-run police department than in a privately run police department, and that there is no more reason to tolerate abuse of employees in a private hospital operating pursuant to a contract with the government than in a city-run hospital. But if these positions are right, the "efficiency" gains derived from private exemption from requirements imposed on government do not support a move to privatization. If any of these requirements are unnecessary, one should relieve governments from having to comply with them; if the requirements are desirable, one should apply them to any entity that performs a service offered in the public interest and supported by publicly generated revenue.

The argument that the private sector is more "efficient" than the public sector can thus be answered by proposing to reform the public sector instead. Some people claim that the incentive system in the private sector makes employees more productive than does the system adopted by government. But even if this is true (and its truth is much debated), the difference between their incentive systems may be attributable simply to the legal rules that require government to operate differently from the way business operates. If schools would be run better if they competed against each other, such a competition could be arranged in public schools as well as in publicly financed private schools. If employees and managers in prisons and police departments could be led to act more efficiently by bonuses or profit-sharing, such a system could be installed in government as well. If private firms run better because they pay their executives more money than the government is permitted to pay, the government could revise its wage scale instead of contracting out its services. After all, it's the taxpayer who pays the bill in either case. Slogans like "competition" or "the profit motive" cannot determine the choice between having services performed by the public or private sector.

Even if the private sector is found to be more "efficient" in some sense of the word, it doesn't follow that privatization would be a good idea. Some people assert, for example, that privatization is desirable because services are cheaper when they are run by private businesses rather than by government. Before transferring services to a private concern, however, we need to find out why they are cheaper (if, indeed, they are). If the services are cheaper because private employers cut the wages or benefits of workers from below the levels offered by government, we need to determine whether such cuts promote the public interest. It's by no means obvious that the public interest is advanced by paying workers less or by providing them less adequate health or retirement benefits. Similarly, if private costs are lower because employees work harder out of fear of being fired, we need to decide whether we want to use public money to create that kind of workplace or whether, alternatively, we think that job security better contributes to a sound working environment. Fostering certain values is often worth the cost. (And—to repeat—if we find the values not worth fostering, the alternative system could be adopted in the public sector itself.)

In my view, the principal reason that privatization has become an attractive idea these days is not "efficiency" but the fact that the reform that can readily be seen as an alternative—transforming government itself— appears to be much more difficult than the process of contracting out to a private concern. Reforming government is a formidable task not only because making the tough choices about the best way to operate services is hard but also because, even after people have decided what to do, they have to get their ideas adopted. This requires dealing with state legislatures, city councils, unions, and interest groups. When confronted with such an arduous task, it's not surprising that people say, "Who needs it? Let's just contract the services out." In the current debate about state and local government services, proponents of privatization have shifted the burden of persuasion to those who favor retaining services in the public sector. The question on the public agenda has changed from "How do we make government better?" to "Why not contract out?"

This is the stance that charter city proponents embrace to the maximum extent possible. It's not just that charter cities would contract out many of their services. (Police misconduct, it has been suggested, might be solved by contracting with the Royal Canadian Mounted Police to patrol the country.[11]) The proposal seeks to contract out the city's legal system and, indeed, the city itself. One problem with this idea is that it cannot actually be implemented. If, as I argue, a charter city cannot guarantee legal stability in the way advocates imagine, if the guarantor country cannot administer the law in the way they think necessary, and if consumer choice is inadequate protection against abuse, investors, business people, and residents are likely to be hesitant to sign on. Posing the issue of privatization in these practical terms, however, does not adequately capture what is at stake in the privatization debate. That this is true can be seen just by looking in a dictionary.

According to *Webster's Third New International Dictionary* (the 1981 unabridged edition), the verb "privatize" means "to alter the status of (a business or industry) from public to private control or ownership." One might think, therefore, that the noun "privatization" would, in a parallel fashion, mean the alteration of a business's status from public to private control. This seems to be how people (including me, so far) are using the term these days. But look what the dictionary definition for "privatization" actually is:

> The tendency for an individual to withdraw from
> participation in social and esp[ecially] political life into
> a world of personal concerns usu[ally] as a result
> of a feeling of insignificance and lack of understanding
> of complex social processes.[12]

In *Democracy in America,* his famous survey of America in the 1830s, Alexis de Tocqueville found that taking an active part in political life was an American's "most important business and, so to say, the only pleasure he knows.... If an American should be reduced to occupying himself with his own affairs, at that moment half his existence would be snatched from him; he would feel it as a vast void in his life and would become incredibly unhappy."[13] Since Tocqueville's time, the decrease in participation in public life has contributed, as Tocqueville predicted, to individual feelings of insignificance and to a sense that no ordinary person can deal with the complex social problems of the modern world. These feelings have led, in turn, to further decreases in participation in public life, generating still more "feeling[s] of insignificance and lack of understanding of complex social processes." This cycle of privatization is likely to accelerate if control of global cities were transferred into private hands. Traditionally, the political world has offered a way to engage with others that is different from private life, a form of engagement known as democracy. The sense of empowerment that we gain when we become participants in the creation of our social and political world will be lost if we withdraw even further into our private lives or commercial dealings. To combat this trend toward privatization—to prevent this kind of de-privation—one would need to revive the sense of public involvement engendered by engagement in political life. I'll call the process of reviving political life "publicization." This is not just an unfamiliar concept in the privatization debate; it's not even a word at all (according to Webster's unabridged dictionary).

Charter city proponents recognize the importance of appealing to public values. They often refer to public notions—for example, calling the executive a governor and the transparency commission in Honduras a government. Indeed, I suspect that, notwithstanding their reliance on market choice, they would reject my characterization of their proposal as privatization. To embrace privatization as their goal would undermine the proposal's legitimacy. Some form of publicization seems essential to city life. It is not surprising, therefore, that they include in their proposal the possibility of eventual local democracy. But democracy comes in many forms, not all of them real. (Shareholder democracy is a prime example of this phenomenon.) Genuine democracy would introduce radical uncertainties in the stability that the proposal finds so critical, and it would not be easy for those in charge of the city to transition to it. Moreover, even if there were dozens of charter cities, all with a more democratic form, another important public value would remain at risk. Charter city proponents make it clear that improving the lives of poor people around the world is the fundamental reason that they want to create these new cities. I credit them for stressing the importance of this public goal. But furthering it requires focusing on existing cities rather than walking away from them. The vast majority of the poor people would not be helped by creating charter cities. On the contrary, it is more likely that the reallocation of investment, business growth, and local talent that would occur if charter cities were built would make the world's poor even poorer.

Our current cities are beset with problems that seem unsolvable. Whether it's the need for clean water, corruption, problems with the environment, or the lack of affordable housing—the list of problems goes on and on. And that's not all. The defects of the current democratic structure in existing cities—if they even have one—are apparent for everyone to see. And the fragility of the rule of law, although less apparent, is equally real. The rule of law requires a careful compromise between political responsiveness (judges are appointed by elected officials or, sometimes, elected) and independence of thought (the role of life tenure)—not a simple matter. It's easy to be overwhelmed by these imperfections of law, democracy, and city life. But it is a fantasy to think that we can start all over again, on vacant land, and this time get it right. There are no shortcuts. Urban innovators should focus their energy not on abandoning our current cities but on addressing their problems one-by-one, city-by-city, nation-by-nation. The task of publicization is to create a public world worthy of its name. Doing so, it seems to me, is a moral imperative. And walking away from this undertaking is a moral failure.

1 http://chartercities.org/

2 http://hbr.org/2010/01/the-hbr-list-breakthrough-ideas-for-2010/ar/1

3 One proposal, hypothetically imagined for India, would be to create a version of the special economic zones now established in China and elsewhere. Like these zones, the city would have different rules but would remain subject to Indian law. Another, much more adventurous idea, again hypothetically, is to create a city in Brazil designed only for Haitians. The new city would be subject to Brazilian (not Haitian) law, although residents would not receive any of the social-service benefits Brazilians receive. The city would have to pay for itself. There would be strict border controls to prevent migration from the new city into the rest of the country. The reason to establish the city—the same justification as for the model discussed here—is to improve the lives of the Haitian population by enabling them to live under a reliable rule of law. http://chartercities.org/

4 Honduras, Legislative Decree No. 4-2011 of March 7, 2011, La Gaceta, Diario Oficial de la Republica de Honduras, at 32,460.

5 "The territory of the State if a legal unit that cannot be renounced or transferred, which means that it cannot be sold, given away, ceded, divided, leased or compromised in any way, because it is a constitutive element of the State.... [T]he National Congress does not have the powers to give concessions that affect the integrity of the

territory, the sovereignty and independence of the Republic, or that limit or diminish the constitutional attributions of the supreme constituted powers..." Certificacion de la sentencia recaida en el Recurso de Inconstitucionalidad 769=11, Sala de lo Constitucional de la Corte Suprema de Justicia [Constitutional Chamber of the Supreme Court of Justice] (October 17, 2012) (declaring unconstitutional decree number 283-2010, which created special development regions known as *Regiones Especiales de Desarrollo [RED]*.) (Guillermo J. Garcia Sanchez translation)

6 http://chartercities.org/

7 Charles Tiebout, "A Pure Theory of Local Expenditures," *Journal of Political Economy* 64 (1956): 416.

8 http://www.tamimi.com/en/publication/publications/section/may-1/employment-in-qatar.html

9 Arthur Corbin, *Corbin on Contracts*, vol. 12, section 1136 (1964), 94.

10 Evan McKenzie, *Privatopia: Homeowner Associations and the Rise of Residential Private Government* (New Haven, CT: Yale University Press, 1994).

11 Brandon Fuller and Paul Romer, *Success and the City: How Charter Cities Could Transform the Developing World* (Ottawa, ON: Macdonald-Laurier Institute, April 2012).

12 *Webster's Third New International Dictionary* (8th ed.) (Springfield, MA: G. & C. Merriam Company, 1981).

13 Alexis de Tocqueville, *Democracy in America*, vol. 1, trans. George Lawrence (New York: Harper and Row, 1966), 243.

The New Urban Brazil and Its Margins

Guilherme Wisnik

São Paulo: Borders and City Centers

In his well-known a tour of Passaic, New Jersey, on a Saturday in September 1967, Robert Smithson sees industrial ruins of that small town—his home-town—in a surprising way. In an impermanent and disenchanted world such as ours, ordinary industrial ruins like that can suddenly take on a trag-ically epic character, where excavators and bulldozers standing in the mud are metaphorically seen as fossilized prehistoric creatures. Thus unlike the romantic, bucolic, and picturesque ruin, Passaic is, according to the vision of the great American artist, the deep embodiment of the suburbs—a bottom-less utopia, understood as a game of abandoned futures. For Passaic is full of voids, Smithson notes, voids that are the opposite of the solid and elegant New York order.[1] There lies, in my view, the most acute perception of the artist in his reunion with Passaic: the urban order of the city's center is kept at the expense of its surroundings, which are generally invisible to most peo-ple. Therefore the entropy of the suburb is necessary for the apparent main-tenance of order in the official city—that is, to build its image.

Urban settlements around Billings Reservoir, São Paulo, Brazil, 2013

This insight is crucial to treating the issue of urban fringes in cities in general and will serve me here as an opening to review the situation of Brazilian cities, especially São Paulo—the largest. The topic of borders, or outskirts, cannot be isolated in relation to the existence of the central areas. In São Paulo, one cannot dissociate its new "landscape of power"[2] along the Marginal Pinheiros—São Paulo's icon as it aspires to the condition of "global city" from the precarious illegal invasions of the watershed protection areas in the south of the city, around the Billings and Guarapiranga lakes, in the border region.[3] These situations are actually closely connected.

São Paulo is a city that has expanded a lot in a very short time. Unimportant during the colonial period, the city began to gain relevance only in the mid-19th century, given its strategic connecting position between coffee production in the countryside and the outlets for such production, via railway, through the port of Santos. This strategic role was decisively reinforced at the turn of the 20th century, when coffee money was reinvested in industry and São Paulo became the major industrial hub of the country. Thus the city that in 1900 had 240,000 inhabitants saw its population multiply in the following decades, reaching 2.2 million in 1950 and 8.5 million in 1980. The 1960–80 period represents an even bigger boom, with a great migration from the northeast that resulted in vast slums and a total lack of control of urban growth in Rio de Janeiro and São Paulo. So the city that already had considerable urban sprawl in the early 20th century achieved a size of no less than 2,200 square kilometers (approximately 850 square miles) by the year 2000, constituting the so-called macro-metropolis of São Paulo, which includes other neighboring municipalities, with a total population of

20 million. One can imagine how the notion of border or fringe, in the case of São Paulo, is absolutely volatile and abstract, since the city has continued to advance on the old surrounding rural areas, engulfing them and conurbating with the surrounding cities.

The urban complex that includes the Marginal Pinheiros (Avenida das Nações Unidas) and the Avenues Faria Lima, Engenheiro Luís Carlos Berrini, and Jornalista Roberto Marinho (formerly Água Espraiada) is, since the 1990s, the new financial hub of São Paulo, where the buildings that house the large multinational companies are located. It is also there that the Octávio Frias de Oliveira Bridge was built, between 2003 and 2008. This is a cable-stayed bridge crossing the Pinheiros River that became the latest postcard image of the city. In contrast to the yellow cables of the bridge, the buildings with metal and mirrored-glass façades give the city an image of affluent opulence, only occasionally disturbed in photographs by the possible appearance of trash in the riverbed or on the banks of the polluted river. The intensification of the occupation and verticalization of this area occurred in the 1990s, amid the emergence of finance capital as a major promoter of the new urban landscape, the widespread privatization that accompanied the neoliberal adjustment of the period, and the rise of "public-private partnerships" *(parcerias públi-co-privadas)* as economic instruments to carry out large urban operations, involving the removal of numerous slums and the clearing of their land for the benefit of real estate speculation and large transnational private capital.[4]

As for the vast region bordering the Billings and Guarapiranga lakes, despite being a protected area, it has been intensely occupied in recent decades, primarily by slums. Precarious and informal, the urbanization of

Countryside house alongside a road in Portugal

this watershed area is one of the most serious problems of the city in social and environmental terms, and is certainly one of the biggest challenges for future urban development policies in São Paulo, at a time when the city faces an unprecedented and dramatic crisis of water supply.[5] Initially occupied by rural lots, small farms, and elite country clubs, the region was the target of an intense irregular occupation by low-income houses during the 1970s, by both poor families who migrated from other regions of the country and, shortly after, families already established in the city but who were progressively expelled from the places they had settled. It is worth noting that the massive occupation of these remote and topographically complicated areas did not happen in a spontaneous or random way. It was prompted by high prices of urban land in more central areas and by acts of the government in the 1990s—violently removing slum dwellers who resided in urban operations areas, such as Avenida Água Espraiada, and unofficially relocating them to watershed protection areas. This policy obviously works against the public interests that the government should, in theory, protect.[6]

It is clear that the establishment of the new financial center around the Marginal Pinheiros is not a coincidence. With good road access, this region had a large stock of cheap land occupied by slums and ready to be expropriated, fueling speculation with huge profits. For as we know, the migration of capital in the city follows the predatory logic by which economic vectors create new areas of urban expansion, causing the decline of the areas abandoned by capital. At the same time, the rapid construction of this new "landscape of power," apparently orderly and without cracks, structurally depends on creating disorder in more invisible areas, such as the slums surrounding the

Minha Casa Minha Vida (My House My Life) complex of social housing
in Santa Cruz do Capibaribe, Pernambuco, Brazil, 2013

lakes. This is well demonstrated in the brilliant study of Mariana Fix on the clearing of the Jardim Edith slum, at Avenida Água Espraiada.[7] One is reminded of Robert Smithson's characterization of the relationship between New York and Passaic in the way that São Paulo's city center and its global media image depends on the entropic breakdown of the borders, which disappear as public image and therefore practically do not exist.

Yet the organization of the urban center and entropic outskirts is an explanatory model that is no longer entirely appropriate for many of the largest cities in the world, including São Paulo. In many cases, we see a situation in which the historic centers degrade as the suburbs become affluent, housing the middle classes and elites who take refuge there in search of greater peace and safety. What has been happening with global dynamics for at least sixty years now in many major world cities is the dissolution of the hierarchical relationship between the center and the outskirts, and between town and country. Incidentally, as noted by Rem Koolhaas in an essay that has become a touchstone in discussions on contemporary, globalized, and trivial urbanity, the "generic city" is "the city liberated from the captivity of center, from the straitjacket of identity."[8] Vastly expanded, the generic city has become a large suburb, a cluster without character, built entirely by the laws of entropy, such as shown in the voracious Chinese urbanization.

Thus, if during centuries of human history, as well defined by Adam Smith, the engine of social relationship was grounded in the clear division of labor between the city and the countryside, today this reality is entirely transformed.[9] It is a huge transformation of both what we understood as city and what we considered the countryside.[10] A compelling reading of this new situ-

Moda Center (Fashion Center) in Santa Cruz do Capibaribe, Pernambuco, Brazil, 2013

ation is offered by the Portuguese geographer Álvaro Domingues, who, when analyzing the death of the countryside in Portugal—the last rural bastion of Europe—formulates the concept of "transgenic landscape," which can be understood as a complementary mirror of Koolhaas's "generic city." The death of the countryside, seen as impermeable to the city, happens because of its incorporation into the urban domain, crossed by services and consumption, transforming it into a technical landscape. This change occurs by means of the extension of the road, technification of agriculture, emergence of agribusiness and commodities, and landscape trivialization, as the area is colonized by consumption and propaganda. In this way, according to Domingues, both the city and the countryside were incorporated into the broader and diffuse urban order, dissolving old polarities. In his words,

> The city's transition to urbanity spawned a profound
> metamorphosis: it went from centripetal to centrifugal;
> from limited and restrained to an unconfined thing;
> from cohesive and continuous to diffused and fragmented;
> from a legible and structured space to a force field orga-
> nized by new spatiality and mobility; from "rural" opposite
> or hybrid to a transgenic that assimilates and reprocesses
> elements that once belonged to either rural or urban spaces;
> from organization structured by the relationship to a
> center, to a system of various centers; from a city with well-
> defined borders, to a blurred conglomeration without
> clear beginning or end, etc.[11]

New corner building at Parauapebas, Pará, Brazil, 2013

Brazil: "The Spectacle of Growth"

Within the discussion of contemporary urban Brazil, the border topic on a national scale is also worthy of reflection. In the last ten or twelve years, while the great capital cities of the southeast had, in general, stagnant growth, the medium-sized cities of the north, northeast, and central-west regions of Brazil grew the most. They grew in both economic and demographic terms and physically expanded their urban area. The phenomenon is associated with the intensification of return migration, whereby individuals and families who had tried their luck in southeastern capital cities in previous decades came to find, in more recent times, better job offers in their regions of origin. Thus the spatial logic of the city centers–outskirts relationship in Brazil is turning. Cities that previously gravitated toward São Paulo, Rio de Janeiro, Belo Horizonte, Porto Alegre, Brasilia, Recife, or Salvador today reflect their own more autonomous dynamic.

Historically speaking, Brazil has predominantly developed along its coastal strip, focused on the trade with Europe. Not coincidentally, its first two capital cities were Salvador and Rio de Janeiro. The construction of Brasilia, in the 1950s and 1960s, represented an explicit attempt to bring development to the countryside, strengthening the country's territorial integration on a continental scale. A further by-product of this effort was the construction of a major highway cutting through the Amazon rainforest (Trans-Amazonian Highway/Rodovia Transamazônica), built during the military regime and inaugurated in 1972.[12] Nonetheless, the urbanization of these remote areas still followed a predatory logic of the pioneer fronts of exploration, with miserable towns created as satellite extractive

Suape Port in the metropolitan area of Recife, Pernambuco, Brazil, 2013

settlements, along with copper, bauxite, and gold mines, and latex extraction regions.

The recent growth of medium-sized cities in the north, northeast, and central-west regions of Brazil, in the states of Mato Grosso, Pará, and Pernambuco, is a new phenomenon linked to several factors: 1) an explicit policy economic decentralization implemented by the Luiz Inácio Lula da Silva administration (2003–2010), unfolding in the form of major infrastructure projects in these regions, such as the transposition of the São Francisco River channels, the Transnordestina Railway, the reconfiguration of the port of Suape, new hydroelectric power plants, such as Belo Monte, and the massive affordable housing program Minha Casa, Minha Vida; 2) the mechanization of mining and agriculture (especially soybeans), linked to the rise of Brazilian agribusiness in the international market; and 3) the massive entry of foreign capital in infrastructure projects such as the Belo Monte HPP, bringing not only money but new people to its surrounding cities. This all happened in the context of high economic growth of the country as a whole, despite the severe crisis that affected Europe and North America, coupled with the rise of the "C Class" to middle-class status, with its incorporation into the consumer market.

Early in his first term as president of Brazil, in 2003, former President Lula da Silva announced that the country would have an unprecedented "spectacle of growth." Despite the public's initial skepticism in relation to that prophecy, what we saw was in fact Brazil's entry in the list of emerging "BRIC" countries, navigating nearly unscathed through the global financial crisis of 2008–2009.

Floating houses (*palafitas*) in Altamira, Pará, Brazil, 2013

In this context, the country plunged headlong into the center of global media sports events, becoming the host of the 2014 FIFA World Cup and the 2016 summer Olympic games. Such events go far beyond the sporting level, having become big business in real estate and construction. For that reason, they ended up accentuating the internal social disparities of the country, serving as a powerful spark to large demonstrations in the streets of many Brazilian cities, in June 2013, before the eyes of the world during the FIFA Confederations Cup.[13]

Although the stadiums and other sports and infrastructure facilities related to these events are built in the big regional capital cities of the country, especially in Rio de Janeiro, the great urban growth of the last decade in Brazil follows another geographic arc, driven both by government policy and the market itself, which forces us to try to understand what is the face of this new urban Brazil—no longer peripheral—resulting from the "spectacle of growth."[14] Under these circumstances, would cities like Sinop, Lucas do Rio Verde, Altamira, Parauapebas, Canaã dos Carajás, Salgueiro, Santa Cruz do Capibaribe, Cabo de Santo Agostinho, and Ipojuca, with their new shopping malls and mirrored buildings, be genuine experiments in the field of contemporary urbanization, or just examples of typical "generic cities"?

I would like to refer to this issue using two contrasting examples. The first, a positive one to some extent, is Santa Cruz do Capibaribe, in the state of Pernambuco. Located in the so-called drought polygon in Brazil's northeastern semi-arid region, this small town is today one of the largest centers of textile production in Latin America. Clothes produced by more than 19,000 small and medium-sized clothing and textile companies (many

Belo Monte Hydroelectric Power Plant in Altamira, Pará, Brazil, under construction, 2013

GROWING DENSITIES

The suburbs of Mexico City contain homes for more than 20 million residents. These colonial
suburbs contrast the steel and glass buildings of downtown. Avenida de los Insurgentes, one of the
longest avenues in the world, runs through Mexico City. What unites such a large city? How does
infrastructure play a role in urban density and identity?

GROWING DENSITIES

Chicago is considered a high-density metro area. In the 20th century, the city was second largest in the U.S., until Los Angeles surpassed it in the 1990s. Today U.S. Census Bureau shows Chicago as one of the slowest growing cities in the country. As populations grow, how do cities change?

GROWING DENSITIES

In 2012, the U.S. Census revealed Los Angeles as the country's densest metropolis. The Long Beach–Anaheim section of the city alone has 7,000 people per square mile. Seven of the top ten densest areas in the country reside in California. How do roads link and divide densities?

How can buildings be constructed to meet the housing requirements of a growing population while focusing on livability and community? The Interlace, designed by Ole Scheeren of OMA, in Singapore is a residential development of 1,040 apartment units connected with communal spaces through a greenbelt. Thirty-one apartment blocks form a hexagonal shape, taking into account air and light flow.

GROWING DENSITIES

How does age influence spaces of the urban? Built for "active adults," Sun City, Arizona, is
a retirement community bisected by a main road cutting through concentric rings of houses. Only
people 55 years of age and older live in these homes. What is the cost of an age-specific city?

CITY MEETS WATER

In 1911, Frederick Law Olmsted Jr. designed a park running adjacent to the Allegheny River. In 1998, the Allegheny Riverfront Park, designed by Michael Van Valkenburgh Associates, was created. The public park includes London Plane trees and trellising vines used to block the sight and sound of city traffic. How can design instigate, facilitate, and negotiate novel and established relations between cities and waterbodies in such a way that a significant water source (and its coastal edge) can gain from its proximity to an urban center, and vice versa?

The Old Port in Marseille was historically the economic center of Provence. As transport moved to
the Grand Port Maritime, the Old Port became neglected. At the end of the 20th century, yacht clubs
and cars inhibited 80 percent of public access to docks. The rehabilitation by Michel Desvigne
Paysagistes emphasizes citizens' accessibility and enjoyment of the waterfront.

The Paris *Plages* (Paris Beach) is a constructed public beachfront on the banks of the Seine.
Five thousand tons of sand, around 100 palm trees, and a plethora of sprinklers run between
five bridges including Pont Neuf, the oldest bridge in Paris. Open from 8 AM to 12 AM, the beach
attracted 3 million visitors in 2012.

The Vinterbad Bryggen in Copenhagen celebrates the interaction between the city and water, transforming the identity of the city and helping to foster and fortify a sense of collective stewardship. As the climate changes and populations increase, can collaborative design interventions provide solutions to issues facing cities around the world?

home businesses) located in the vicinity of the town are sold nationwide and exported to the world. With the rise of this textile economy since the 1990s, the town has more than doubled its population in twenty years, from 38,000 to 87,000 inhabitants, and increased by five times gross domestic product in the last ten years . With 120,000 square meters of built area—a vast area compared to the size of the town—Moda Center is the nervous system of Santa Cruz, concentrating more than 10,000 stores and hosting restaurants and hotels.[15]

On the other hand, we have the dramatic example of Altamira, in the state of Pará, located in the Amazon forest, on the edge of the Trans-Amazonian Highway and by the banks of the Xingu River. Housing the hydroelectric power plant of Belo Monte (still under construction) as well as indigenous and riverine communities, it concentrates many problems such as flooding, high rates of migration, deforestation, water pollution, car and motorcycle traffic, violence, and social disparities. In short, it is a town greatly affected by the predatory logic of extraction and the negative impact of the large energy infrastructure on local life and the environment, generating an uncontrolled boom of construction and consumption that does not translate into education, human development, and social equity—that is, in urbanity.

The administrations of former President Lula da Silva and current President Dilma Rousseff, both of the Workers Party (PT), have held office in Brazil since 2003 and have managed to accomplish greater decentralization of investment in the country while putting forth a welfare policy around food (Program Zero Hunger) and social housing (Minha Casa, Minha Vida). In addition, they created the Ministry of Cities (Ministério das Cidades),

Streets of Altamira, Pará, Brazil, 2013

responsible for implementing urban reform and addressing the demands made for the past two decades by the Landless Workers' Movement (Movimento dos Sem-Terra—MST). Unfortunately, the Ministry of Cities has served only as a political bargaining chip for the government rather than being a real locus of reflection and strategic actions that recognize and affirm cities as the true sites of democratic formation. Minha Casa, Minha Vida has also proved to be a disaster from the urban point of view.

Implemented by the consortium created between a government bank, Caixa Econômica Federal, and the largest construction companies and contractors in the country, the program builds houses in marginal areas of cities—often linked to local real estate interests—that are entirely devoid of urbanity (services and transport).[16] Thus social housing, by making use of an architectural and urban model that is extremely anachronistic, ends up serving as an urban disruptor, as can be seen in the case of Altamira and numerous other cities along the route of the paradoxical Brazilian "spectacle of growth" of the past decade.

The large developments of single-story or ranch-style houses of Minha Casa, Minha Vida—symbols of the new urban Brazil—push cities to their edges. If inhabitants can now have televisions, refrigerators, and cars, they are nevertheless not being formed as citizens of a political community that understands the *urbs* as *civitas,* who recognize public space as the mediation arena of the conflicts of urban life. On television, or over the Internet, they can see Brazil as a postcard image that will be broadcast to the entire world during the Olympic games in Rio de Janeiro. This is the other side of the "spectacle of growth" that reaches them, showing itself as a predictable growth of the spectacle.

1 "Passaic seems full of 'holes' compared to New York City, which seems tightly packed and solid, and those holes in a sense are the monumental vacancies that define, without trying the memory-traces of an abandoned set of futures. Such futures are found in grade B Utopian films, and then imitated by the suburbanite." Robert Smithson, "A Tour of the Monuments of Passaic, New Jersey," in Jack Flam, ed., *Robert Smithson: The Collected Writings* (Berkeley: University of California Press, 1996), 72.

2 Reference to the concept created by Sharon Zukin in *Landscapes of Power: From Detroit to Disney World* (Berkeley: University of California Press, 1991).

3 Marginal Pinheiros is a section of Highway SP-015 that runs through the city of São Paul. The name of this section comes from the fact that the expressway runs along the Pinheiros River. It is one of the most important roads in São Paulo, linking the north and south, beginning at the triple border of Campo Grande, Cidade Dutra, and Socorro, and ending at the border of Vila Leopoldina and Jaguaré. It provides access to many important highways of the state of São Paulo, including the Anchieta Highway and the Imigrantes Highway via the Bandeirantes Avenue; the Raposo Tavares Highway and the Régis Bittencourt Highway via the Francisco Morato Avenue; and to the Castelo Branco Highway via the Cebolão–a complex of roads linking Marginal Pinheiros, Marginal Tietê, and the aforementioned highway. There are several bridges connecting each side of the river, such as the Octavio Frias de Oliveira Bridge.

4 See Mariana Fix, *São Paulo cidade global: fundamentos financeiros de uma miragem* (São Paulo: Boitempo, 2007).

5 Since 2014, the city of São Paulo has faced the worst water supply crisis in its history, seeing its reservoirs (the Cantareira, Guarapiranga, and Alto Tietê systems) reduced to less than 10 percent of their capacity.

6 See Mariana Fix, *Parceiros da exclusão: duas histórias da construção de uma 'nova cidade' em São Paulo: Faria Lima e Água Espraiada* (São Paulo: Boitempo, 2001). These urban operations, and the related removal of people, took place during the administration of Paulo Maluf, São Paulo's mayor between 1993 and 1996.

7 See Fix, *Parceiros da exclusão.*

8 Rem Koolhaas, "The Generic City," in Rem Koolhaas and Bruce Mau, *S, M, L, XL* (New York: Monacelli Press, 1995), 1249–50.

9 See Adam Smith, *The Wealth of Nations*, 1776.

10 See Giulio Carlo Argan, for example, in *L'Europe delle capitali,* 1964. For Argan, the city is the fundamental unit of civilization and history, a concrete body of persons who live in the same space, share the same symbols, and see the same scenery.

11 Álvaro Domingues, *A rua da estrada* (Porto: Dafne Editora, 2009), 13; translation by Melissa Harkin.

12 The Trans-Amazonian Highway (official designation BR-230 and official name Rodovia Transamazônica) is 4,000-kilometer highway, the third longest in Brazil. It runs through the Brazilian states of Paraíba, Ceará, Piauí, Maranhão, Tocantins, Pará, and Amazonas, from the proximities of Saboeiro until the town of Lábrea.

13 See Guilherme Wisnik, "Invisible City," *Artforum* (May 2014). See also Ermínia Maricato et al., *Cidades rebeldes: Passe Livre e as manifestações que tomaram as ruas do Brasil* (São Paulo: Boitempo, 2013); and Andrew Jennings et al., *Brasil em jogo: o que fica da Copa e das Olimpíadas?* (São Paulo: Boitempo, 2014).

14 This set of issues resulted in the exhibit "Brazil: The Spectacle of Growth" in the Tenth International São Paulo Architecture Biennale, in 2003. Curatorship by Guilherme Wisnik (Chief Curator), Ligia Nobre and Ana Luiza Nobre, Co-curatorship by Paula Santoro, and research by Carolina Sacconi, André Godinho, Isabela Mota, and Yuri Quevedo. See *Monolito* no. 17: *X Bienal de Arquitetura* (São Paulo: Editora Monolito, Oct./Nov. 2013).

15 Largest wholesale clothing mall in Brazil, with 10,000 stores, 6,000 parking spaces, and six food courts. Source: http://www.modacentersantacruz.com.br/, accessed on August 20, 2015.

16 See João Sette Whitaker Ferreira, ed. , *Produzir casas ou construir cidades? Desafios para um novo Brasil urbano* (São Paulo: LABHAB/FUPAM, 2012).

INDEX

ILLUSTRATION CREDITS

Cover, Dan Istitene/Getty Images
17, Mack Magagane, "Light Hours," 2009
18–19, Maciej Dakowicz
20, 21, Iwan Baan
22–23, Maciej Dakowicz
24–25, Antoine Rose
27, New York City Department of Transportation
28–29, © Artists Rights Society (ARS), New York / VG Bild-Kunst, Bonn / Artist: Ralf Witthaus / Photo: Harald Neumann
30–31, © Alex S. MacLean
32, Mimi Mollica
36, 37, © Hilary Koob-Sassen
57, Judith Parrott
58–59, © Alex S. MacLean
60–61, Maciej Dakowicz
62–63, Ian Lambot
64–65, Islemount Images / Alamy Stock Photo
66–67, Claudia Jaguaribe
68–69, © Alex S. MacLean
70–71, Etienne Frossard
72, Nigel Henderson (1917–1985), © Tate, London 2016
81, ZUS
82, Stad in de Maak
88, Wikimedia Commons: Creative Commons Attribution/Share Alike License: https://commons.wikimedia. org/wiki/File:Le_Panthéon_(Paris).jpg
89, Arash Khamooshi for *The New York Times*
90–91, Mimi Mollica, *Everything's Good,* 2012
92–93, Leonardo Finotti
94, Ahmed Mater, 2012
95, Artichoke, 2009
96, Yak Films, TURF FEINZ RIP RichD Dancing in the Rain Oakland Street YAK FILMS, 2009, Oakland, U.S.A. Source: https://m.youtube.com/ watch?v=JQRRnAhmB58
97, Musée du Louvre, Département des arts graphiques, RF 5282.18, Recto.
98, Bibliothèque nationale de France, Département estampes et photographie, RESERVE QB-370 (17)-FT 4
99, Bibliothèque nationale de France, département estampes et photographie, EST RESERVE HA-80 (2)
101, *Révolutions de France et de Brabant,* 52. The Houghton Library, Harvard University
103, Bibliothèque nationale de France, Département estampes et photographie, RESERVE FOL-QB-201 (119)
108, 109, Michael Arad
110, Google Images, 2011

111, Joe Woolhead, courtesy Handel Architects
112, Jin Lee, Courtesy 9/11 Memorial and Handel Architects
113, Eduardo Muñoz / Reuters Pictures
114–15, Ralph Larmann, 2014
116–17, Janet Echelman, 2015
118–19, Camille Zakharia
120, ©2016 Artists Rights Society (ARS), New York / VG Bild-Kunst, Bonn / Artist: Ralf Witthaus / Photo: Harald Neumann 2011
121, 124, 125, Joe Woolhead, courtesy Handel Architects
128–36, courtesy of the artist Krzysztof Wodiczko and Galerie Lelong, NY
137, Iwan Baan
138–39, Ahmed Mater, 2012
140, Richard Rowland, 2011
141, Mimi Mollica, 2000, part of the portfolio, "Un Tocco di Kalsa"
142–43, Yannis Behrakis / Reuters Pictures
144, Mathew Micah Wright
147, Jacques Gréber, Ville de Marseille, plan d'aménagement et extension, Paris, 1933. Ill. 57
148, Archives départementales des Bouches du Rhône
149, Getty Centre collections: 84. XM.126.82
154, German Federal Archives: Bild 101I-027-1477-32
155, Jacques Gréber, Ville de Marseille, plan d'aménagement et extension, Paris 1933, ill. 18
156, Marche – *Le magazine français*
157, German Federal Archives: Bild 101I-027-1480-02
158, Jacques Gréber, Ville de Marseille, plan d'aménagement et extension, Paris 1933, ill. 55
159, German Federal Archives: Bild 101I-027-1477-29
160, German Federal Archives: Bild 101I-027-1480-39A
169, Mimi Mollica, "Sicilian Immigrants," London, England
170, Polly Braden, "What time is it here?" China Between, 2007, Xiamen, China
171, Marc Domage, 2008, *Tree Huts,* Paris, France
172–73, Ioana Marinescu
174, 175, Mimi Mollica
177, 178–79, Maciej Dakowicz
180, Carlo Allegri / Reuters Pictures
182, 183, Tali Hatuka
184, Takeaway, Wikimedia
185, Jonathan Rashad, Wikimedia
182, Tali Hatuka
196–97, 199, 200, 201, 203, Loïc Wacquant
213, Charlie Koolhaas

214–15, Frank Augstein, AP Images, 2016
216–17, 218–19, Iwan Baan
220–21, Drew St. Lawrence
222–23, courtesy Rijksoverheid
224, Mimi Mollica
241, Pascal Rossignol / Reuters Pictures
242–43, Hannes Zander
244–45, Sayler/Morris, "Fieldnotes from the Gowanus," 2011
246–47, Harish Tyagi/EPA, 2015
248–49, Iwan Baan
251, Homer Sykes, 1981
252, Mirrorpix Photo Archives
253, Chris Marker and Pierre L'homme, La Sofra, 1963
254–255, Mohammed Al-Kouh, 2016
256, Morton Broffman, 1965
273, Trent Parke / Magnum Photos
274–75, Ioana Marinescu
276–77, Brian Harkin for *The Guardian,* 2014
278–79, Adam Magyar, *Hong Kong V,* 2007–2008
280–81, Polly Braden
282–83, Sean Pavone, 2012
284, Chris Marker, "Untitled #95," Passengers, 2008–2010
285, Chris Marker, "Untitled #198," Passengers, 2008–2010
286–87, Jonas Gratzer, 2013
288, ©Randy H. Goodman, IRAN: Women Only, Tehran, Iran, 2015
296, Luciana Travassos / São Paulo Urbanismo, Municipality of São Paulo
297, Cássio Vasconcellos, from the series "Aérias #2" (Aerial #2), 2010–2014
298, Álvaro Domingues, *A rua da estrada* ("The street of the road"), 2009
299, 300, 301, 302, Tuca Vieira
303, 304, Iwan Baan
305, Pablo Lopez Luz, Barcroft Media
306–7, 308–9, 310–11, Iwan Baan
312–13, © Alex S. MacLean, *Subdivision Divided in Two,* 2004
315, Annie M. O'Neill
316–17, Anne-Christine Poujoulat / AFP, 2013
318–19, Marcus Smith, France This Way, 2015
320, Linda Kastrup / Scanpix
321, Iwan Baan

329

CONTRIBUTORS

Mohsen Mostafavi is Dean of the Harvard University Graduate School of Design and the Alexander and Victoria Wiley Professor of Design.

Michael Arad is a Partner at Handel Architects. In 2012, he won both the AIA Presidential Citation for his work on the National September 11 Memorial, and the Liberty Award for Artistic Leadership by the Lower Manhattan Cultural Council.

Jean-Louis Cohen is the Sheldon H. Solow Professor in the History of Architecture at New York University's Institute of Fine Arts.

Diane E. Davis is the Charles Dyer Norton Professor of Regional Planning and Urbanism and Chair of the Department of Urban Planning and Design at the Harvard University Graduate School of Design.

Keller Easterling is a professor, architect, and writer at Yale University.

Gerald Frug is the Louis D. Brandeis Professor of Law at Harvard Law School.

Chantal Mouffe is Professor of Political Theory at the University of Westminster.

Erika Naginski is Professor of Architectural History at the Harvard University Graduate School of Design.

Michelle Provoost is an architectural historian. In 1994, she cofounded the office of Crimson Architectural Historians, and since 2008 she has served as Director of the International New Town Institute in Almere, the Netherlands.

Robert J. Sampson is the Henry Ford II Professor of the Social Sciences at Harvard University and Director of the Boston Area Research Initiative at the Radcliffe Institute for Advanced Study.

Saskia Sassen is the Robert S. Lynd Professor of Sociology, and chairs The Committee on Global Thought at Columbia University.

Richard Sennett is University Professor of the Humanities at New York University, Professor of Sociology at the London School of Economics and Political Science, Chair of Theatrum Mundi, and Distinguished Visiting Scholar at the University of Cambridge.

Erik Swyngedouw is Professor of Geography at the University of Manchester.

Loïc Wacquant is Professor of Sociology and Research Associate at the Institute for Legal Research, Boalt Law School, University of California at Berkeley.

Guilherme Wisnik is Professor of Architecture and Urbanism at the University of São Paulo.

Krzysztof Wodiczko is Professor in Residence of Art, Design, and the Public Domain at the Harvard University Graduate School of Design.

ACKNOWLEDGMENTS

First of all, thanks to Melissa Vaughn for meticulously editing the texts in this volume. I thank Gareth Doherty for his overall coordination and curation of the photographs, and for seeing the book through to publication. Thanks to Suryani Oka Dewa Ayu, Hamed Bukhamseen, and Peter Sealy for their dedicated and careful research on images and captions. Suryani Oka Dewa Ayu was responsible for many of the captions. Thanks also to Meghan Sandberg and Christine O'Brien for securing image permissions. Thanks to Jane Acheson, Kate Bauer, Shantel Blakely, Suneeta Gill, Miguel Lopez Melendez, Theresa Lund, Anna Lyman, Jennifer Sigler, and Rachel Tolano. Thanks to Carolyn Wheeler for proofreading, and Tobiah Waldron for the index.

And I thank Lars Müller and Martina Mullis of Lars Müller Publishers for their continued professionalism and friendship.

Ethics of the Urban
The City and the Spaces of the Political

Editor: Mohsen Mostafavi
Editorial coordination: Gareth Doherty
Editorial assistance: Suryani Oka Dewa Ayu (captions and images)
and Hamed Bukhamseen (images)
Text editing: Melissa Vaughn
Proofreading: Carolyn Wheeler
Index: Tobiah Waldron
Design: Integral Lars Müller/Lars Müller and Martina Mullis
Production: Martina Mullis
Lithography: prints professional, Jan Scheffler, Berlin, Germany
Printing and binding: DZA Druckerei zu Altenburg, Germany
Paper: Munken Lynx, 130 gsm, and Terra Print Gloss, 90 gsm

© 2017 Lars Müller Publishers
and the President and Fellows of Harvard College

Lars Müller Publishers
Zürich, Switzerland
www.lars-mueller-publishers.com

ISBN 978-3-03778-381-8

Printed in Germany